AF477796

Institutional
Realism

Institutional Realism

Social and

Political Constraints on

Rational Actors

Robert Grafstein

Yale University Press   **New Haven and London**

Published with assistance from the
foundation established in memory of
William McKean Brown.

Designed by James J. Johnson. Set in
Univers and Times Roman types by
DEKR Corporation, Woburn, Massachu-
setts. Printed in the United States of
America by BookCrafters, Inc., Chelsea,
Michigan.

*Library of Congress Cataloging-in-Publi-
cation Data*

Grafstein, Robert, 1948–
    Institutional realism : the social and
political constraints on rational actors /
Robert Grafstein.
        p.   cm.
    Includes bibliograhical references
and index.
    ISBN 0–300–05164–6 (alk. paper)
    1. Social choice.   2. Social interac-
tion.   3. Social institutions.   I. Title.
HB846.8.G727   1992
302'.13—dc20   91-40363

The paper in this book meets the guide-
lines for permanence and durability of
the Committeee on Production Guide-
lines for Book Longevity of the Council
on Library Resources.

10   9   8   7   6   5   4   3   2   1

To My Mother and Father

Contents

Figures

Preface

Institution is an appropriately imposing term for an imposing social entity, namely, a collection of people whose behavior and behavioral dispositions assure, in the aggregate, the institution's persistent influence on social outcomes. To some, a characterization of this kind represents an overly reductionist view of institutions, which are better appreciated as distinct structures, totalities, or systems transcending any mere collection of individuals. The predominant view, however, is that institutions need to be demystified even further. An institution, in this analysis, is a human construct, the product of choice, decision, affirmation, and recognition.

In the course of developing the doctrine of institutional realism, this book argues against the conventionalist approach, particularly in its rational choice incarnation. Yet in the latter case, it argues as a friend: although an institution's influence on people goes beyond any construct's, this influence is shown to be entirely consistent with the full rationality of the institution's members. Thus sharing the stage with a fair amount of philosophical analysis are rational choice models reflecting a game theoretic conception of institutions.

My wide-ranging intellectual debts are indicated, if not always fully discharged, by the citations in the text. Often the debt is proportional to the degree of criticism. Partners in conversation, panel discussants, and anonymous journal referees are too numerous (or impossible) to mention. During my graduate student days, David Easton and Adam Przeworski had a lasting impact on the way I think and do not think about many of the topics covered in this book. Jack Knight and Ian Shapiro read the entire manuscript. Their suggestions led to substantial improvements, although obviously the responsibility for any remaining faults is mine alone. It has been a pleasure to work with my editor, John Covell, whose patience is greatly appreciated, and the manuscript editor, Richard Miller, who is responsible for many stylistic improvements. Finally, my wife and son have had very little to do with the content of this book, but everything to do with the person who wrote it.

Introduction

Institutions are puzzling. If they are just human creations, how can they coerce us? If they are not, what else could they possibly be? In this book I attempt to resolve this puzzle by answering the second question. In doing so, I have to wage an uphill battle against the dominant view in the social sciences, and the philosophies covering them, that institutions are ultimately conventions of human behavior. As such, proponents of this view imply, institutions are no more puzzling than any other human artifact. Like alarm clocks, they can thwart our immediate desires. Yet like a broken alarm, institutions in principle can be replaced when their performance disappoints us.

The analogy with ordinary inventions, however, is faulty. People do not produce institutions in the sense assumed, and institutions have greater power to constrain than the analogy grants. Their power over us represents more than the fulfillment of our plans, our ability to arrange things so that we choose to subordinate immediate satisfaction to the realization of longer-term gains. The standard conventionalist account, in short, expects too much of individuals and too little of institutions. It does so because conventionalism in the end is unable to comprehend social objects that are social forces in their own right.

Without turning institutions into supernatural entities, the account I propose allows them the requisite degree of independence to act as real constraints even on the decisions of fully rational individuals. This account is based on realism, a view that institutions as physical objects exist independently of our beliefs about them. I define institutions as four-dimensional wholes, with human individuals (specifically, four-dimensional segments of individuals' lives) serving as their parts. This definition, of course, suggests the ontology associated with institutions, not their appropriate sociopolitical description. Still, this ontology plays a crucial role in solving the problem of institutional constraint by allowing for a physical realization of the constraining mechanisms without divorcing institutions from the people who comprise them.

Ontological clarity brings additional rewards. In its absence, the presumption that different approaches to the study of institutions represent different views of the same institutional phenomena is just wishful thinking. In my opinion, however, the current academic debate over the nature of institutions is far from pointless. Emphasizing the conventionalist conception, Samuel Huntington (1968:10), for example, argues that "[political] institutions are the behavioral manifestation of the moral consensus and mutual interest." In this view, the entry of the newly mobilized into politics weakens institutions to the extent the values and interests of these latest participants differ from those that the existing institutions express. New institutions reflecting these new participants have to coalesce. More likely, says Huntington, existing institutions simply decay under the pressure of the new orientations.

Adopting the opposite view that institutions are independent constraints on individuals, Adam Przeworski (1975) concludes that the same mobilization should strengthen institutions insofar as additional people are brought under their dominion. The newly mobilized adapt to the changed conditions under which they must now lead their lives, thereby expressing the power of the institutions themselves. The disagreement between Huntington and Przeworski is partly empirical, yet it also reflects a deeper disagreement over what the phenomenon of institutionalization represents.

A full and convincing solution to this empirical question requires a resolution of the broader theoretical question. The disagreement between Huntington and Przeworski, moreover, is not just academic. As both appreciate, it has important implications for understanding the limits we face in trying to preserve, control, or even dissolve the institutional restrictions under which we find ourselves.

Institutions matter. The historian Robert Brenner (1986) argues that because of the way precapitalist societies institutionalized property relations, rational lords and serfs operated so as to preserve that system rather than undermine it, say, with innovations in technology and production. Brenner's claim contrasts with orthodox Marxism's insistence that an independent and unrelenting drive to expand the forces of production inevitably bursts their feudal integument. Institutional constraints, he counters, were a stable fact of life for our rational ancestors. From the standpoint of institutional realism, unfortunately, Brenner cannot leave well enough alone. Having explained the domination of institutions over productive forces, he tries, reasonably enough, to account for the preservation of these institutions. His account, however, betrays the heavy hand of conventionalism. If activity within institutional constraints is explicable as the product of rational choices by participants, then (says the conventionalist) the existence of the constraints must be explicable on the same model of choice. So Brenner (1986:49) adds that parties to the institution "have as one of their conscious goals" maintaining the institutional framework. Though this explanation, even on its own terms, must overcome such hurdles as free rider problems, the point to notice for the present is the stretching of ordinary psychological explanation that is so characteristic of conventionalism.

Congress offers a parallel and more contemporary example of institutional constraint. Various technical results from social choice theory might lead one to expect that legislative decisions would be much less stable than they actually are. Kenneth Shepsle and Barry Weingast (1981) have shown that the institutional structure of Congress—its committee system—creates order despite the instability suggested by the underlying preferences of the members.

As we will see in chapter 3, Shepsle and Weingast's conventionalism then prompts them to explain this institutional constraint as the product of decisions made by the very participants who are ostensibly constrained by it. Demanding pro forma consistency, conventionalism has actors implicitly select their own restrictions. "Stop us before we choose again," the participants seem to plead. But how, in the end, can self-imposed restrictions accomplish this? Conventionalism answers by equipping participants with bigger ideas, iterated hierarchies of belief, deeper commitments, and increasing levels of organization. What it cannot abide are institutional arrangements that do not result from continuing and deliberate acts of collective or individual will.

Institutional realism, of course, does not deny that the basis of any explanation is itself in need of explanation. But it does deny that institutions as institutions can be explained in the same manner as conventions. They are not self-policing, either in the ordinary game theoretic sense that the traffic game's solution—everyone drive on the right—is self-policing or in the more subtle game theoretic sense that institutions represent some agreed-upon solution to a still larger game.

Conventionalists invoke these overarching choices about choices not simply because they are caught up in the analytic momentum of their micro-level analysis. They recognize, quite rightly, that their failure to bring the social phenomenon of institutions under the sway of the choice model raises awkward questions about their ability to understand these institutions and, ultimately, the choices made within them.

My competing thesis insists that institutions are typically conditions of choice, not objects of choice. Their structuring of alternatives can be a brute fact of life for those who live within them, much as physical situations can be brute facts of life for everyone at large. This thesis, then, brings the infinite regress of the conventionalist analysis to an end. It thereby short-circuits the increasingly ornate psychological axioms needed to support the analysis of strategic institutional interaction. And aside from allowing more realistic assumptions in the ordinary sense, the competing thesis in its rational choice form handles specific behavioral anomalies that frustrate even refurbished forms of conventionalist rational choice theory, most important, the infamous paradox of not voting.

1.

The idea that the organization of our social life is a matter of convention now seems, well, natural. As the doctrine of divine right of kings lost credibility, there was a Copernican revolution in reverse, looking to human beings and, in particular, the human mind as the source of such social order as one finds in the world. The regularities of social life exist, in this view, because day in and day out people reaffirm and even tacitly agree to their continuation. The social order people find is the order they put there. This is not to say such regularities are inconsequential. But they depend on people's collective beliefs and desires. Given a different set of underlying agreements and understandings, the conventions would be different. The teleology of divine intervention has been replaced by the social construction of the social world. Yet in a sense, social order continues to be seen as supernatural, as something imposed on natural objects and processes.

If social order is imposed, the conventionalist reasons, there must be an imposer. In the end, ordinary people are the profane source of social order, imposing and maintaining it even if they did not originally design it and even if they do not like or anticipate all its consequences. This is particularly true of political order, since politics is the vehicle through which members of society can actively consider what sort of social structure they want to have. To Durkheim (1958), who had a flawless instinct for capturing this mirror relation between mind and society, the state accordingly should be viewed as society's brain.

Yet how can one reconcile the conventional character of institutions with their social efficacy? Though supposedly willed into the world, institutions are not inert artifacts. They structure interactions, stabilize social outcomes, and help determine what the feasible courses of action are. They are the way things are done if they are to be done. Evidently, the institutional tail can wag the societal dog.

Marx clearly was aware of this problem. His letter to P. V. Annenkov in 1846 (Marx and Engels 1968:670) nicely illustrates the tension plaguing conventionalism: "What is society whatever its form might be? The product of men's reciprocal action. Are men free to choose this or that form of society? By no means." Marx goes on to justify this negative conclusion by asserting a chain of "correspondences" in which the social form of activity, the product of previous generations, is inherited as a constraint on succeeding activity. Yet what exactly is transmitted that can play such an independent role? If the social form is a product of previous generations, why are subsequent generations less privileged by being condemned to submit to it?

Or consider those previous generations. From what Archimedean point do people decide upon the social order in which they are embedded? What does a socially unstructured collective decision look like? What precisely is the object of such a decision? It is unclear how an account of the decisions that create institutions, or an account of the beliefs that reaffirm them, can avoid appealing to the very constraints of social order that were supposed to be explained.

There are three leading and sometimes overlapping strategies in social science for understanding institutions. One strategy is to characterize all supraindividual entities like institutions as an observer's abstraction from the mass of social interactions (e.g., Easton 1979, 1990). This obviates the ontological question, but what remains unclear is how abstractions from the world interact with it. Another strategy, associated with structuralists, systems or organization theorists, and Marxists, among others, is to posit distinct social structures having the power to organize and define social interactions (e.g., Althusser and Balibar 1970). This approach either must treat institutional constraints as inexplicable or, at a minimum, will fail to explain how these constraints are actually realized and, therefore, what sort of human product these constraining institutions must be. Instead of expunging the conventionalist ghost from the social machine, the ghost becomes the social machine.

One might also mention in this context those who explicitly treat society as a social construction (see Berger and Luckmann 1964) and those postmodernists who find in society a construction without a constructor (e.g., Foucault 1970). All seem to want the logical closure that comes with positing a force or subject behind society, yet without appealing to what they rightly see as an old-fashioned and outmoded view of the individual. The term *social* in social construction, as we shall see, covers a multitude of sins, whereas social inquiries inspired by postmodernism often seem to replace one kind of methodological placeholder, the individual subject, with another, whether a free-floating language, discourse, problematic, or episteme.

The third and dominant strategy, which is probably the most forthright, explicitly treats institutions as conventions, that is, regularities of behavior reflecting (1) an organization's routinized patterns of interaction compensating for the individual's inability to act in a fully rational manner (e.g., March and Simon 1958), (2) norms expressing the values or interests of society (e.g., Parsons 1954), or (3) individually rational choices (e.g., Schotter 1981).

The organizational approach is more enlightening about the limits of individuals than the strengths of institutions. If the institutional routine is not just another way of describing individual behavior, then how do institutions work and what precisely are they? One indication that something is wrong with the normative consensus approach is its tendency to produce circular, not to mention strained, explanations (e.g., democratic institutions reflect democratic values). The interest approach has similar liabilities (procapitalist policies reflect capitalist class interests).

The problem with the rational choice approach, as currently practiced, is its attenuated sense of institutions as persisting constraints on human beings, constraints operating independently of their will, to borrow Marx's phrase. What makes these neutered institutions seem credible are the incredible cognitive powers imputed to those participating within them. In the end, rational choice theory defines institutions as though they are subject to a continuing recall by their participants.

The so-called new institutionalism (see March and Olsen 1984, 1989; Shepsle 1989) is one important response to the problems facing extreme conventionalism. It has made its mark in economics, political economy, history, and political theory, all areas where the significance of institutions has never been more appreciated. In contrast to cruder versions of conventionalism, institutions, according to the new institutionalism, are not required to emerge by design. Nor are they seen merely as tokens of earlier decisions. They are factors to be considered by those who must coexist with them. Equally important, this updated institutionalism submits to the rigors of modern science. Institutions are not invoked as a deus ex machina but arise from the actions of individuals.

Unfortunately, the new institutionalism, for all this, only perfects the conventionalist revolution. Peel away all the refinements it has introduced, and what remains is a crucial premise common not only to conventionalism but to the theocratic doctrine that conventionalism replaced: social order has a purposive source. The regularities of this order are ultimately defined, even under the new institutionalism, by the way individuals define themselves and their society. At its core, the new institutionalism is a new conventionalism and inherits its inability to provide a full account of institutional constraint.

Since rational choice theory is the most conspicuous target of my criticisms as well as the framework for my own analysis, it might be useful to state in condensed but more explicit form the rational choice issues at stake. In the standard rational choice analysis, the process by which institutions persist is just a recapitulation of the process by which they first emerged. To talk in discrete terms for simplicity, at the end of every institutional period or cycle each participant is supposed to recalculate the pros and cons of continuing with the arrangement or seeking some other. Every vote for a candidate or for a piece of legislation, every Sunday spent in church, is tantamount to contract renewal, and this implicit contract renewal parallels the initial selection of the institution over all other possibilities. In this sense, participants never leave the analytic high ground of the state of nature.

At best, the only difference between choice within an institution and choice prior to its existence is that the institution has a history in the former case, and this improves projections of the institution's future course. Institutions are always objects of choice and never true constraints that rational actors may understand but not redefine or remove at will.

According to institutional realism, however, institutions are, like rules of the game, ultimately conditions within which—not on which—actors operate. Universal rationality does not mean that the constraints that other actors' choices present to us, or that ours present to them, were chosen as such or must now be objects of choice. The characterization—or ideology, as I will later call it—under which choices are made does not necessarily coincide with the relevant institutional constraints other choosers in fact represent.

I grant that there are often good practical reasons for assuming that rational actors have a broad understanding of their institution and even for assuming considerable homogeneity in their beliefs, behavior, and perceived alternatives. Yet for conventionalists, this breadth and homogeneity become more than methodological postulates. In the end, conventionalism must exaggerate and homogenize the cognitive capacities and interests of institutional participants because this is the only way the institution will remain their creation. The institution's independent existence would threaten conventionalism itself.

Institutional realism, by contrast, can let actual behavior rather than postulates guide psychological imputations. More important, it can address anomalies that no methodological doctrine could explain away. As it turns out, even decision makers fortified with inflated psychological powers cannot always overcome the preinstitutional isolation that conventional rational choice theory analytically imposes on them. By more fully embedding rational actors within their social context, institutional realism is better positioned to handle these recalcitrant cases.

In short, a survey of the existing forms of institutional analysis suggests the following. When social science respects the power of institutions to constrain, it largely ignores their status as human products. When social science emphasizes the role of participants in the creation of institutions, it does so at the expense of institutional constraint. Together these problems reflect the failure of social science to resolve the delicate problems of institutional ontology.

These problems can only be solved by an unconventional analysis of institutions. It will be one in which institutions are treated first and foremost as found objects, not human inventions continually reinvented. It will also be one in which a social order can be selected only within a social order, not de novo. These are difficult claims to characterize in a plausible way, let alone justify. Conventionalism is not regnant without reason. To state the difficulty in summary form, any substitute for conventionalism must, like the new institutionalism, satisfy the demands of rigorous science. There can be no appeal to mysterious entities or forces, nor any implied transcending of the laws of physics. In this book, I present a scientifically credible analysis of institutions, indeed one that in some respects, I believe, better meets the demands of science than do its predecessors.

2.

Just because institutions are now regarded as centrally important does not mean that they are well understood. Current public uncertainty about institutions parallels academia's profound uncertainty about the nature of these social entities and, accordingly, about their relation to ordinary human beings. I have suggested that a serious analysis of institutions is impossible without a careful consideration of their ontological status. Simply put, the question of institutions is a species of the question, What exists?

If fighting conventionalism is an uphill battle, it might seem tactically unwise to start it so very far from the summit, which is to say, with the question of institutional ontology. To make matters worse, both ends of the intellectual spectrum may well think this larger question to be misconceived. First of all, it may seem misconceived to philosophers who think ontological issues are relatively unimportant or even pointless. I disagree; the reasons for my disagreement are spelled out in chapter 1, where I also name names. I have tailored that chapter to analytical critics of ontology, despite the influence of the continental mode among social and political philosophers. Perhaps after the very sympathetic analytical treatment of continental themes by Richard Rorty (1979), this approach will represent less of a deterrent to those outside this tradition. Continental enthusiasts may also be less than pleased by my general acceptance of scientific method, as opposed to particular social scientific theories. Even those who officially dislike philosophical kibitzing about social science often deplore its current emulation of the natural sciences. I will not undertake a general defense of scientific practice in this book.

At the other end of the spectrum, practitioners of science may find my initial focus on ontology misconceived, rejecting it as an example of what Karl Popper (1961:26–34) calls methodological essentialism. Methodological essentialists believe that in order to characterize and study the objects of science, one must understand their essences or essential natures. Essentialism, Popper objects, has not been the strategy of natural science and should not be the strategy of social science (in fact, he uses institutions as an example). The false issue, in other words, is what institutions are; the real issue is how they behave and how they relate to other items of social scientific interest.

Some might go even further than Popper. Social science ought to proceed autonomously, guided by data and norms of theorizing specific to the discipline. Outside advice, according to this view, is usually unsolicited, unheeded, and unwarranted.

I take these objections seriously, especially since I am not about to propose either first philosophy or essentialism as a solution to the puzzle of institutions. There are also practical reasons to be leery of attempts to integrate philosophy and social theory. It is difficult for the reader, not to mention the writer, to keep in balance areas of research that often differ so markedly in substance, approach, and even style.

I have two specific reasons for recommending an explicit ontology of institutions. First, the systematic study of the main social scientific approaches to institutional phenomena will show not only that all are fundamentally flawed but that there is a deeply rooted pattern to their mistakes. Both the ambiguity plaguing their formulations and their often outré theoretical assumptions serve, in effect, to duck the ontological implications of their conceptions. Although social scientists are not obligated to scratch whenever philosophers itch, philosophy can be a useful tool for diagnosing preexisting problems. As Nelson Goodman (1972:168) has characterized their respective roles, "The practical scientist does the business but the philosopher keeps the books." Sometimes, only a careful audit will reveal that business is not as good as it seemed to be.

Second, the philosophy informing this study is continuous with science. Insights about ontology and related philosophical issues influence the ontological analysis of institutions and this, in turn, influences the more refined conception of institutions presented in the remainder of the book. The first chapter offers a philosophical analysis of problems independently generated within social science; subsequent chapters resolve these theoretical and empirical problems in light of that opening analysis. Philosophy, in short, grounds the institutional analysis; the institutional analysis gives the philosophy its point.

Ultimately, the philosophical quandary that social theorists con-

front is how to understand the relation between conventionally imposed descriptions and the things described. The conventional dimension of institutions reflects, in part, our ability to categorize the socially
relevant objects of the world in alternative ways. These categorizations, I grant, are not simply glosses on the underlying social or
physical mechanism. Nor do they create and control that mechanism.
If mere categorization were able to accomplish this, institutions would
hardly deserve their reputation. The problem is to reconcile the fact
that institutions are in some sense human products subject to human
categorization and the fact that they continue to constrain their producers.

3.

In the remainder of the introduction, I want to spell out a bit
more carefully the general path the book follows. The first stage in the
analysis of institutions, we have seen, is to characterize a particular
approach to ontological questions. The version of realism I recommend
eschews certain customary posits of realist theorizing, namely, internal
relations (for example, causality in a strong sense) and properties (if
only because their status in limbo between description and object begs
the interesting questions). Deprived of these obvious devices, the
analysis of institutional constraint has to proceed with more care than
would otherwise be necessary.

My argument in chapter 1 assumes that any social entities of
interest are going to have systematic effects on individuals, and vice
versa. I propose to think of institutions as entities whose impact on
the individual promotes behavior leading to their reproduction. If these
entities are relatively stable, as are institutions, they will be reproduced in part through psychological processes. To say institutions have
an impact on individuals, in other words, is not to say they have the
same kind of impact as a car hitting a tree.

It is one thing to recognize the individual's crucial mediating role,
but quite another to be bowled over into supposing that institutions as
such must be meaningful to their participants or effectively decoded
by them. Although institutions induce behavior that generates institutions in a way that must make psychological sense, institutionally
relevant behavior need not be intentional, intended, or even recognized as such. When institutions have their own ontological identity,
social reality and conceptions of it do not automatically operate in
tandem, *pace* the common view of conventionalists. Chapter 1 begins
weaning the institutional context from individual psychology.

Realism assures us that those reciprocal influences which we are
then in a position to attribute to institutions and participants are physically realized in ways that, in principle, are comprehensible to sci-

ence. As aggregates of human beings, institutions are, unproblematically, entities determined by their participants. As distinct physical entities, institutions can be distinct social forces. The resulting interactions between individuals and institutions, it turns out, are compatible with some plausible assumptions about individuals. The persistence of institutions is neither miraculous nor accidental.

Since the conceptions of participants do not literally constitute institutions in the strong sense of that philosophically loaded term, there can be alternative conceptions of those selfsame social entities. For all the talk of realism, then, what emerges in these pages is a conception of institutions consistent with many conventionalist insights of modern social theory and antirealist philosophy of (social) science. To some extent, the result is realism in sheep's clothing. Or to give it a more positive slant, we can call it domesticated realism. Yet this bow to conventionalism is not at the cost of wildly exaggerating the creative and cognitive powers, or concerns, of human beings.

Once the book's philosophical assumptions are laid out, along with the resulting distinction between institutions and conventions, the remaining chapters accomplish two things. One, they document the failure of particular social scientific theories to reconcile the dual status of institutions as products and constraints. The principal focus is the popular rational choice approach, including the new institutionalism and David Lewis's (1969) seminal work on conventions. There is a sidelong glance at sociological approaches, Marxist theory, and recent neo-Weberian discussions of the state.

Two, the remaining chapters develop an alternative conception of institutions, which I have labeled *institutional realism*. This includes a detailed proposal for integrating a reconstructed rational choice approach into this more robust institutional analysis. As it turns out, rational choice theory, with its instrumentalist, "as-if" approach to belief and preference, offers the best way to translate into workable form my concern with externals, that is, with the persistence of appropriate behavioral output from a given range of institutional input. The theory's agnosticism about psychology makes it the perfect tool for focusing on institutional realities. In this case, an indifference usually justified by an esoteric philosophy of science (but cf. Tsebelis 1990:31–39) is theoretically motivated.

The modifications I recommend in the theory are designed to capture the way in which individuals are embedded in institutions. These modifications not only strengthen the conception of institutions developed here but also hold considerable promise for empirical research. I argue that the resulting model of human behavior is, nonetheless, a legitimate form of rational choice theory. In my book, this is good, given the theory's well-known virtues: perspicuousness and formal clarity, the power of a deductive apparatus, the promise of analytic generality reaching beyond the statistical generalizations of behavioralism, the outline of an actual mechanism by which outcomes occur, and a meticulous attention to the macro-micro relations so important to this book.

A significant recent development is Marxist rational choice theory (e.g., Roemer 1982). It should ward off charges that the rational choice approach is politically biased. Though rational choice theory has also been widely criticized for its synoptic approach to human decision making, for present purposes this is one of its best assets. By relying on its understanding of human behavior, we are giving individuals all the intellectual resources they need to confirm a conventionalist view of institutions. If any approach can save conventionalism, or reveal its inherent limitations, rational choice is it.

I apply the ensuing conception of institutions, in any case, to prisoners' dilemma problems, which the standard rational choice analysis expects institutions to solve. The proposed modification of rational choice theory comes into its own here. Since the proof is in the pudding, I focus this institutionally sensitized version of rational choice on the persistent problem of explaining why rational voters participate in mass elections, and conclude that the resulting model rationalizes positive turnout even from large electorates.

I also consider one other challenge posed by standard (that is, conventionalist) rational choice theory. Assume that fully rational agents will make efficient use of all the information they have about their environment. At equilibrium, their rational expectations about the social order and the actual behavior of the social order should converge. Social regularities thus become transparent and conventionalism is rescued. Among these social regularities, institutions, if anything, should exhibit the sort of patterns that can be anticipated; and if they can be anticipated, fully rational actors will do so. How, in the face of rational expectations, can institutional realism assert the distinct efficacy of institutionalized regularities of behavior?

By affirming the possibility of social order without institutions in a full-bodied sense, rational expectations theory becomes the individualistic analog of Marxism. When one finds institutional effects that survive even rational expectations, one truly deepens the idea that institutions structure the choices for rational agents.

If institutions do not simply reflect the rational decision making of participants, neither can one expect rational decision makers simply to reflect institutional arrangements. There may be slack between the two. On the macro side, this requires clarifying the role of institutional rules in providing relevant information to the participants. Rules are featured in most accounts of how institutions operate and are understood by participants, but their status under my ontological assumptions is certainly delicate. On the micro side, I treat ideology as a particular way of framing decisions in order to clarify the alternative "semantic" relations between fully rational decision makers and their institutionalized environments. The selfsame institution can coexist with alternative conceptions of it.

Ideology in this sense is not just a substitute for information, the standard rational choice interpretation, but it also determines basic, alternative categorizations of social experience. Yet even though ideologies influence people's understanding of their institutional environment, having them, I conclude, is entirely consistent with rational choice. This is fortunate. Not only is ideological thinking an important component of institutional realism; it squares with basic experimental findings in psychology as well.

The contrast between the ideological influences recognized by institutional realism and the transparency of institutions envisioned by conventionalism reintroduces those important practical issues raised by the debate between Samuel Huntington and Adam Przeworski, including the prospects for controlling or even dispensing with institutions. Presumably, transparent institutions are easier to master. It is also worth noting that academic interest in institutions and their control occurs at a time of—perhaps because of—the declining authority of institutions in the West. What freedoms do we gain from this decline and what exactly do we lose? What sort of collective decisions about our institutional framework is it possible for us to make? These are primarily questions for political science, since politics tests the limits of freedom within and from institutions. In the final chapter I examine what institutional realism says about these limits.

Rational choice theory is especially helpful in unpacking the political dimension of this issue: the possibility of using institutions to shape institutions. Existing applications of the rational choice method to state-of-nature theory, constitutional choice, and collective decision making offer enormous opportunities for exploring this dimension. They also offer additional insights into the current limitations of conventionalist analyses of institutions. The conclusions I reach concerning the political control of institutions are somewhat pessimistic, as against those who would hope to deinstitutionalize social life or turn institutions into pure objects of collective choice. Perhaps these conclusions can still be counted optimistic insofar as to be fully human, in my view, is to be part of institutions.

Institutions represent—in a sense, *are*—our connectedness. But while this, arguably, is a nice thing to say about institutions, it is also indefensibly vague. By the end of the book, its real meaning will have been cashed out in terms of a particular conception of institutions coupled with a specific model of rational choice. They are combined in order to make better sense of the subtle relation of individual part to institutional whole.

What emerges in these pages, then, is a conception of institutions capable of doing justice to the ways in which participants and institutions influence one another. In terms of existing intellectual markers, once again, this conception avoids the reification of abstract institutional structure, yet resists the extreme methodological individualism one associates with most rational choice theory. A word of caution, however: the apparent safety and obviousness of adopting a middle-of-the-road position are deceptive.

True, there is nothing easier than to resolve the conflict between these conceptual extremes simply by declaring that institutions and individuals affect one another. The problem with this direct resolution is twofold. First, a simple agreement to split the difference overlooks the stubborn obstacles to a coherent solution. The parties to such an agreement cannot begin to see why the conceptual extremes ever appealed to anyone. Second, and more important, those who fail to appreciate the genuine analytical considerations fueling these extremes are bound, in the end, to embrace them. As we will see, researchers who have sought to make progress by leapfrogging toward the middle have actually wound up tracing a closed loop.

1.

Philosophical Preliminaries

Do institutions exist? Do they exist, that is, in the same sense as knives and forks, daisies, the current American president, and quarks and supernovas? For some, the very question mistakenly conflates social constructs and natural objects. For others, it represents a towering irrelevance. And still others, particularly among the philosophically sophisticated, do not see it as wrong so much as wrongheaded. To them, traditional questions of ontology and existence have been put to rest by a formidable array of thinkers including Hilary Putnam, Nelson Goodman, Jacques Derrida, Martin Heidegger, and Richard Rorty.

Clarifying one's ontology—what one claims to exist—ought to be an uncontroversial way to start any study. Ontology, after all, is literally everything there is to discuss. Yet ontology is the issue underlying the troubled distinction between conventions and institutions. Reflecting doubts nonrealists both articulate and defend, conventionalism strains to avoid a commitment to institutional entities, entities that institutional realism happily embraces.

The idea of a mind-independent world composed of objects not necessarily of our own making thus faces renewed challenge that finds expression in contemporary social and political theory. Doubt is not just aimed at the concepts of truth and knowledge, as with old-fashioned skepticism. Rather, much of contemporary theory and philosophy rejects the ontological ballast that, for many, gives these notions meaning. According to this more recent view, there are no objects to be truthful or knowledgeable about.

Modern skeptics renounce what they often describe as metaphysical realism, a belief in objects existing independently of worldviews and methods of reasoning. To them, Gertrude Stein's complaint about Oakland applies to reality generally: there is no there there. The modern alternative is to fill the void by defining truth and knowledge about reality as entirely relative to our worldviews or accepted standards of deliberation and judgment.[1]

My aim in this chapter is not to present a sustained argument for ontological realism applied to institutions. Indeed, to those already positively disposed toward realism, the message of the following two sections might well be gratuitous. In those sections I do hope, nonetheless, to clarify what my realism does and does not entail, and to weaken, however slightly, the conviction of too many astute social and political theorists that this is a position no reasonably well informed person could hold. With this breathing room secured, I will explore the role ontological realism plays in conceptualizing the distinction between a convention and an institution.

An institution, I have said, is a physical aggregate of participants organized in such a way that their behavior, in the aggregate, serves to reproduce the relevant regularity of behavior. This happens because the remaining aggregate which each participant encounters acts as an unavoidable constraint on his behavior. In turn, rational adaptation to this constraint determines a behavioral disposition that helps constitute an analogous constraint on other participants.

What realism about institutions accomplishes, then, is a certain easing of the pressure felt by theorists to develop what are ultimately psychological explanations for institutional persistence. If institutional realism is correct, a theorist does not risk losing the objects of her analysis whenever she relaxes the assumption that participants must always supervise them. Realism generates a corresponding openness to the possibility that institutions can exist on their own without getting regular checkups from their members. Realism per se does not prove that theories inspired by conventionalism are wrong, or that institutionally realist theories are correct. It creates an analytically level playing field in which each theory can be judged on its own merits, unhampered by any presumption that the realist approach is intrinsically unattractive or self-refuting or that the conventionalist approach is unavoidable.

Not that I plan to be so noncommittal in this book. Here realist considerations will be used to motivate a particular, positive conception of institutions. Although it will be fully developed later, this conception plays an important background role even in this initial chapter. Technically, I understand an institution as a game rather than as a solution to some broader, contemporaneous game or social problem. The game's structure, which constitutes the constraints on institutional participants, is determined by their behavioral dispositions.

In advancing his goals within those constraints, each player helps reproduce the institutional structure, wittingly or unwittingly.

Although it is consistent with the full rationality of the participants, institutional stability will not require these players to prefer the existing structure to untold numbers of imagined alternatives. To anticipate an important formal consideration, the reproduction of the institution does not even assume that participants factor in the transaction costs of organizing alternative arrangements.

1.

I ask what it means for institutions to exist, since it is not a foregone conclusion that they do exist. Common sense, intuition, and ordinary language provide insufficient guidance. Indeed, it is by no means unusual for scientists to challenge the ontological import of what were once commonly employed concepts, terms, or symbols (such as *witch*). Nor do these challenges typically send respondents into a metaphysical tailspin. Ontological questions are easily understood, however, because other parts of the critic's ontology are held fixed. In other words, it is easy for us to make sense of questions about particular ontological claims insofar as these questions take ontology in the larger sense for granted.

Thus we may deny there is a god Ra, even though the ancient Egyptians believed in it, but we usually understand this denial as a specific claim about the referential impotence of an existing hieroglyphic token used by actual people. Similarly, when we say that the residents of Salem were wrong about there being witches, we are not denying the existence of the very individuals they persecuted or some of the unusual behavior that might have provoked the apprehension of the community. And the claim that lipoproteins are only a recent discovery is perfectly credible without imagining that their first moment of existence coincided with the moment scientists or the typical user of the language first conceptualized them.

Ideally, the question of institutional existence would be pursued in this framework. One would worry about whether these specific things really exist and, insofar as fairly theoretical entities are at issue, one would pursue this question by seeing how the positing of institutions coheres with other knowledge—in particular, whether they are part of the best social scientific explanation for certain regularities of behavior or other social phenomena. Given the physically oriented definition of institutions I will soon offer, establishing the sheer claim of existence turns out to be relatively easy. The real trick is to show that positing the entities I define as institutions solves some existing social scientific problems.

Social entities defined this way, unfortunately, face a broader skepticism about ontology, a skepticism particularly virulent among social and political theorists. This deeper skepticism comes at a price, nonetheless, since it is less easily understood than a focused doubt about a particular concept. What does general ontological skepticism mean? It is not equivalent to a "linguistic idealism" which says words or social interpretations are all there is. That would just be an implausible ontology. Nor does it treat all objects as mental creations, the view of old-fashioned idealism. Finally, it is not a proposal to banish every linguistic form purporting to have ontological significance, such as *There exists* and *There are*. Rather, it claims that although reality does not typically consist of mental entities, it is nonetheless constructed, not found. Institutions, in particular, are social constructs; accordingly, there is no separating institutional reality and concepts of it, since this reality is nothing more than the correlate of our credible social concepts.

In principle, antirealism of this sort might be applied only to institutions and other social objects. Certainly, it is much more plausible in this arena. Social objects are relative newcomers in the universe and, while not immune from the laws of nature, have distinctly nonphysical properties. Yet the idea that social objects have no independent ontological standing, an idea that seems to license their special methodological treatment, is profoundly rooted in a more general skepticism about ontology.

Consider Nelson Goodman's (1984:36) example of a constellation of stars. Are we to believe, asks Goodman, that a given constellation exists before human beings carve it out of the multitude of stars in the sky? No, "a constellation becomes such only through being chosen from among all configurations." Since constellations have been socially significant objects of mythmaking and storytelling, this is a particularly apt example for social scientists.

It is not, however, a particularly good illustration for antirealists. Constellations may be pure constructions, but their construction presupposes stars as building materials.[2] This example, in short, can be construed to make an ontological point *against* all those who find that the social construction of reality challenges, rather than presupposes, realism: the whole notion of conceptual imposition requires the existence of things on which we impose our concepts. This distinction, moreover, defangs some of social constructionism's broader claims about the tenuous, concept-laden status of social objects.

Followers of Wittgenstein, for instance, emphasize the role of the electoral context in defining a vote; and so-called constitutivists argue that the identity of the vote is determined, is "constituted," by the concepts and intentions voters bring to it (e.g., Taylor 1985). When isolated from the voter's intentions and beliefs, they argue, voting loses its social identity and is demoted to meaningless behavior. For this reason, social objects depend on meaningful recognition for their social efficacy. When they lose their perceived significance, they automatically forfeit their standing as distinct, socially important entities.

I do not question the contextualist thesis about voting and other social behavior, particularly in light of the contextual role I assign to institutions. But I would warn its purveyors: dependence on context does not change the fact that the act of voting itself is the vote, not the electoral context or the voter's intention. These contextual influences do not make the idea of an independent ontology suspect. The physical act—in a word, the behavior—is still the political event of voting, even if it can be truthfully described as such only by virtue of its context. There are not two things, the marking of the ballot and the vote, but one thing which can be characterized in different ways.[3]

Charles Taylor (1985) seems to appreciate this point despite the far-reaching claims often made for his constitutivist position. Although he (1985:34) insists, for example, that chess depends on the constitutive rules players understand themselves to be following—how the knight moves and so forth—he also recognizes that even in the absence of this understanding it "would still, of course, be the activity of pushing a wooden piece around the board . . . but this is not chess any longer."

To the realist, Taylor's attractive distinction boils down to this. Suppose the notion of a game includes its players. Since the original players, with their particular understanding, are no longer pushing the pieces, the substitutes now innocently moving them represent a physically and therefore ontologically distinct group. After their arrival, one may no longer be justified in describing their otherwise similar movements as chess play. This redescription, however, in no way undermines realism. The apparently magical notion of constitution merely recognizes that the ontology of chess includes not only the actions but also the brains of players. Even if behaviors are held constant, different brains can mean a different game, or no game at all.

Having made this concession to the constitutivists, I would demand one from them. The behavior of the substitute players is as it is, notwithstanding psychological differences of otherwise great importance. Therefore it could be true that the newcomers will continue to reproduce gamelike behavior, perhaps under a different label, *and* that this collection of behaviors will continue to have no less of a social impact than its original counterpart had. It could be true insofar as the relevant social object, in this case the gamelike collection of behaviors, is an entity distinct from specific beliefs or intentions.

Distinct existence may not be a sufficient condition for social efficacy, but to the realist it does satisfy a necessary condition. Constitutivism, on the other hand, has transformed an empirical claim about the conditions under which social arrangements matter into a planted axiom. Having defined institutions in terms of the meanings participants attach to their behavior, the constitutivist puts institutions on a relatively short psychological leash. Existence becomes a question of meaningfulness. Yet if the objects of participant conceptualization and belief can exist independently of these contextual factors, then this leash begins to look arbitrarily short, pre-Copernican.[4] Perhaps, the key to the institutionalization of behavior is precisely its independence from specific psychological supervision by the participants.

Faced with this demotion of its central vision, strong constitutivism is induced to radicalize its otherwise unpretentious idea of social construction. Unwilling to accept that our verdict on social construction is contingent on the results of ordinary social science, constitutivists portray the reality studied by ordinary science as itself an example of construction. In this way, the limited issue of realism in the social sciences spills over into a debate concerning more general issues of metaphysics, and a rather mundane point becomes the basis for an entire philosophical vision.

Continuing the debate along those lines, Goodman (1984) applies conventionalism to the stars that constellations connect, to voters and the ballots they mark, and so on down the line, from the largest configurations of objects to the smallest. According to this full-fledged conventionalism, there is no genuinely foundational material out of which constellations, votes, and chess games are constructed, no background collection of objects from which the creators of worlds can carve out their objects and kinds. When it comes to the atoms of our system, in short, there is no distinction between categorizations and things categorized.

This thoroughgoing notion of construction is a double-edged sword: if there is no background or building materials, it is difficult to see in what sense constellations or anything else are constructed. Certainly there is not construction in the sense of "selection" from a given population of objects. Goodman's answer to this rejoinder is to declare flat-footedly that it is equally correct, though contradictory, to say that our interpretations of the world both correspond to and are worlds. I read this response as a reductio ad absurdum of the basic position. Designed to avoid the supposed mistakes of idealism and realism, Goodman's doctrine of "irrealism" surrenders to both, by regarding worlds as interpretations and as the things interpreted. And the problems facing Goodman's irrealism are not idiosyncratic. He is simply more resolute, rigorous, and clearer than many of his better known counterparts.

2.

Antirealists might object that the problematic inference that reality and interpretation are redundant counterparts is a two-way street. When world and true interpretation mirror each other, what is to be said for taking the *world* seriously as a collection of independent objects?[5] There are in fact many ingenious arguments for believing in the continuing virtues of realism. Some have contended that so-called metaphysical realism is an empirical claim that helps us explain the achievements of science and other cognitive successes (e.g., Devitt 1984; Field 1986a). Attacks against realism, it is also argued, take an excessively linguistic view of science. Actual scientific theorizing is intertwined with a lot of nonverbal, experimental interaction with things (see Cartwright 1983; Hacking 1983).

I believe that there is an important assumption unifying these distinct defenses. For the version of metaphysical realism I support, questions about ontology are questions for science, not first philosophy. No one can prove philosophically that there is an independent reality beyond what is disclosed when scientists examine and exhibit our relations with it. But this is not because scientific theory is a linguistic substitute for the genuine article, ontology. For modern realists, science is just the refined means for advancing the original, philosophical project of talking about belief-independent objects.

> Now how is all this robust realism to be reconciled with the barren [philosophical] scene that I have just been depicting? The answer is naturalism: the recognition that it is within science itself, and not in some prior philosophy, that reality is to be identified and described. The semantical considerations that seemed to undermine all this were concerned not with assessing reality but with analyzing method and evidence. (Quine 1981:21)

The term *metaphysical* thus proves to be misleading. The proposed version of realism renounces the unenviable task of apodictically demonstrating the existence of an independent reality. It looks instead to the physical and social sciences to adjudicate specific existence claims, the original point of ontological questions. Understood thus, philosophical realism plays largely a negative role. It clears away those ontological prejudices that prevent too many theorists from confronting institutions as they are, as opposed to laboring under the supposition that institutions must be demoted to constructs or conventions in order for them to be intelligible.

To some, this negative approach forfeits realism itself, insofar as our specific understanding of reality is determined to be the correlate of our credible concepts, now understood as scientific concepts with scientific credibility. "Reality" becomes a pointless conceptual adjunct to scientific posits. A realist defense would throw the irrealists' criticism back at them: why do you think you can step out of science's formulation of ontology in order to question whether it delivers on the original promise of realism? That the realist knows no better argument than a scientific one for the reality of the posits of science only means that the realist's argument has been refined, not that it has been forsaken. The modern interpretation of metaphysical realism adds nothing, in the end, to what science says because on this topic there is no better way to say it. The realist is still justified in being concerned about the reality of what is, as best science understands what is.[6]

3.

In institutional realism, the existence of an object, even a social object, is independent of culture.[7] This does not preclude institutional realists from using participant beliefs or intentions to pick out objects of interest. In fact, consistent with realism one can argue that such objects as the act of voting are specifiable only by virtue of the beliefs and intentions of the voters. Yet regardless of how they are specified, these objects exist independently of the particular specification. Specification within a culture or by observers is in part an act of discovery, not of creation. Social life does not begin at conception.

The picture I want to convey is one of observers and participants living in a common world, albeit a world to which they may have different reactions, bring different concerns, and which they may experience at different locations in differing, limited segments.[8] Each institutional component of this world is a sum of spatiotemporal regions, specifically, spatiotemporal segments—time slices—of human beings.[9] Institutions, then, are physical wholes composed of human parts. The pertinent segments of these human parts extend over the times in which people do whatever is relevant to the particular institution, be it voting, staying married, obeying, commanding, or signing or adhering to a contract. There is no harm, and a great deal of convenience, in defining these segments themselves as whole human beings extended in the space and time occupied during their institutional participation. Thus an electoral institutions is composed of flesh-and-blood candidates campaigning, voters voting, electoral officials supervising, and registrars registering, among others.

From another angle, institutions are collections of social relations understood in terms of relational descriptions such as *votes for, obeys, is subordinate to, is married to,* and the like. Just as *husband* is true of flesh-and-blood individuals and need not imply a separate entity called husbandhood, so too can relational descriptions such as *is the husband of* apply to pairs or n-tuples of individuals without additional ontological commitments. Compounding all the human time slices making up these relations yields a physical aggregate of human life called an institution—an aggregate, one might say, that gives new meaning to the notion of body politic. An important point to note for later discussion is that in relation to each participant an institution is a distinct, albeit not a discrete, entity.

Although this characterization captures much of what the language of institutional rules, norms, and roles is meant to convey, there is a crucial difference. The institutional arrangement described in those terms is understood by conventionalists to reflect the beliefs and attitudes of the participants. Human agency defines the institution. Indeed, even those students of institutions who are inclined to spurn the methodological individualism anchoring this psychologization of institutions are apt to take its underlying conventionalism to a higher level: against individualists they argue that institutions can act, have preferences, achieve goals, and so forth.

Institutional realism, by contrast, can understand institutions to be *conditions* under which institutional participants operate. They need not be actors, agents, or otherwise higher-order supervisors in people's lives, but can simply be constraints to which agents submit, a collection of behavioral channels they run either well or indifferently.

Clearly this represents only a first step toward a serious analysis of institutions. To say an institution is an aggregate is to say far too little. But before discussing the details, I want to address an opposite concern, that I have already said too much. I have defined an institution in terms of specific flesh-and-blood individuals, whereas some definitions focus on certain abstracted behavioral relations among them. If one follows my broader approach, an institution apparently consists of foot scratching, breathing, digesting, and other irrelevant activities (cf. Easton 1979:35–45).

This objection correctly recognizes that in order to describe, one necessarily must abstract from detail. It is unnecessary, however, to abstract from detail by invoking abstract entities. Talk of (behavioral) systems or "levels of analysis," which was popular among social theorists in the 1950s and 1960s, only obscures the crucial ontological distinction between things and their descriptions. Thus I say yes to levels of *analysis*. Some characterizations of an object are appropriately more general than others. Fido can truly be described as a dog without mentioning how many fleas he has. Yet I say no to *levels* of analysis. When Shylock asks, "hath not a Jew hands, organs, dimensions . . . ?" he correctly understands that having a social identity is fully consistent with being a physical object. Analysis at a different "level" remains an analysis of the selfsame thing described in a different way. Different levels of analysis, then, do not entail different levels of reality.[10]

A related objection to this particular ontology is that an institution is not simply a matter of what is, but of what can be. Institutions dictate the possible ways participants can act. Since much of this book will focus on institutional constraint, I do not want to condense that more comprehensive discussion here. For now, let us say that the possible actions and reactions of the participants in an institutional relation, such as master and slave, are inscribed in the bodies of those actors and any other relevant parties. As with levels of analysis, the behavioral dispositions of each can be understood in terms of a direct description of the people involved. There is no need to commit oneself to an increasingly complex hierarchy of levels of reality.

Finally, it might seem as though I have purchased freedom from conventionalist restrictions at a very high price, namely, by enshrining as "objects" oddly gerrymandered collections of disparate people. Defined in this way, an institution might not seem to be a true object, let alone a constraint. It becomes an artificial symbol in the fight against conventionalism.

Institutional realism actually rests on a doctrine that can be called ontological egalitarianism. Following Quine (1981), Field (1985), Hellman and Thompson (1975), and Noonan (1980), I am supposing that the world consists of four-dimensional spacetime, which is the kind of universe much of modern physics seems to confirm (e.g., Friedman 1983).[11] The denizens of this universe are basically *any* of its spatiotemporal regions, however disconnected, gerrymandered, or otherwise artificial. Does this mean I propose to treat as an object the total region occupied by, say, my shoes, Julius Caesar's thumb in 46 B.C., and the moon? Yes, it is an object according to this egalitarian view, though a scientifically uninteresting one. By the same token, the physical behaviors that count as voting, though important to political science, are also physically heterogeneous, and are artificial to the physicist and perhaps to the members of a tribe in New Guinea.

Even the institutional realist will not find all these spacetime objects to be equally interesting, useful, comprehensible, or morally significant. There are more objects in this universe than any finite language-users could describe, let alone care about. Still, all exist, and the universe itself does not play favorites. It is indeed with this in mind that I began the chapter by asserting that institutions exist in the same sense as supernovas, presidents, and daisies.

Similarly, relational descriptions tying objects together—*son of, slave of, president of, votes for, interrogates*—are not, according to this doctrine, ontologically superior to other collections of objects. They are just a few of the myriad overlays one can place on the world, again some more interesting than others. Thus the idea of real relations, internal relations, or constitutive relations does no better than other attempts to grant a privileged ontological status to particular parts of the world. The world itself does not distinguish among them.[12] Most important, they may not even be distinguished by agents in the world.

The egalitarian approach to ontology thus aids institutional realism in two important respects. One, absent egalitarianism, the definition of institutions as aggregates of particular time slices of human beings would fail the most cursory test for face validity. If, on the other hand, such aggregates exist whenever their components do, the issue of institutional existence becomes relatively straightforward. The only real question is the scientific utility of the definition.

Two, the egalitarian approach implies a great degree of ontological homogeneity in the world insofar as everything is equally a region of the same underlying material. This proves useful for explaining how seemingly abstract objects like institutions can constrain concrete human beings. Specifically, institutions can operate as constraints without being compact objects. Their influence on individual behavior does not have to parallel the impact of a shove on someone who falls down the stairs. The power of institutions can be more subtle and diffuse.

At first blush, ontological egalitarianism might even seem attractive to the conventionalist, since it provides a common backdrop legitimating the idea of alternative interpretations of reality (Newton-Smith 1982:113–14). Understood this way, egalitarianism apparently grounds the idea of culture-specific ways of characterizing the world. Yet it would be a mistake to infer from this specific agreement that the egalitarianism informing institutional realism is inconsequential. Egalitarianism goes to the heart of conventionalism's quandary over institutions.

For it is one thing to believe that since conceptions of reality can categorize and recategorize reality as needed, social concepts are in principle infinitely varied. It is quite another thing to think that the categorized and recategorized pieces of the world are constituted, come into and out of existence, with each categorization. Conventionalism provides, perhaps, one plausible account of how institutions are created. In the end, it will leave us dumbfounded as to how these creations have any effect on their creators. When institutions are created and destroyed at will, they are too humble to accomplish the tasks for which they are presumably created. Starting with the next chapter, we will see conventionalist analyses of institutions wrestling with this dilemma.

4.

Which human aggregates are worth recognizing as institutions? Conventionalism tends to invoke institutions in order to explain and characterize the regularities of behavior associated with social and

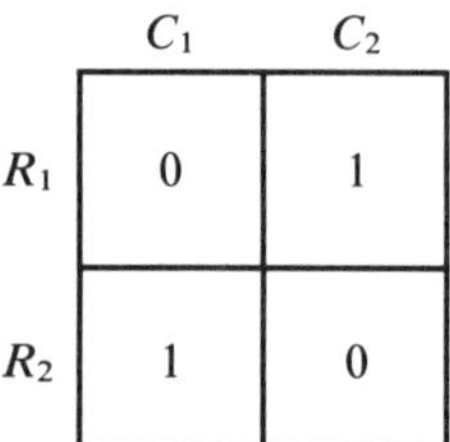

Figure 1. Convention Problem

political order. There is no reason not to accept this view. The effect of the institution on behavior and behavioral dispositions, I stipulate, is to reproduce the original situation again and again. An institution thus comprises both recurrent situations and regularities in the responses to them. This means that institutional realism takes as its *explanandum* what the concept of a convention, loosely speaking, is also designed to explain. The overlap is important: if realism refuses to acknowledge even this part of the original conventionalist project, it does not so much challenge conventionalism as change the subject.

To the conventionalist, however, the macro-level regularity of behavior associated with social order is handily specified and explained by anchoring it in the psychology of the participants. To Hobbes, for example, social order is the product of a desperate agreement among individuals in the state of nature. To Locke, civil society and the institutions of the state arise serially rather than simultaneously, but they reflect roughly the same motivation attributed by Hobbes, namely, individual interest. To Talcott Parsons (1968), the Hobbesian problem of order cannot be solved by purely self-interested, purposive agents. Only shared norms and their superordinate values allow people to institutionalize their interactions on the basis of stable, complementary expectations. Insofar as this normative hierarchy is internalized by the relevant parties, it dictates appropriate modes of conduct, which both reflect and help reproduce the norms themselves.

Following David Lewis (1969:12), consider a situation in which two people, R and C, are induced to establish a small bit of social order, a conventional regularity of behavior in response to a mundane problem: they have been cut off from a phone conversation they would like to resume. If just one of them calls back, they are both happy; whereas if both call or fail to call, they are unhappy. Let R_1 and C_1 denote calling back by R and C respectively, and let R_2 and C_2 denote not calling back by R and C respectively. This sets up a matrix of possible outcomes: with a '1' in a box denoting happiness for both and a '0' denoting unhappiness for both (fig. 1). R and C are, in effect, trying to coordinate their behavior. A convention, any convention, about who calls back would be useful to them. Indeed, Lewis suggests that under circumstances such as these, conventions will arise, persisting as long as the problems they solve recur. Strictly speaking, institutions differ from conventions, even in the conventionalist account, since they are not directly self-policing. Yet as we will see, the implied coordination of intent and belief is still the backbone of the conventionalist's institutional analysis.[13]

What does institutional realism find wrong with Lewis's conventionalist account of social order? The answer is not that institutions have been defined as aggregates of people whereas conventions are behavioral regularities in equilibrium. While some might consider the latter to be properties or similar abstractions, there is a way to translate the one characterization into the other. Suppose a regularity of behavior deserves to be called an institution. Then this regularity of behavior can be described in terms of the recurrent collection of events comprising it. And these events can be described in terms of the human time slices composing them, the individual actions over time.[14] So from the institutional realist's perspective, the emphasis on regularities does not distinguish a convention from an institution.

Yet conventionalism, as we have seen, defines these regularities of behavior in terms of participant preferences and expectations. The convention about phoning, for example, arises when a particular behavioral regularity meshes with the expectations and preferences of the agents responsible for it. Their expectations and preferences, in turn, are determined by some combination of interests and norms. Conventions, then, are not just recurrent social situations. They are stable regularities of behavior that develop because of the way people intentionally respond to those recurrent situations.[15] What is stabilized, in effect, are the expectations people bring to their situation. When their expectations are stable, their responses become predictable. This ensures that their situation will recur, since each occurrence stimulates the intentional reproduction of the symptomatic regularity.

Looking at the way behavioral regularities mesh with individual expectations and preferences, institutional realism asks whether this tight fit is necessary to explain the regularities. In an electoral institution, for instance, particular regularities of behavior are produced and reproduced by the participants. Conventionalists emphasize the responsibility of human agents for this result, their essential contribution to the creation and re-creation of the institution as an intended object of their actions and deliberations. By contrast, institutional realism emphasizes the extent to which this reproduction can take place in ways not requiring conscious human supervision or implicit understandings and agreements—in a word, decisions to reproduce the regularities.

In explanatory terms, institutional realism focuses on the extent to which institutional regularities of behavior become a stable occurrence as a result, at least in part, of the institutional aggregate itself. The conventionalist, of course, has a different explanation for this stability. Elections, to return to politics, take place because each participant expects others to engage in the relevant behavior and knows that these expectations are generally shared. Institutional realism has to find another way to make sense of this arrangement, using the regularity of behavior to help explain its own existence.

Consider William Connolly's (1981:7–18) observation that a well-documented regularity about elections such as Duverger's law survives even if voters enter the booth blindfolded and pull levers at random. Under these bizarre circumstances, winner-takes-all rules would still tend to produce two-party systems. This example, he argues, shows the vacuity of the nonconventionalist approach by underscoring the distance between one of the best social scientific laws and the meaningful electoral process it purports to explain: what is not even an election by most people's definition, including the participants', remains subject to social scientific electoral analysis.

Institutional realists would see a different moral: the weakness of the epistemic requirements for institutional stability. An electoral institution can survive even when participant psychologies are essentially ignored. The institution persists, in other words, despite these enormous psychological changes.

I want, then, to join conventionalism in ascribing to institutions a characteristic ability to reproduce their own constraints, but to limit the amount of the institution that participants are required, as matter of definition, to recognize or intend. Institutional realism does not find it necessary to define an institution by the participants' beliefs and intentions in order to make sense of its constraints on the individual. Whereas the center of gravity for conventionalism is the alleged psychological substratum of the behavioral equilibrium, the center of gravity for the institutional analysis is the behavioral equilibrium itself. The persistence of the regularity as a whole does not, for that reason, become a miracle. Rather, something in the operation of the regularity—and not just the agents' psychologies—must help account for its stability.

To clarify the differences and similarities between institutions and the conventions for which they are often mistaken, it will be helpful to have a more explicit definition of a conventional regularity of behavior. Lewis's (1969) analysis provides the contemporary foundation for much of the articulate conventionalist theorizing about institutions and, therefore, is a useful place to begin.

Lewis defines a convention as a regularity of behavior concerning a recurrent situation for which it is true, and is common knowledge, that (1) everyone conforms to the regularity, (2) everyone expects everyone to conform, (3) everyone prefers to conform, and (4) everyone prefers that everyone conform.[16] Thus a universally understood rule about which party to a phone conversation calls back is conventional in Lewis's sense since any of a number of rules will equally satisfy everyone, so long as each knows—and knows that each knows—about the rule. Red and green traffic lights are also conventional since apparently there is nothing natural or unavoidable about this particular assignment of roles to the two colors. It does not matter which color plays which role, so long as one color, any color, is assigned one and only one role by all drivers. Conventions arise and persist only because people want them to persist.

But what remains of this basic analysis when its conventionalist underpinnings are stripped away? To answer this question, let us first explore what happens when Lewis's original definition is modified by substituting a common belief requirement for the common knowledge requirement. Here are the new criteria: each individual (1) conforms to the regularity, (2) expects everyone to conform to it, (3) prefers to conform to it, (4) prefers that everyone conform to it, and (5) believes everyone prefers to conform to it.

Since I respect Lewis's right to define conventions as he pleases, I will not call this belief-based system a convention. The result, nonetheless, would certainly be convention-like save in one respect. The fact that there is conformity does not, in this case, directly or necessarily determine the beliefs needed to produce the regularity. The beliefs must be efficacious, but unlike knowledge they do not have to be accurate. A participant's beliefs about others can be wrong but still produce the appropriate behavior.

The resulting regularity is still clearly the product of the individual psychological states of the participants. Still, it is progress to recognize that common knowledge contributes nothing to the actual mechanism of the convention itself. Belief is sufficient, so long as everyone has the relevant preferences.

Belief suffices, but there are reasons why conventionalists might still consider knowledge to be the definitive psychological state. As people acquire beliefs about the current social state of affairs, they presumably learn of opportunities for coordination equilibria, as when one person calls back and one does not. They can take advantage of these opportunities by establishing conventions. The existence of the recurrent situation, therefore, helps explain why people develop beliefs about it and respond accordingly. Without getting mired in some rather difficult issues, let us say participants under these circumstances have warranted true beliefs about their situation; and having warranted true beliefs is, on many accounts, what constitutes having knowledge.[17] So knowledge ensures that people are successfully connected to the situations that generate conventions. They are not distracted by alternative interpretations.

The knowledge requirement, in short, plays two related roles for Lewis. First, there is certainly no point to defining conventions that cannot or will not be generated. Knowledge provides a coherent and fairly elegant explanation for their existence. Second, since beliefs vary among individuals but knowledge is knowledge, the identification of the behavioral regularity at issue becomes easier when the definition incorporates a more homogeneous psychological state than belief. For the conventionalist, remember, the identification of the regularity is ultimately at the mercy of the underlying psychology.

The telephone game illustrates the point in more concrete terms. One might think that R and C are successful so long as they act differently. Yet as Lewis notes, this represents a misunderstanding of the necessary conditions for success. Let R_1' and C_1' denote calling back by R and $C,$ respectively, when the person calling back is also the original caller; similarly, let R_2' and C_2' denote calling back by R and C, respectively, when the person who calls back is not the original caller. The resulting coordination game is identical to the first, except that equilibrium arises when R and C act the same way, not differently.

The moral, Lewis says, is this: "What is important about the combinations we are interested in is not that they are—under some description—uniform but that they are equilibria" (1969:12). So long as both parties want to resume their conversation, their actions need not enjoy a common or univocal social description. What matters is the equilibrium defined by their intentions and beliefs, not the actual sameness of their actions.

At first sight, Lewis undermines his definition of conventions, which requires participants to have knowledge of everyone's knowledge of everyone's knowledge concerning the regularity of behavior. In this framework, participants cannot remain indifferent to the way actions are described among themselves. For all practical purposes, common meanings are crucial.

What saves Lewis's analysis of conventions from contradiction is, in fact, his conventionalism. Evidently, the equilibrium that concerns him is an equilibrium of intention, belief, and reasoning on the part of R and C. The conditions characterizing a coordination equilibrium, in other words, are not external patterns of behavior but internal psychological states (this point will reemerge in chapters 4 and 5). These internal states are the real forces at work. However it is externally described, what is in equilibrium is ultimately the particular combination of beliefs and intentions generating the behavior. The observed regularities are as they are; their sole function is to cue the participants.

By displacing equilibria to the minds of the participants, Lewis can remain indifferent to the alternative ways a set of actions can be described. He sidesteps another problem as well. Were equilibrium defined in behavioral terms, his argument for being indifferent about the sameness of action would seem to demonstrate the superfluity of even this supposedly more basic concept.

To see this, note that the actions constituting such an equilibrium are the same only under some particular description. Likewise, a regularity of behavior is a diverse set of physical events that are in equilibrium only under some particular description. After all, the events that are judged to be recurrent or static under one description actually undergo numerous changes and reorganizations. For example, the people participating in equilibria—the same people to whom we ascribe a continually held set of beliefs and intentions—are continually reconstructed in a biological sense. So the notion of equilibrium, understood behaviorally, is as externally imposed as the idea of same action. And this is to say nothing of the complexity and flexibility allowed by the equilibrium concept itself, as a glance at modern macroeconomics will show.[18]

By psychologizing the concept of equilibrium, Lewis attempts to immunize himself against this argument. In his view, the observer's potential disagreement with the participants shows precisely why the participants' own identification of the relevant regularity has to be taken seriously. They are the ones who produce the regularity and they produce it, in part, because of the way they define it.

We have already seen, though, that this particular explanation for the knowledge condition is unpersuasive as a *definitional* requirement. The sheer persistence of a regularity of behavior does not require participant knowledge (warranted true belief). Rather, it depends only on the production of behavior that, for whatever reason, is sufficient to encourage all agents in their belief that continued production of the appropriate behavior is to their advantage. Lewis's insight shows how easy it is for an arrangement that fails to satisfy the criteria for a convention to mimic one (see Millikan 1984).

It seems to me, then, that the important reasons why conventionalists would be inclined to restrict the definition of conventions to situations where the participants have knowledge really reduce to one. The principal function of the knowledge requirement is to secure an exact correspondence between the beliefs of the participants and the regularity whose continuation provokes those beliefs. Knowledge guarantees that subjective belief and objective conditions will not go their separate ways, which could happen were there a gap between participant psychology and the convention. The possibility that objective conditions might have a life of their own does not have to be confronted and therefore does not have to be explained.

That one particular pattern rather than some other constitutes the continuing regularity is not an independent datum to the conventionalist. It is determined by the knowledge and preferences of the participants. Since the common knowledge condition guarantees that the regularity already exists in potential psychological form, the regularity qua regularity contributes to its own reproduction only in a passive sense. The series of events in question simply realizes the pattern or regularity that participants impose on them. Their expectations are confirmed and therefore the pattern continues. The regularity is operative, then, insofar as these participants act on the information that their expectations have in the past been fulfilled. In that sense, of course, a deer shot by hunters has an operative role insofar as the hunters will continue to go hunting because their expectations on this occasion were fulfilled.

The specific identity of the regularity as a particular pattern—say, calling back when your call has been cut off—counts as a regularity only because it is the pattern recognized or internally represented by the participants. Any additional explanatory weight one might have been tempted to ascribe to the regularity as such becomes an artifact of the common knowledge condition; the identity of the regularity has no distinct causal efficacy in Lewis's scheme.

Put another way, the problem the knowledge condition addresses is that any series of events realizes many regularities. If it is warm every Friday night when Ted and Sally meet at the park, this regularity of air temperature exists as an "external" datum in whatever sense the regularity they did pick out exists. After all, it is conceivable that the air temperature, rather than the day of the week, could have motivated them.[19]

In the conventionalist view, the participants are responsible for causally activating one of the patterns. The events making up the regularities, rather than the regularities themselves, do all the "external" work there is to be done, by providing a basis for the common knowledge developed by participants (which helps them meet the requirements for the definition of a convention) and by being among the causes of the behavior in question.

Lewis (1969:64–68) comes close to acknowledging this point. The knowledge sustaining a convention, he points out, can be *in sensu diviso.* Under this weaker condition, when the relevant situation occurs, each participant is merely prompted to believe of each of the other participants that he or she will at that time behave in a way which, by our lights, conforms to some particular regularity. Since there are no intertemporal beliefs, this is a regularity that need not know its name. The participants are not required to recognize the string of situations or instances of the regularity as linked under a description or pattern.

What sort of convention does this weakening permit? Imagine a series of situations concerning each of which the following is true. As in the matrix in figure 1, each participant distinguishes two kinds of action both for himself and for everyone else en masse; thus for each participant there are four possible outcomes. Each prefers two of the outcomes to either of the others and expects one of the two will occur. In each of the recurrent situations, however, the alternatives defined by the participants are different than in previous situations. Thus for the first occurrence, the alternatives might be to walk in the warm night air or not; in the second occurrence, they might be to meet in the park on Friday night or not; ad infinitum.

Lewis (1969:67), I gather, would consider this a convention so long as (1) observers can characterize each set of choices in terms of a regularity, and (2) in each situation there is common knowledge of everyone's preferences and expectations. But surely, there is no regularity in any active sense. And all that common knowledge really accomplishes here is to ensure that the disintegration of the convention does not go one step further. That would occur, for example, if in each situation participants had differing conceptions of the alternative actions but, for whatever reason, were still able to predict the behavior of other participants, relative to their conceptions, and prefer the outcomes designated as coordinated by observers (see the discussion of ideology in chapter 5). Common knowledge, by contrast, means that although no one identifies a regularity over time, one can still speak at each instance of *a* pattern. Yet this so-called pattern has no effect on the future. Indeed, it has no future.

There is one way in which the definition of conventions is commonly liberalized without blatantly jeopardizing its conventionalist underpinnings. Though conventionalism glorifies the psychology or conceptualizations built into social life, in practice it demotes them by refusing to attribute to participants an *explicit* or *conscious* psychology, as opposed to a subconscious, implicit, or tacit one.[20] So long as the imputed knowledge, preferences, and decisions to conform are tacit or latent, they can be plausibly "stretched" to cover the regularity as a whole.[21] In a way, the conventionalist's recognition of latent knowledge can be considered testimony to the limited applicability of the idea of conventions strictly understood.

Lewis (1969:63–64) does recognize the extent to which the knowledge supporting a convention can be nonverbal or even "potential." The latter is an understandable relaxation of the definition, but one that is grist for the institutional realist's mill. When do appeals to potential or explicit knowledge simply become empty gestures on behalf of an unnecessarily limited view of social order?

5.

To sum up, conventions are human products. They are patterns instrumentally selected to perform some needed task and are registered in the common consciousness of the participants. Like green and red lights, they have no social identity in themselves but are defined by the purposes they serve. These purposes, however, can be served with much weaker assumptions about the participants' psychology. What I would call institutional regularities can be maintained without the active intervention of comprehensive knowledge or beliefs. I would even say the same for the purposes themselves, that is, participant preferences and the choices they motivate. These need not take entire regularities of behavior as their object.

Why do conventionalists hesitate to acknowledge this within their characterization of conventions? The answer is that a convention, as a social object, is not merely explained by the participants' knowledge and beliefs; it is defined by them. Conventionalism, as a result, is forced to overestimate the role of individuals in producing the regularities that serve their purposes. The institutional realist is free to embrace the possibility of stable equilibria that are unintended and even unnoticed by the participants.

Once this distinctly conventionalist restriction is cast aside, regularities are liberated from the immediate plans, meanings, and supervision of the participants. If institutions are important, this weakened role for participant psychology signals a commensurately stronger role for the regularities themselves. Though unrecognized as such by the participants, stable regularities may provide just the right information and opportunities for choice to ensure their own persistence. While participants would still produce this kind of regularity in the literal, physical sense, it would not necessarily be the intended object of their actions. Accordingly, a common preference for this kind of regularity would not be required for its survival. No longer a mere creature of the people whose behavior sustains it, an institution would be a fact about their collective lives, about the way things are done, which participants might even recognize but still could not literally choose.

Although the real issue between the psychology of conventionalism and that of institutional realism is the assumed scope of the participants' beliefs, implicit or explicit, I do not want to overdramatize this contrast by insisting on restricted scope as a necessary condition for the existence of an institution. Institutions in any serious sense of the term will not disappear just because participants have become less ignorant. Yet limited scope remains an important consideration. For to recognize the *possibility* of beliefs with limited scope is to acknowledge that one must make sense of the idea that institutions do some of their own work.

I do not deny, of course, that some conventions arise in the intelligent way Lewis (1969) describes. Paul Revere's famous convention, "one if by land, two if by sea," is a clear example, and Lewis offers many more. Yet this should not deter us from pursuing the original project, namely, to explore the extent to which convention-like behavior can be nonconventional in the strict sense. Indeed, some have already expressed grave doubts about the utility of invoking full-blown conventions to explain what is ostensibly the most important example, language. Thus Millikan (1984:69) notes how much people can do, linguistically and otherwise, without having the full complement of knowledge Lewis requires, and conversely, how biologically "inefficient [having full knowledge] would be, if we take having intentions and beliefs to be real modifications of the nervous system!"[22]

We now have the beginnings of a concept of institutions that generalizes the idea of convention by broadening the kinds of psychology consistent with it. Having an ontological foundation allows institutions to assume an identity independent of the beliefs or intentions of the participants. This independence is worthwhile, in turn, only insofar as these liberated institutions do some work on their own. This requirement is both the most intriguing aspect of institutions and the most questionable. After all, if institutional regularities are fairly abstract entities relatively detached from the psychological forces operating within those who ultimately choose and behave, what sort of work can these regularities possibly do?

More pointedly, since the participants will be the proximate cause of any behavioral regularity associated with an institution, whether they know it or not, what good can positing institutions accomplish? If this objection were just an expression of blanket reductionism, it would not have to occupy us for long. There is every reason to maintain and perfect higher-level sciences. Considered in a more practical vein, on the other hand, as a reflection of Ockham's warning not to multiply entities beyond necessity, the objection carries considerable weight. Purely philosophical responses will not suffice.

The concept of a convention, by contrast, provides relief from these perplexities, albeit by indulging strong psychological assumptions. A conventional regularity is in the end a passive product, not a producer. The knowledge conditions assure us of that. So conventional regularities do no work on their own, and this fact, at the very least, allows theorists to avoid confronting the awkward question of how more "active" regularities could have an effect.

Put another way, conventional regularities are assured a distinguished role insofar as they are distinguished by their producers. They are not merely creatures of the observer. This seems to protect them from the kind of skepticism with which Marx, for example, approached observer-dependent concepts of society. "Men can be distinguished from animals by consciousness, by religion or anything else you like. They themselves begin to distinguish themselves from animals as soon as they begin to *produce* their means of subsistence." (Marx and Engels 1947:7).

Does this mean that institutions are less efficacious, less likely to persist, or less important in the life of a society than conventions? Not at all, provided that (1) the relation between individuals and institutions parallels or functionally simulates the relation between individuals and conventions, and (2) institutional entities have the required effect on society even when they are relatively invisible to the participants. Starting with the next chapter, I will show that there are particular social scientific problems which the positing of institutions helps resolve.

Institutions help account for their own persistence insofar as they become the conditions under which individuals produce behavior that reproduces the regularities.[23] These institutional conditions, in general, are disaggregated: participants need not have an overview of the institution as a whole. A participant, instead, can perceive an institution through its parts. As Marx and Engels (1968:97) observed, "Men make their own history, but they do not make it just as they please; they do not make it under circumstances chosen by themselves, but under circumstances directly encountered, given and transmitted from the past." Or, I would add, transmitted in the present.

People are encountered, individual committees meet, messages are received, congregations assemble, ballots are counted, and information is acquired. This disaggregation of impact is perfectly compatible with the view that participants are being affected by an institution. They are no more required to confront the institution as a whole than a victim of a stabbing is required to come in contact with every square inch of the knife. Nor must their understanding of the parts they do encounter agree with anyone else's.

As I noted above, I do not mean to preclude full comprehension in institutional settings, whose very stability may help make full comprehension possible. For institutionalization, in the end, is not a condition of required ignorance but the collective inability of participants to assume complete and unmediated control over social outcomes, even under otherwise ideal conditions. Full knowledge can be superfluous or ineffective insofar as individuals must still act within the confines of existing institutions. A convention requires the knowledge of the population in order to survive. An institution, on the other hand, does not rely on the complicity of its participants. It may, but need not be, maintained behind their backs.

The contrast between conventionalism and institutional realism is thus partly substantive and partly methodological. It is substantive to the extent that conventionalism adopts an unrealistic attitude toward institutions and is forced, therefore, to make sense of social order by beefing up the psychological resources it imputes to social actors. It is methodological to the extent that this indulgent psychology amounts to explanatory overkill. These substantive and methodological considerations interact in a philosophically subtle way. This is best seen by considering an important challenge to the strategy of institutional realism.

Why does the mere possibility of leaner psychological explanations of institutional phenomena justify their adoption? A leaner psychology, after all, is not necessarily a correct psychology. Two things can be said in response. In making psychological inferences to the best explanation of human behavior, one must be guided by the ordinary canons of simplicity. So long as one forsakes appeals to clairvoyance, even when introspection may seem tempting, one cannot claim to know what the psychological facts of the matter are and must, instead, assume that leaner is better. Nor is introspection the only route to psychological insight I recommend shunning. To boil down a complicated judgment, I will assume that hermeneutics "as a name for an epistemology . . . is perhaps merely a verbal placebo" (Dunn 1978:153). For present purposes, in short, I will view language, belief, and the like as additional elements in the scientific explanation of behavior. "Linguistic action . . . has no special status" (Stalnaker 1984:4).

More substantively, by giving institutional regularities of behavior precedence over any allegedly independent psychological considerations, institutional realism converges with some interesting developments in the philosophy of language and mind. Perhaps, in this more recent view, there is no language of thought, so-called Mentalese, defining individual-specific meanings that are then expressed through action (Dennett 1978). Perhaps even the proposed identification of states of the brain with linguistic structures like sentences is neuro-physiologically doubtful (Churchland 1986). Perhaps psychological content is a matter of external similarities among people rather than internal correspondences, let alone intersubjective identities (Stich 1983; Field 1986b). And perhaps the whole conventionalist study of psychology is more deeply flawed than its methodological shortcomings might indicate (Schiffer 1987).

When it comes to institutionalized behavior and its supposed psychological sources, the institutional realist is inclined to echo Quine's assertion, "We have been beaten into an outward conformity to an outward standard" (1969:5), with the outward standard, in this case, supplied by institutions. If so, institutions do not recapitulate psychology, nor are the mechanisms leading to institutional stability psychological in the conventionalist's folk-psychology sense.[24]

My concern with the stability of institutions, incidentally, does not reflect an unacknowledged conservative bias. Explanation and understanding in science seek truths about change, but, to return to my initial discussion of Goodman, it is change relative to a stable background. A definition of institutions centered around their status as persistent objects does not cause institutions to be more stable, unstable phenomena to disappear, or change to be thwarted. One merely does self-consciously what essentialist appeals to substance and conventionalist appeals to knowledge and preference get on the cheap. To investigate change, one needs to know what changes. To appreciate the fortuitous, one needs to know what is expected. Indeed, I suspect, to appreciate human beings in all their richness, one needs to grasp the institutional continuities in their social environment.

2.

The Sociological Solution

The doctrine of ontological egalitarianism pressed in chapter 1 is a double-edged sword. While it eases the justification of an institutional ontology, it makes the sheer existence of institutions less interesting since existence per se is seen as less of an achievement. Demonstrating the utility of positing institutions is properly left to each individual social science, which must usefully connect them to important phenomena. In the present case, the phenomena in question are the constraints that social and political circumstances exert on individual behavior. The issue is whether institutions of the sort posited in chapter 1 are needed to explain these constraints.

No social scientist seriously questions John Donne's counsel that no man is an island. In fact, most crucial instances of constraint are likely to be accepted as such by nearly all parties to the controversy over institutions. Later I will show, for example, how electoral institutions influence rational turnout in mass elections. As between conventionalists and institutional realists, there is no quarrel about the turnout, nor is there much dispute that the electoral context is significant. But somehow there remains serious disagreement over what recognition of the "social embeddedness" (Granovetter 1985) of voters entails.

For this reason, it is unlikely some decisive piece of evidence, say, a clearly observable institutional constraint, will force all reasonable observers to acknowledge institutions as worthy components of social scientific explanation. Too many alternative explanations are available purporting either to avoid the appeal to institutions altogether or to appeal to them in an ontologically noncommittal way. Institution-like phenomena are no guarantee of institutions.

Nor is it sufficient, in my view, to follow some of the philosophers discussed previously, who would be the first out of the gate in indicating that turnout could not count as such in the absence of a meaningful electoral context. When I say electoral institutions play a role, I mean something more than this. The problem is that most of the social scientists who are *not* institutional realists also seem to recognize an additional explanatory role for institutional context. Many of them, however, are either mute on details or provide details that are unconvincing and implausible.

Institutional realism cannot rest content with producing instances of institutional constraint. It must show that current attempts to explain these constraints, or explain them away, are unsatisfactory. I will show the need for an alternative by tracing some of the main approaches to institutional explanation within social and political theory, concentrating of course on those inspired by conventionalism. In this chapter, the focus is on the account of institutions developed within sociology (excepting the rational choice version, which is addressed in chapters 3 and 4).

1.

Although standard sociology has a conventionalist theory of institutions, it cannot be accused of identifying them with conventions as strictly defined by Lewis (1969). In the case of conventions, actors must create a regularity to which each has an independent, untutored interest in conforming. Institutions, at least by one standard conventionalist view, address the quite different Hobbesian problem in which actors seek to establish a regularity when each has an independent, untutored interest in seeing everyone else conform. A regularity entailing respect for the possessions of others, for example, is not self-policing the way the convention of driving on the right is. What links the analysis of conventions to the analysis of institutions is the insistence of conventionalism that any social order emerging from the state of nature, or rediscovered by subsequent generations, somehow remains a tool of participant desires and beliefs.

Although it does not equate conventions and institutions, conventionalism cannot fully distinguish the one, which actors control, from the other, which presumably control actors. It cannot unleash institutions from their participants, for that would grant institutions a distinct status as social entities, and conventionalism does not have a viable social ontology. Sometimes, of course, conventionalists make a concession to institutional reality by recognizing unintended consequences. This still leaves the participants in charge of their immediately intended actions. Since the unintended consequences remain meaningful, moreover, whatever has escaped can always be snared again. The leash is only temporarily broken. In effect, the institution's conceptual dependence on acting subjects guarantees their prerogatives as holders of the leash.

In thus dodging the implications of institutional realism, conventionalism must strain to assure for social actors the conceptual powers necessary to sustain the ontological subordination of institutions. This strain, indeed, is one of the characteristic features of conventionalism, which is forced to impute to social actors an implausibly comprehensive psychology covering whatever phenomena would otherwise count as evidence of institutional constraint.

Consider the work of Emile Durkheim, who as a champion of methodological holism insists that "social facts are to be treated as things" (1964a:xliii). A great deal could be said about the "learned ambiguity" (Harris 1968:473) of his strong pronouncements on this topic, not the least of which is the very ambiguity of the notion of fact as both the (linguistic) representation of an unyielding social reality and the independent reality that is represented (see Durkheim 1964a:xliii–xliv). The crucial point is that this methodological insecurity about social objects translates, in Durkheim's case, into a social scientific analysis that, even at its most holistic, never sheds the trappings of the conventionalist program. His famous *conscience collective* (1964b), supposedly epitomizing the influence of social facts as things, is not only mentalistic in terminology but, in the end, mentalistic in its operative significance. His core ambiguity, as Parsons (1968:343–68) forcefully argues, is never fully resolved.

Talcott Parsons's own sustained attempt to resolve this ambiguity within a conventionalist framework involves a profound exploration of the nature of institutions. There are few comparable efforts to make sense of the conventionalist problem of order in a systematic way. Although his style of grand theory, not to mention its substance, has been out of favor, the issues and problems his work raises in this respect are not being ignored because they have been solved.[1]

Parsons (1968), I noted earlier, explains institutions as tools to resolve the Hobbesian problem of order. Given the anarchy of purposes in a state of nature, a stable body of reciprocally expected behavior can arise only if shared norms and values guide the residents. Whether Parsons is right to dismiss the prospect of order in the absence of norms is, of course, debatable.[2] His own particular motivation for doing so, however, is as methodological as it is substantive, dictated in the end by deeply conventionalist considerations.

As a conventionalist, Parsons believes that social objects are constituted by acting subjects, either the social actors themselves or observers. When the observer is a social scientist, her special task is to encompass within her constitutive "frame of reference" the frame of reference of the social actors she studies, a frame constituting their social, as opposed to their physical, world.[3] What from the observer's standpoint amounts to objective facts—physical environment, genetic endowment, and the like—must be understood by the social scientist as data filtered through the social actor's frame of reference (1968:46). Thinking and acting subjects are not just behaving in a world viewed independently by social scientists. Through their acting and thinking, they are constituting the world that social scientists qua social scientists purport to study.

To act in a socially meaningful manner is to make choices and selections according to normative standards, to constitute this social world rather than some other. "I wish to use the term 'value' . . . to designate the creative element in action in general, that element which is causally independent of the positivistic factors of heredity and environment" (Parsons 1935:306; cf. 1968:81).[4] Values are independent of these factors since value-guided selections cannot constitute a world they are already part of. Values, rather, are at the pinnacle of a hierarchy of standards by which actors make choices: when the standards for selecting standards for selecting standards cannot themselves be justified in any meaningful way, the limits of intelligibility have been reached. These limits are designated as values.

The Parsonian value scheme, in short, is not justified as an empirical fact. Rather, this scheme is a function of the way social facts are—and must be—construed. True, the "*empirical* significance of selective or value standards as determinants of concrete action may be considered problematical and should not be prejudged" (Parsons and Shils 1951:64). People's concrete actions may escape normative supervision, as when people are physically coerced, hormonally driven, or simply out of their minds. Still, imputed values are crucial to defining the interface between social actors and any social world they inhabit. Accordingly, "as soon as a certain consistency of choosing can be inferred from a series of concrete acts, then we can begin to make statements about the value standards involved" (Parsons and Shils 1951:78). Parsons and Shils are apt to find norms behind any pattern of social behavior.

When Parsons argues that the Hobbesian problem of order cannot be solved without appealing to values and norms, he is in effect doing little more than expressing his understanding of what the problem of order is. The problem of order is the problem of social order, and the problem of social order is the problem of explaining stable, constitutive choices by residents of the state of nature. This stability is logically attributed in Parsons's conception to stable and shared standards of choice.[5]

Since these standards both explain and constitute social order, social order, as the embodiment of those standards, must be understood as a normative order. Small wonder that Parsons's so-called pattern variables, which give individual choices their systematic, societal significance, "could equally be employed to describe actual behavior as well as normative expectations" (Parsons and Shils 1951:79).

Pattern variables link action, subjectively guided by "felt" values (Kluckhohn 1951:396), to social order of societal scope. Since the typical social world constituted and explained by value hierarchies is fairly complex, this link would seem to strain the subjective powers of the individual actor. The typical conventionalist solution, as noted in chapter 1, is to invoke the idea of tacit beliefs and values. This allows them to shoulder a greater burden in explaining institutional phenomena.

Here the stretching of the actor's constitutive powers is accomplished the same way. Pattern variables, it turns out, "enter at the concrete level as five discrete choices (implicit or explicit) which every actor makes before he can act" (Parsons and Shils 1951:78). So "the emphasis on choice, choice alternatives, patterns of choice, etc., . . . should not be interpreted to mean that the actor always deliberately and consciously contemplates alternatives and then chooses among them in the light of the value standard . . . In a figurative sense, it might be said that the value-orientations . . . come to make the choice rather than the actor." (Parsons and Shils 1951:70).[6] This is an odd dénouement for the process of meaningful constitution.

Parsons, according to many critics, fosters an "oversocialized conception of man" (Wrong 1962). Though this complaint has considerable merit, I have been arguing for the opposite judgment. What Parsons produces, in effect, is an overindividualized conception of society, one in which stable social structure must meaningfully mirror the standards and patterns of choice ascribed to individuals. Another word for this result is conventionalism. The near equation of society and normatively grounded structure (e.g., Parsons 1951) reflects the socialization of the individual but also the leashing of society.

There is little disagreement over the tendency of Parsonian sociology to establish a correspondence between individual values and norms and, in turn, between societal values and norms: "The value-pattern defines the situation and gives the appropriate expectations for *all* phases *both* of the system process, *and* each unit process" (Parsons, Bales, and Shils 1953:252). To Wrong and others, this relation is testimony to the excessive influence Parsons attributes to society. I see conventionalism, rather, as the dominant force. "If the structure of social systems were solely a function of the 'free choices' of their component actors, their main structural outline would be capable of description in terms of the patterns of value-orientation alone" (Parsons 1951:168).[7] And similarly, "If we had a completely adequate dynamic theory of human motivation it is probable that . . . the use of structural categories . . . would be unnecessary, for such categories are only . . . introduced to fill the gaps left by the inadequacy of our dynamic knowledge" (Parsons 1954:341).

In his later work, it is fair to say, Parsons increasingly sees society as governed by distinct, self-regulating open systems (such as systems of culture, personality, organism). "Our position . . . derives particularly from Durkheim's statement that society—and other social systems—is a 'reality *sui generis*'" (Parsons 1971:7). How can Parsons reconcile a conventionalism preaching the human constitution of social order and a cybernetics affirming the homeostatic autonomy of the social system?

Here is one answer. Social order can enjoy a two-sided existence as a social system and as a set of values because the self-regulating properties of the system, which is an abstract entity, must be implemented through the actions of concrete human beings in a physical world. Cybernetic processes do operate by their own logic, but their outcomes dictate certain patterns of behavior by human beings who act by human standards, otherwise known as norms and values. The relation between social system and values is not one of equivalence but the logically weaker one of implication.

If these were the conclusions demanded by Parsons's later appreciation of cybernetics and evolutionary systems, then he did largely break free of his original conventionalism.[8] This is not, in my view, the best way to break free, but at least it recognizes that the systemic properties of society—or as I would prefer, the general truths about it—need not reflect the subjective perspective of individual decision makers. That Parsons had come to abandon his relentless, indeed heroic conventionalism would say volumes about the prospects for less systematic versions.

Yet the truth is, Parsons balks. First, he reaffirms that all systems "are abstractly defined relative to the concrete behavior of social interaction" (Parsons 1971:4). I do not believe he means simply that systems are abstract rather than concrete *entities*. From the beginning, he carefully distinguishes abstraction from strictly ontological notions.[9] Rather, he is reaffirming conventionalism by demoting systems to a second-class reality (or by not promoting them to first class).

If, in other words, the issue for Parsons were just one of general philosophy of science—the observer constitutes the observed reality—then so-called concrete individuals would not be accorded preferred status over systems. They would be equally abstractions or "products" of observation. The motive for the inequality is a specifically conventionalist sense of social order: social systems are and must be the product of individuals and their subjectively defined interactions.

A second indication that Parsons balks is all the more important for its otherwise strange character. Social systems, he argues (1951), must address specific functional exigencies. The famous four in his original list are goal attainment, adaptation, integration, and pattern maintenance. Suppose that there is primarily one-way influence between these system processes and their execution by individuals who are proximately guided by shared values and norms. If so, the ultimate values controlling an individual's normative hierarchy would no longer be imposed on the world, in good conventionalist fashion, but would be derived from their role in performing system-level functions. Conversely, these system-level needs would no longer respond to a meaningfully constituted world, in good conventionalist fashion, but would confront social problems that may remain unrecognized by social actors and unfiltered through their individual conceptions of reality.

Suppose, on the other hand, that Parsons is still a conventionalist, believing social reality must be meaningful and that meaningfulness is constitutive of reality. The existence of systems as described above would certainly strain this conventionalist identity, whose defense would force Parsons to take conventionalist principles to their logical limit. This indeed is what his defense does:

> Beyond these systems are the environments of action itself, standing above and below the general hierarchy of factors that control action in the world of life. . . . Below action in the hierarchy stands the physical-organic environment. . . . In principle, similar considerations apply to the environment above action—the "ultimate reality" with which we are ultimately concerned in grappling with what Weber called the "problems of meaning." (1966:8; cf. 28 and 1971:5)

Parsons (1966:11) is aware of the problems he is solving with this appeal to the supernatural. A normative hierarchy, he believes, is not self-legitimating in the sense that it "simply *is* right or wrong." Likewise, normative order is not "adequately legitimized by necessities imposed at the lower levels of the hierarchy of control," say, necessities arising because "the stability or even survival of the system is at stake." Legitimation of the normative order, instead, "is always related to, and meaningfully dependent on, a grounding in ordered relations to ultimate reality."

The idea of ultimate reality, for all its strangeness in a social scientific context, represents an understandable extension of conventionalism. On the one hand, the objective exigencies of the social system stand outside values and norms. On the other hand, these system processes must fit into the conventionalist framework. The resolution is clear. The connection between the normative hierarchy and the system is deposited outside the system's boundaries and turned into a given with respect to the system. If objective factors are a parametric condition for meaningful social interaction, meaningful normative factors become a parametric condition for what is objective.

The subjectively meaningful dimension of social life connects to an actual environment of the social system, albeit the special environment labeled ultimate reality.

To sum up, the price Parsons pays to maintain his conventionalism is threefold. One, as typical of conventionalists, he must depend heavily on implicit values and norms. Two, he comes close to equating social and normative order. This is much less typical of conventionalists, although the formula often repeats itself, substituting interests or preferences for values and norms. Three, he invokes ultimate reality to incorporate system-level activity into the conventionalist framework. This, of course, is even less typical, though in many respects it is a logical extension of the principles motivating the first two strategies. The appeal to ultimate reality is the symptom of a problem many face.

Thus far I have discussed the Parsonian analysis of social order without specifically addressing his conception of institutions. In brief, Parsons recognizes how rare it is for common values to be internalized perfectly, so he does not expect general conformity to arise purely from the congruence of free choices. Institutions take up the slack. A potentially deviant individual is kept in line by the (threatened) sanctions controlled by other actors. The general preponderance of "correct" expectations that any actor faces constitutes an institutional role, with institutions defined as structured sets of roles.

For present purposes, there is only one noteworthy aspect to this analysis. When actors enter an institution, they face what to them seems to be a fact of life: Conform or get hurt. For these actors, the institutional role is neither psychological nor subjective. It is a Durkheimian social fact which they ignore at their peril. What appears to each actor as a fact, however, is from the observer's standpoint a fact constituted by the expectations, motivations, and intentions of those actors whom the occupant of an institutional role faces. These other actors, who control sanctions, have internalized correct expectations about this occupant's behavior.

The problem with this explication of institutional constraint is its amiable conventionalist assumption that deviants are special cases, whereas the social facts they face result from a largely successful process of socialization. Why should this be true? In principle, every institutional participant might be a potential deviant but conform only on the mistaken assumption that everyone else has internalized correct values. Each would conform under the threat of sanctions, but the threat and implementation of sanctions would also result from the threat of sanctions. The institution would be a socially effective sham.[10] Empirical evidence about this is beside the point: the very possibility indicates a certain looseness in Parsons's argument for the normative basis of order.

Rational choice theorists also have wondered about the possibility of an institutional sham. A sham, they argue, is unlikely to survive because actors who see the big picture would renegotiate undesirable institutional structures. Though equally conventionalist, rational choice theory typically finds institutions to be even more precarious than does sociology (see Harsanyi 1969).

In any case, the Parsonian message is that the need to supplement normative order with the institutionalization of roles does not threaten conventionalism. Behavioral conformity is still attributed to the individual motivations of all the interacting members, well socialized or not, without any residue representing the institution's distinct contribution. The institution remains an external, social fact only from the subjective point of view. Social facts ultimately are dissolved into psychological facts: "As dynamic [motivational] knowledge is extended the *independent* explanatory significance of structural categories evaporates" (Parsons 1951:21).

2.

Sociology is not without theorists who are willing to embrace a more active conception of social structure than Parsons proposes. In practice, however, they tend not to explain how structural constraints are in fact activated. According to Peter Blau (1970), for example, the proportion of an organization's personnel that is administrative corresponds to its degree of internal differentiation, which in turn is a function of its size. Yet this structural generalization does not explain the how or why, and certainly not in structural terms. Perhaps these changes in administration occur for the mundane reason that existing administrators decide to change the organization in response to the problems that increased size entails (Turner 1977). If so, structure is an alternative description of a familiar process fully consistent with a nonstructural, conventionalist approach. As Anthony Giddens (1984:181) observes, "The causal relations supposedly at work are obscure" (see also Hechter 1987).

The obvious way for structuralists to explain social phenomena is to show how one thing, a social structure, influences another thing, individual behavior. I think the reluctance to put explanations in this form reflects a reluctance to acknowledge structures as full-blown entities, while the reluctance to acknowledge them as entities reflects some uncertainty about what these entities could possibly be.[11]

When Blau confronts this problem, his apparent ambivalence over the status of structures is resolved, ironically, in what should now be familiar Parsonian form—the factotum of analytic abstraction. Specifically, social structures are "observable aspects of social life" (Blau 1977:2) that are nonetheless "abstraction[s] from . . . observable patterns, which are the empirical foundation of the abstracted structures" (1977:1). Their asserted observability notwithstanding, structural premises are also "fundamentally arithmetic" (1977:245). Evidently, indifference to the role of individual psychology in the explanation of social order is not the same as finding a substitute for it.

The so-called microsociologists have the opposite task—to render plausible more individualized accounts of ostensibly social structural phenomena. Giddens (1984), for example, in his study of the "constitution of society," develops a conventionalist conception of what he calls "structuration," albeit one more cognitive and less normative than that of Parsons. Structure, in this view, is a combination of rules, defined as social conventions (Giddens 1981:170), and resources. It "exists only as memory traces, the organic basis of human knowledgeability, and instantiated in action" (1984:337).

His desire to avoid an ontological commitment to structure per se is laudably explicit. For Giddens, social life does not literally have a social structure. Rather, social practices "exhibit" structural properties, which exist only through their "instantiations" in time and space. Those instantiating social practices having the "greatest time-space extension within [societal] totalities can be referred to as *institutions*" (1984:17). The requirement of instantiation means that structure "has no existence independent of the knowledge that agents have" (1984:28). Institutions, in particular, must be "followed and acknowledged by the majority of the members of society" (1971:164). This explicit operationalization of the conventionalist program shows the oddity of the program all the more: one might wonder, for example, whether run-off elections are permitted when determining which institution has majority support.

What is the institutional realist to make of Giddens's conventionalist structuration theory, which might be more properly called a destructuration theory? The first thing to notice is that paralleling—indeed compensating for—his clear statement on structural ontology is his continuing ambiguity on other ontological matters. Properties, in particular, have an ambiguous role quite reminiscent of the sociological treatment of analytic abstractions as both abstract entities and impositions by an observer. The concept of system, as we have seen, is similarly ambiguous.

In one of its sense, a property connotes description: to say something has the property of redness is, for most purposes, equivalent to saying it is red. According to this reading, a social property characterizes a social thing but is not itself a social thing since it has no causal efficacy: "The structural properties of social systems do not act, or 'act on,' anyone like forces of nature to 'compel' him or her to behave in any particular way" (Giddens 1984:181). In more positive terms, "only individuals, beings which have a corporeal existence, are agents" (1984:220).

Insofar as a property is not merely a description but an independent entity of some kind (technically speaking, a universal), it can provide the constraint associated with social structure, much as the property of redness, to some, explains how the term *red* can properly apply to certain objects: "Structure thus refers . . . to the structuring properties . . . which make it possible for discernibly similar social practices to exist across varying spans of time and space and which lend them 'systematic' form" (1984:17).

How can properties satisfy both functions? The answer, for many, is that they do not. "There are those who feel that our ability . . . to see one concrete object as resembling another, would be inexplicable unless there were universals. . . . And there are those who fail to detect in such appeal . . . any explanatory value" (Quine 1961:102). Alternatively, if these structuring properties were explanatory, they presumably would represent conditions capable of affecting specific behavior, contrary to Giddens's earlier assurances.[12]

For Giddens, this little conundrum evidently is resolved by appealing to the "duality of structure." Agents, he affirms, are the only forces in the world capable of generating the observed social patterns. Yet agents do not create social systems; they can only reproduce or transform them, "remaking what is already made in the continuity of *praxis*" (1984:171). Agents thus reproduce the social conditions that make this reproduction possible. The duality of structure means, then, that structure is not merely a constraint; it also enables, much like the structure of language.

The picture Giddens presents, I gather, is this. The social world cannot be made to order. Individuals seeking to act must do so under circumstances in which other actors also make or have made choices. So each actor works within, not just on, these circumstances. This leads to the tautology that these circumstances will change or stay the same depending on what the new generation of actors decides.

At the level of tautology, the picture is unexceptionable. But the nature of the circumstances—the structure—within which each actor operates remains unclear. A social structure, on the one hand, typically transcends the collection of actors each agent is in contact with. At best, each confronts only a fragment of the structure. When that structure transcends the actor's immediate acquaintances, on the other hand, the larger structure has its effects in ways Giddens has not fully illuminated.

To be clear, Giddens strongly rejects the suggestion of W. I. Thomas that "if actors define situations as real, then they are real in their consequences." The factual basis of structural phenomena, he observes, also involves "linking the very idea of of mutual intelligibility and coherence of situated interaction to 'facticity' on a broadly based institutional level."

What this comes to, however, even I think after Giddens's more detailed discussion of constraints applied to lower-class school boys, is the view that social forces "are nothing less than mixes of intended or unintended consequences of action taken in specifiable contexts" (1984:220). But either these unintended consequences can operate as coherent forces or undetected conditions, in which case we are on the road to institutional realism, or they will eventually be lassoed by individual intentions and beliefs, in good conventionalist fashion. The idea of the unintended does not begin to uncover the process by which intended actions and consequences can give way to an institutionalized arena in which unintended consequences form systematic connections lying *between* the horizons of individual understanding.

Giddens also recognizes the importance of unacknowledged conditions, although these "are always to be interpreted within the flow of intentional conduct" (1984:285). Yet anyone who takes institutional ontology seriously will surely say that it is the other way around: intentional conduct is to be interpreted within the flow of unacknowledged conditions. Mediation by intentional conduct, however necessary, does not make it the anchor for institutions. The duality of structure, in short, turns out to be unclear or trivially true.

The premium that Giddens places on human knowledge issues in an appeal, which one now expects, to tacit knowledge, routinization, and a "practical consciousness" embodied in social action.[13] The patterned order of relationships "is 'real' (i.e., structurally stable) . . . precisely because [actors] accept it as such—not necessarily in their discursive consciousness but in the practical consciousness incorporated in what they do" (1984:331). This psychological stretching, he recognizes, is necessary to maintain the credibility of his conventionalist understanding of the "massively complex overall process of institutional reproduction" (1984:303). The conventionalist's insistence on channeling the flow of institutional structure through intentional conduct again takes its toll.

Michael Taylor (1988:95) similarly objects to Giddens's deflation of social structure into a "medium of action": "structure typically emerges as a result of, and is maintained or transformed by, the actions of individuals. But it is not *the same thing* as these actions." Playing the literalist once again, I question Taylor's own attempt to reconcile structural constraint and the causal role of individually rational actions.

What he has in mind for the former is not subsisting "*abstract* structures—that is, sets of relations defined independently of specific relata," but rather "*specific* structures, that is, structures with specific relata, or those parts of them which impinge on, say, the attitudes and beliefs in question" (1988:93). This is unclear because Taylor's formulation seems to reject the kind of distinct ontological status for the impinging structure that his objection to Giddens presupposes, again from my literalist standpoint. I certainly have no problem with the rejection of abstract structure. Yet Taylor gives us little sense, in the alternative, of what structure is and why anyone would appeal to it over and above the rational actions of the so-called relata.

3.

In making the reproduction of social order central to his analysis, Giddens consciously borrows a theme pursued by Marx. With its emphasis on the constraints of economic structure, Marxist theory is perhaps better equipped than other sociological theories to tell us about the institutional nexus among acting individuals.[14]

"Men make their own history, but . . . they do not make it under circumstances chosen by themselves" (Marx and Engels 1968:97). From the beginning, Marxists have used the concepts of social structure and institution to help characterize those circumstances which people do not choose so much as choose within. Such circumstances, of course, are not miraculous; they are determined by what people are and how they behave. Still, Marx insists, no one can simply circumvent them at will, say, by using the state of nature as an analytic platform for making revolutionary decisions. Because workers and capitalists are always choosing among structured alternatives does not mean they typically choose among alternative structures. Summarizing this view, Marx (1970:20–21) writes:

> In the social production of their existence, men inevitably enter into definite relations, which are independent of their will, namely relations of production. . . . The totality of these relations of production constitutes the economic structure of society, the real foundation, on which arises a legal and political superstructure. . . . At a certain stage of development, the material productive forces of society come into conflict with the existing relations of production. . . . From forms of development of the productive forces these relations turn into their fetters.

At first sight, Marx's emphasis on constraint ("fetters") offers a sharp contrast to the conventionalist's emphasis on individual choice. Yet one important link remains: these constraints apply prior to communism. After communism, there is "production of the form of intercourse itself," and in this conventionalist heaven it is "impossible that anything should exist independently of individuals" (Marx and Engels 1947:70). There are institutions before communism, and conventions after it. I want to show briefly that Marxist theory has been unable to reconcile these two claims. It does not supply a useful alternative to the conception of institutions proposed here.

Marx really discusses two kinds of constraint. In the first, which I shall call the internal version, production by members of society occurs within and is ultimately fettered by the relations of production, as those between manager and worker. In the second, external version, the society itself is articulated into economic and political institutional levels whose relation of mutual constraint has been a constant object of Marxist theorizing.

For reasons of space, I will focus on the internal version, though an analysis of the external case would reveal parallel problems (see, e.g., Parijs 1984). In particular, the mechanisms of external constraint have typically been understood functionally, with one level of structure explained by the way it functions to preserve other, usually economic levels. The typical complaint, with which I agree, is that this kind of explanation only makes sense if there is an underlying mechanism to carry out the imputed functions. But once these mechanisms are delineated, the appeal to functions carries no additional explanatory weight (see Elster 1980).[15] I now turn to the topic of internal constraint.

In *The German Ideology* (Marx and Engels 1947) and elsewhere, Marx left to his followers a strong admonition to study the real, biological creatures who *produce* their social and political world, including their relations of production. There is nothing here to worry a conventionalist. Marx also argued, however, that these same relations of production and other social structures constrain producers independently of their will, fettering the development of their productive forces. "This crystallization of social activity, this consolidation of what we ourselves produce into an objective power above us, growing out of our control, thwarting our expectations . . . . is one of the chief factors in historical development up till now" (Marx and Engels 1947:23).

What are these objective forces thwarting our expectations? What kind of power can they have over us and how is this power effective? It is not enough to appeal, as some do, to particular answers like the division of labor. It is insufficient not because the division of labor is empirically unimportant but because this kind of answer does not explain why there is a deep difference between the social constraints people face before and after communism. After all, this division is apparently no different in kind than the division of labor in legislatures analyzed by Shepsle and Weingast (1981), who are not institutional realists by any stretch of the imagination.

At the very least, Marx's conception of institutional constraint still needs clarification, which unfortunately Marx does not supply (Cohen 1978; Elster 1985). The next best alternative is to examine

Cohen's reconstruction, which includes an admirably detailed and careful attempt to clarify the Marxist conception of the issue.

One understanding of constraint suggested by Gerald Cohen can be inferred from his definition of a social description: "a description is social if and only if it entails an ascription to persons . . . of rights or powers *vis-à-vis* other men" (1978:94).[16] The implied individual-to-individual analysis is bound to appeal to conventionalist intuitions. Moreover, it renders the claim that social relations constrain—fetter independently of our will—trivial and uncontroversial. We all know that no one is an island, no one an unmoved mover. There is only one problem: the institutional component, if it exists; is as uncertain as ever.

Cohen's discussion of social structure holds more promise. According to his description of the Marxist view, an economic structure, in particular, determines each person's "objective place in the network of ownership relations" (1978:73). With an eye to unpacking the notion of constraint, Cohen carefully excludes consciousness, culture, politics, and even actual behavior from his definition of objective structural place: "these exclusions are required to protect the substantive character of the Marxian thesis that class position strongly conditions consciousness, culture, and politics." *X,* in other words, can constrain *Y* only if *X* is distinct from *Y.* Stripped of all this flesh and blood, a social structure, "like a number . . . is an abstract entity" (Cohen 1978:236). Recall that this is not the first time abstract entities have been invoked to explain institutions.

In affording social structure a clear ontological status, Cohen accedes to the basic requirement for making sense of institutional or structural constraint. No longer a mere reflection of participant expectations and beliefs, an institution becomes an object in its own right, one capable of exerting a distinct influence. The drawback is the specific kind of ontological status Cohen provides. Whether or not abstract entities are dressed up with social descriptions, the sense in which they constrain or causally interact with the more mundane objects of the world is still unclear after the twenty-five hundred years of analysis since Plato (e.g., Field 1980). Abstract entities do no better for Cohen than for Parsons or Giddens.

Cohen (1978:235) recognizes the problem in order to dismiss it. Though the divorce rate, he argues, is a number—which is an abstract entity—it nonetheless explains à la Durkheim other things such as a fear of marriage. Now the sense in which a number, as opposed to a numeral, explains some phenomenon is, under the most direct interpretation, the sense in which the number causes that phenomenon (see, e.g., Salmon 1984).[17] Yet that is precisely what is so difficult to understand. As a result, when describing the influence of divorce rates one is more likely to fudge by saying something like "the fact that" the divorce rate is such and such prompts fears about marriage. This need to fudge helps confirm the decision made back in chapter 1 to eschew abstract entities.

The whole issue comes to a head when Cohen (1978:131) considers the arrival of communism, an epoch in which structural constraint is finally eliminated or at least greatly reduced. "Activity under communism . . . is not unstructured, but it is also not pre-structured. . . . One might say: *the form is now just the boundary created by matter itself.* The structure displayed by communism is no more than the outline of the activities of its members, not something into which they must fit themselves." There are regularities under communism, but not regularities that constrain.

Presumably, any patterned collection of matter, human or not, has a form and is therefore structured in some sense. This includes communism, which under Cohen's interpretation must therefore consist of abstract structural forms existing alongside the communists. To avoid this awkward and pessimistic result concerning the possibility of eliminating structural constraint, Cohen distinguishes activities that are pre-structured from those that are merely structured.[18] Everything, therefore, hinges on the notion of pre-structuring, which is his formulation of the idea of active structural constraint.

All Cohen tells us about pre-structuring, however, is that in its absence, individuals "face one another and themselves 'as such,' without the mediation of institutions. For institutions represent 'fixation of social activity, consolidation of what we ourselves produce into an objective power above us'" (1978:133). So Cohen's analysis comes full circle. To explain institutional constraint, he posits structures. Yet if structures explain, they explain too much insofar as they cease to be limited to class societies. To recognize the freedom of communism, therefore, Cohen is forced to confront the sense in which structures, conceived as abstract entities, do not necessarily constrain. Yet if structures per se do not constrain, then the mere positing of them fails to solve the problem of constraint.

Cohen's final suggestion is that in the constraining case, individual relations are mediated by institutions. This brings us back to square one, that is, without a serious understanding of how institutions in the Marxist view constrain, though perhaps with a better sense of why it would be worth finding out. And Cohen's case is neither unique nor unrepresentative.

To Przeworski (1985:80), for example, class struggle operates within and on its own institutional constraints: "Under conditions that are objective in the sense that they are inherited and are thus given at any moment, concrete actors enter into conflicts to preserve and transform in a particular manner these conditions." The possibility of transformation is so open that, at the limit, a time can come when there are no longer objects of transformation acting even as temporary institutional constraints: "While certain ways of dividing activities emerge as the result of freely formulated choices, this division is no longer an institution. The choice is no longer 'what will I become.' . . . The 'what' itself becomes the object of individual making." (1985:245–46).

Yet somehow these malleable institutional constraints "are invariant relations among places-to-be-occupied-by-individuals rather than among specific individuals: the substitution of one individual for another does not alter these relations" (Przeworski 1985:92). Since structure is not treated as an attribute of recurrent interactions, the Marxist approach, Przeworski notes, is essentialist about social structure; hence for Marxism the world somehow gives a privileged status to some descriptions of individuals over others. How these individuals are supposed to alter a relational description declared to be independent of its own occupants is unclear, as are the reasons for the eventual disappearance of these structural essences. Thus Marxism leaves "to an uncertain future the ancient vision of a world set free" (Lichtheim 1961:406). The reasons for this uncertainty are theoretical as well as practical.

4.

To Marxists, politics is the primary tool for eliminating the institutional constraints of capitalism. It provides an external point of leverage for refashioning economic institutions, just as it does for preserving them. The problem of eliminating what I have called the internal constraints of economic institutions is indirectly related, then, to another focus of intense Marxist debate—the autonomy of political institutions, also known as the state. Insofar as the state reflects the balance of socioeconomic forces, the growing strength of workers will ultimately translate into politically induced changes in the economy. On the other hand, insofar as the state is relatively autonomous, seizing the political arena through ordinary democratic means will not produce fundamental changes.[19]

The Marxist discussion of external constraint, I noted earlier, illustrates the problems facing a conventionalist conception of social order more than it solves them. Since neo-Weberian analyses of the state often analyze specific examples of relative autonomy in much greater detail, they might also be expected to fill in some of the theoretical gaps left by Marxist discussions. Without commenting on the historical value of these studies, which is where they make their major claim, I suggest that they do not appreciably improve existing theoretical frameworks for making sense of constraint.[20]

Consider Theda Skocpol's (1979) examination of the role of states in social revolutions. From the standpoint of institutional realism, she starts out promisingly enough: "an adequate understanding of social revolutions requires that the analyst take a nonvoluntarist, structural perspective on their causes and consequences" (1979:14). *Pace* the usual view, social order does not depend on consensus support among the lower classes, and for the same reason its overthrow does not depend on consensus dissatisfaction.

An institution is not a continuing plebiscite. "Differently situated and motivated groups have become participants in complex unfoldings of multiple conflicts. These conflicts have been powerfully shaped and limited by existing socioeconomic and international conditions" (1979:17). In order to make sense of this complexity, the analyst must focus on "the institutionally determined situations and relations of groups within society. . . . To take such an impersonal and nonsubjective viewpoint—one that emphasizes patterns of relationships among groups and societies—is to work from what may in some generic sense be called a structural perspective" (1979:18).

Skocpol emphasizes the structural constraints impersonally molding the conflicts of actors, whose subjective understanding and choices become less significant. One does not have to be a conventionalist to ask, What are the mechanisms of this constraint? By way of an answer, Skocpol quotes approvingly from Gordon Wood's study of the American Revolution. Wood [1973:29] writes:

> It's not that men's motives are unimportant; they indeed make events, including revolutions. But the purposes of men, especially in a revolution, are so numerous, so varied, and so contradictory that their complex interaction produces results that no one intended or could even foresee. It is this interaction and these results that recent historians are referring to when they speak disparagingly of the "underlying determinants" and "impersonal and inexorable forces" bringing on revolution.

It is striking that Engels, in his letter to Bloch (Marx and Engels 1968:692–93), took up this identical theme when trying to explain how the historical forces identified by Marx operate. Still more striking is that Engels in turn has been disparaged by the so-called structuralist Marxists, who are horrified by the individualist implications of his explanation (Althusser 1970:120–28). Thus Skocpol clarifies her "structural perspective" using an idea attacked by structuralists.

Few doubt the existence of unintended consequences.[21] The real problem, once again, is the uncertain status of the mechanisms that take over once the boundaries of individual intention are crossed. The realist institutional ontology developed in chapter 1 can, in principle, confront this problem even if corporeal bodies alone are conceivable as forces, as Giddens plausibly insists. Unfortunately, theorists typically think in terms of ordinary corporeal bodies and therefore are apt to associate institutional ontology with abstract entities. Since this association brings more credit to abstract entities than to institutions, many structuralists understandably find a straightforward appeal to unintended consequences to be the most attractive option.

The appeal to unintended consequences, unfortunately, states a problem but does not solve it. Worse still, this astructural statement of the problem is essentially conventionalist. So conventionalism and structuralism begin to look embarrassingly alike whenever their adherents, for differing reasons, avoid embracing an institutional or structural ontology. Structuralism without structure, in sum, is pretty much conventionalism with structuration.[22]

Traces of this convergence do show up in Skocpol's own summary of her explanation of stability and revolution. From her structuralist perspective, she does not find the legitimacy of the state to be an important part of the explanation. This voluntaristic notion does indeed imply that the continuation of a state depends on the results of an ongoing evaluation by citizens.[23] Yet rather than eliminating voluntarism, Skocpol simply restricts it to the elites. What is really at issue with the survival of a state, she suggests, is "support or acquiescence not of the popular majority of society but of the politically powerful and mobilized groups" (1979:31).

Similarly, her structuralist analysis of the British government's response to the Great Depression takes on a decidedly conventionalist cast. In exploring the ways in which the structures of this government shaped policy, Weir and Skocpol (1985) emphasize recruitment patterns, bias against policy innovations, and the "contentious blend of viewpoints" on the government's Economic Advisory Council (1985:128). Correct or not, their explanation seems fully consistent with the sort of approach recommended by Giddens (1984) and Harré (1981), who is a fairly ardent microsociologist. The underlying details concerning how *structures* constrain, which Weir and Skocpol certainly agree they do, are not explicitly developed.

In the same vein, Stephen Skowronek's (1982) historical examination of the American state duly notes the impact of structural context. Struggles to change states are said to be "rooted in and mediated by preestablished institutional arrangements" (1982:ix). This is because "an established state structures a set of power relationships among its discretionary officers, and it provides an operating framework through which these officers attempt to maintain order" (1982:169). Yet Skowronek, in the end, is likewise unclear about the extent to which a statist or structural analysis entails more than the recognition that actors in social institutions must work with the resources and people they find. Although he certainly does not embrace the conventionalist sense of institutional transparency, the opacity he finds does not translate into an identifiable institutional realism.

Evidently, Skowronek believes that there is a two-way process in which individual actors maintain an institutional order and the order maintains them. In practice, the role of these situated individuals is much clearer than the framework or order they attempt to maintain. "Government officials do not respond automatically with the appropriate institutional innovations [although the] intervention of government officials is the critical factor in the state-building process." Rather, an "official's response to environmental disruptions will involve a distinctly political calculus of the impact of potential innovations on the particular arrangements that support him in office" (1982:12). Thus, "after 1896, the old rules of institutional politics no longer compelled such respect. . . . Government officials seeking to maintain or enhance their positions faced an uncharted universe of political and institutional action" (1982:169).

I have difficulty distinguishing this analysis from the voluntaristic approach with which it is often contrasted. Individuals calculate whether to maintain the arrangement nominally constraining them, whereas the break from charted territory to a world of uncertainty seems to result from a lapse in the feelings of legitimacy or respect that institutions command. The former idea, we shall see in the next chapter, is heartily embraced by a supposedly a-institutional rational choice theory. The latter idea, not to put too fine a point on it, is traditional sociology.

In order to show the influence of an institution, say conventionalists of all stripes, it is not enough to show that individuals situated within institutions behave in some respects differently from their counterparts outside. That only demonstrates that individuals within institutions face somewhat different individuals. What is left out of the equation—should be left out, say conventionalists—is the structural constraints that are neither the reflection nor the object of human choice. Skowronek might reply, How can I reveal what is invisible, what can only be seen in the behavior of individuals? Precisely, says the conventionalist.[24]

Conventionalists insist that a philosophically respectable social science cannot live with institutions; in practice, conventionalists have a difficult time without them. Those adopting a structural perspective recognize that they cannot live without institutions; but in practice, structuralists have a hard time with them. The explanation, I have suggested, is that few are willing to abide or acknowledge the ontological burdens institutional analysis brings. And those that do, like Cohen (1978), correctly accept an expanded ontology but mistakenly embrace an otherworldly one.

I can anticipate the reaction from structuralists: What more is there, they will ask, to structural constraint than finding a pattern in the ostensibly conventionalist details? At the risk of seeming pedantic, I respond that this question still does not tell us how patterns, interpreted literally as abstract entities, constrain. If, on the other hand, they are not to be interpreted literally, then institutional realism offers one way to unpack the pattern metaphor in a nonvoluntaristic manner.

3.

The Rational Choice Solution

Although many of the infirmities that plague sociological theory also afflict rational choice theory, the latter requires somewhat
more careful scrutiny. For despite the opposition of rational choice
theory to the sociological tradition (Harsanyi 1969), it is, in some ways,
rooted in a more radical brand of conventionalism.[1] The sociologist
Talcott Parsons resolves the Hobbesian problem of order by invoking
values and norms to restrict the free play—the "double contingency"—
of voluntaristic interactions. As a result, individual choices embody a
normative institutional structure that Parsons's conventionalism does
not successfully dissolve. Rational choice theory, by contrast, forces
institutions to earn their way, proving their utilitarian worth as the
products of collective action. Any institution emerging from this rational choice process is guaranteed to satisfy conventionalist criteria.

Although some regard the rational choice approach as less profound than its sociological cousins, its intense interest in the emergence of institutions means that in many respects it poses a deeper
challenge to institutional realism. This is especially true in light of the
"new institutionalism," a version of the theory focusing on institutional
effects (Shepsle 1989). Still another reason why the rational choice
approach deserves special scrutiny is that a suitably modified version
of it can be used to mold institutional realism into a social scientifically
recognizable form. Rational choice theory, in short, represents institutional realism's toughest test and greatest opportunity.

The opportunity can be outlined in a few short steps. Within
rational choice theory, situations involving socially interdependent
actors are modeled using game theory (von Neumann and Morgenstern

1953). In those social situations characterized as games, participants try, as proper rational actors, to maximize their expected payoffs. They do so, however, knowing that these payoffs depend not on their individual choices alone but also on the choices of the other participants. In fact, the rules of the game precisely describe the payoffs associated with each possible collection of participant choices.

If an institution in the realist's sense were modeled as a game, the game rules would model its structure. I do not mean a structure in the inert though common sense in which, say, the distribution of demographic characteristics is considered part of the social structure. Rather, an institutional game structure determines who qualifies as a player as well as the possible paths his behavior may take. The structure, then, defines the ways in which the choices of different individuals may combine to produce social outcomes. Although players, in this view, try to run the institutional maze as intelligently as possible, the institutional structure gives them the initial opportunity and defines the available routes. It is something they confront rather than manipulate or choose. In brief, the interdependence of the players—their roles—are institutionalized.

Of course, this is not the way rational choice theorists see things. Consider, for example, a voting institution. The usual rational choice story is that agents submit to the voting rules of this institution because, on the whole, they prefer its outcomes to those of any conceivable alternative arrangement. The institution ultimately is selected by its members; this preference is in turn a by-product of their preference for the stream of benefits that the institution produces.

In some situations, this picture makes intuitive sense. If, for example, the voting institution is simply a committee with a small membership directly voting on policies, these members may well treat the institution instrumentally, as the standard theory assumes. The resulting situation is roughly analogous to the explicit conventions whose existence was acknowledged in chapter 1.

In larger legislative bodies having complex committee systems as well as other less formal structures, the idea that each member prefers that whole institution, literally and specifically, to a host of imagined alternatives clearly stretches the rational choice format, not to mention the assumed cognitive capacity of the membership. Yet if one is willing to take an instrumental view of psychological assumptions—an approach with which I have no quarrel—then one might continue to hold to the standard theory, although deeper problems with it will emerge in this chapter.[2]

In this intermediate case, the standard theory and institutional realism have alternative explanations of the same phenomenon. The former sees institutional regularities as continuing objects of choice, whereas the latter sees them as constraints to which individuals must adapt. As we will see, the practical difference between the two is at this stage subtle and indirect.

Finally, when an institution calls for a mass electorate to select people who will implement policies, the resulting arrangement does not simply increase the complexity of the institution by orders of magnitude. For even if participants generally understood and supported the institution, they might not be rationally motivated to reproduce it. This famous paradox of not voting will be addressed in chapter 6. In the meantime, I observe that the standard theory's assumption that members can remain intellectually detached from the institution within which they are supposedly embedded here works against the persistence of the institution.

In the remainder of this chapter I will trace through the standard rational choice analyses of institutions, adding refinements and formal detail as necessary, to show how the standard conception of institutions attempts to preserve a conventionalist foundation. In this guise, rational choice theory represents a major challenge to institutional realism. Contrary to appearances, however, the conventionalist strategy adopted by rational choice theorists is similar to that of sociology and inherits a parallel set of problems.

1.

Before there was game theory, there was rational choice theory. And similarly, before games can be played, there must be rational individuals to play them. A rational individual will be defined as one who behaves as if she maximizes expected utility. This notion of utility is not meant to carry any psychological baggage; hence "as if." Rather, an agent maximizing utility behaves in a way that can be characterized by a family of mathematical functions satisfying certain intuitively plausible axioms about the choices the agent is prepared to make (e.g., Hernstein and Milnor 1953).

If, for example, an agent prefers alternative X to alternative Y, and alternative Y to alternative Z, the agent, if rational, will prefer X to Z. This is the axiom of transitivity. Given three alternatives ordered this way, the agent is said to maximize utility so long as the agent's utility function reaches its maximum when the agent chooses alternative X over all others, and similarly so long as the value of the function is higher when Y is chosen over Z. The agent is said to maximize *expected* utility when the ordered alternatives can be lotteries, that is, collections of outcomes each occurring only with some (subjective) probability.

Although this brief description ignores many significant complications, one critically important ambiguity lurks in the notion of expectation. Suppose, by way of illustration, that visiting a doctor is positively correlated with being terminally ill. If so, then in a sense agents who avoid checkups thereby increase their expected utility. Yet clearly, the association between expected illness and checkups would not deter a truly rational decision maker. Standard rational choice theory precludes this form of stupidity by assuming, explicitly or implicitly, that decision makers factor in the expectations associated with their actions only for those outcomes, or features of outcomes, that are actually brought about—caused—by the agent (Lewis 1981). According to the standard view, in other words, calculations of expected utility only recognize the causal, as opposed to the merely stochastic, dependence of outcomes on actions.

A rational decision problem is thus defined by the standard theory as follows. Agents envision the various relevant ways the world might be, on the condition that they be causally independent of the agent's actions. In the example just considered, the agent might distinguish between being terminally ill and not being terminally ill. Since the independence requirement is met in this case, the decision maker acts by considering the actual consequences of a checkup, disregarding any statistical relation between going to the doctor and being terminally ill. In order to underscore their causal independence from acts, the possible states of the world are often called states of nature.

Now let us transport this theory into a game theoretic setting in which the possible states of nature involve the decisions of other human beings. For each actor in a game, the situation is as before, except the alternative states are now defined, in part, by decisions outside the actor's control. How any actor fares in this situation is contingent on what others have decided. The social interdependence of the actors is thus recognized in two ways. First, the states of nature determining the results of each action incorporate other decision makers. Second, actors maximize expected utility by anticipating that the other decision makers are also, independently, trying to anticipate the expected utility calculations of each participant.[3] One might think that these calculations would result in an infinite regress of "If I think that they think that I think . . ." The whole point to game theory is to show that this regress actually leads to an equilibrium of calculations, meaning further reflection fails to change the decision about what is rational to do. In what is called a Nash equilibrium, no individual player can unilaterally improve her situation.

Consider the famous prisoners' dilemma, which is shown in bi-matrix form in figure 2. The utilities for agents A and $B,$ who face alternatives $\{A_1,B_1\}$ and $\{A_2,B_2\}$ respectively, are structured so that $0 < x < y < 1.$ According to the standard analysis, each agent winds up with a payoff of x: since each concludes that A_2 (resp. B_2) is preferable to A_1 (resp. B_1) regardless of the other player's behavior, their joint

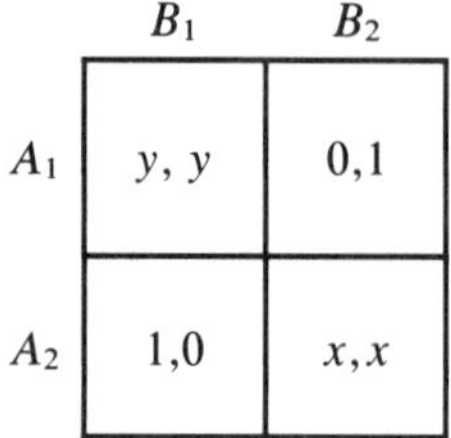

Figure 2. Prisoners' Dilemma

outcome is (A_2, B_2). This outcome is socially inferior to (A_1, B_1), but the independence of the players precludes any joint manipulation of the result. For no matter how attractive it may be, a preferable outcome that cannot be achieved through independent calculation cannot be achieved. At any rate, since (A_2, B_2) is the unique equilibrium, additional calculations by the players will not lead to a different result.[4]

From the standpoint of institutional realism, games such as prisoners' dilemma can characterize situations in which there is an inevitable social interdependence among the agents. This inevitability is painful for conventionalists, since they believe that what is social is synthetic and therefore subject, in principle, to control or revision. The prisoners' dilemma nicely illustrates the way in which standard game theory attempts to make social interdependence safe for conventionalism.

Note, first of all, that whereas the outcome of a game is a collection of possible *actions,* equilibrium strictly speaking is a psychological phenomenon defined by the stability of each agent's rational calculus.[5] Seeing no reason to change any contemplated action, the agent is not condemned to an infinite regress in thought.[6] Some versions of game theory do recognize possibilities for social coordination. Aumann (1987), for example, allows independent agents to witness jointly the outcomes of randomizing devices used in the formulation of their mixed strategies. Yet in the end, each of these outcomes is a suggestion no agent is required to accept. Social coordination remains a possibility, not a condition of choice.

Since each of the decisions composing a social outcome is the prerogative of a single player, the collection of these decisions cannot as such be stabilized. No one person or collectivity chooses it and, according to conventionalism, this means a social outcome must remain something of an artifact. Once the game is played, after all, it is a done deal: any further contemplation of alternative scenarios is pointless. All maneuvers and causal distinctions, then, must ultimately register in the minds of the participants (or a disembodied umpire).

The way these factors are currently built into game theory thus reflects its conventionalist orientation.

The interdependence reflected in the existence of parallel rational decision making has also been given a conventionalist treatment. In the standard view, for example, rational players facing the prisoners' dilemma will not allow their decision making to be influenced by the symmetry of their situation, which is to say, their common social condition. Players who *were* influenced by their common condition might reason as follows. If we are both rational and this is common knowledge, then we should not expect to find ourselves in the asymmetric positions (A_1,B_2) or (A_2,B_1). By the symmetry of our situations, the argument continues, what is rationally prescribed for the one is rationally prescribed for the other. This suggests our real choices are between (A_1,B_1) and (A_2,B_2). If so, the argument concludes, we should expect to come to the same conclusion that the former outcome is better than the latter (see, e.g., Rapoport 1966:141–42).

Alternatively, suppose neither of us can be sure that the other is identically rational (Hardin 1982:151–52). Still, each of us may believe that our two decisions will be highly correlated, at least in the sense that the chance of an off-diagonal outcome is negligible. This does not guarantee that the expected utility of A_1 (resp. B_1) will exceed the expected utility of A_2 (resp. B_2). Though low, the probability of outcome (A_2,B_1), may be sufficiently higher than the probability of (A_2,B_2), for instance, to preclude A's choice of A_1 (see Jeffrey 1981:485). But under some circumstances, the suboptimal result is inappropriate.

Yet according to the standard view, players will not take this symmetry into account since their rational calculations allow them to rise above any apparent interdependence in their decisions. The inter-player correlations, however high, can be disregarded since neither player's choice has any power to affect the choice of the other, who in fact may have already acted. Thus in selecting A_2, player A is not biasing the game toward (A_2,B_2) over (A_1,B_1) so much as biasing it toward (A_2,B_2) over (A_1,B_2). In fact, in the standard view, A_2 (resp. B_2) remains preferable when players expect a perfect statistical relation between their choices. Even this relation cannot nullify the objective causal independence of the two players' actions (see Harper 1985:221–23).

There is still another way games seem to reflect the common social condition of the players. A game does not consist merely of calculating individuals trying to anticipate the decisions of others. The impact of these other decisions is determined by the *rules* of the game, which define how alternative collections of decisions combine to establish outcomes. It is built into the rules of the prisoners' dilemma, for example, that player A must decide without knowing what player B has decided, and vice versa. These rules, I have suggested, can reflect the specific social situation of the participants, something individual players might understand and use, but not something they create or control within the game.

How can standard game theory make sense of rules without surrendering its conventionalist conviction that social constraints are the products of human choice? One answer is to treat the rule-bound context as a physical rather than social feature of the game, in which case its independence becomes conceptually less awkward.[7] This explicit solution goes back to von Neumann and Morgenstern (1953: 41–43), who describe the fundamental rules as a "physical background" from which solutions to the game emerge out of the rational decisions of the players.[8] As we saw in the prisoners' dilemma, this contrast between player choices and physical givens also surfaces as the idea that rational players can and do bracket out interplayer correlations when making their decisions. Since these correlations are not physical facts dictated by the rules of the game, they need not be incorporated in the players' decisions about the best way to behave given their physical circumstances.[9]

Von Neumann and Morgenstern, in short, take a straightforwardly conventionalist approach to game theory. And the manifestations of this are not limited to the internalization of equilibria or dicta about the proper interpretation of player interdependence. Von Neumann and Morgenstern's definition of the most fundamental notion of game structure, the "extensive form" of the game, is likewise rooted in conventionalism. As they define the extensive form, it includes both the details of the basic decision tree—the possible paths the game can take—as well as each player's information about the actual course of the game. The specific way they introduce information, however, converts the entire structure of the game into a homogeneously psychological phenomenon.

To an institutional realist, the idea of a game structure reinforces a crucial distinction between the game agents are playing and beliefs about the game these agents might have. The game structure constitutes the conditions to which each player must adapt. To the conventionalist, by contrast, this distinction is a problem, since an unperceived structure must be understood as having an independent identity. The concept of information camouflages this problem by bridging the gap between objective structure and the players' opinions about it: though information is, in a sense, subjective, it is also about the game. By introducing the idea of information, then, von Neumann and Morgenstern substitute a psychological notion for the awkward concept of structure.

Yet the notion of information also creates a problem. For if the definition of a game includes both the game and player information about it, game theory introduces a degree of reflexivity not easily accommodated in formalizations. In the end, von Neumann and Morgenstern resolve these related problems in superconventionalist fashion by defining the entire game in terms of information.[10] The unfolding of a game—the making of choices and so forth—appears in their axiomatization as the successive refinement of information concerning what the actual course of play is (1953:67). When the game is finally completed, its full identity is secured by assuming that there is an umpire who has the information that such and such is the way the actual game played out relative to all the possible ways in which it could have been played (1953:71).

For all practical purposes, von Neumann and Morgenstern collapse the crucial distinction between the game's structure and information about it. The structure becomes a perceived structure, which means no one has to worry about what an unperceived structure is. Arguing in its defense, Aumann (1987:8) observes that "this 'outside observer' perspective is common to all differential information models in economics (as well as to all extensive games that are not games of perfect information)." The use of an outside observer to anthropomorphize the facts about the game is not the troubling issue, however, but is only symptomatic of the real difficulty—namely, the use of the concept of information to disguise the awkward relation between the facts of the game and conventionalist definitions of the game in terms of the subjective perspective of the players. Indeed, Aumann connects this generalized conventionalism to the specific, paradigmatic understanding of conventions by Lewis (1969), adding that "'outside observer' referred to above is thus a surrogate for the ignorance of the system as a whole—the lack of common knowledge—of the signals received by each player."[11]

The classic von Neumann–Morgenstern axiomatization, in sum, does not so much model the game as model shifts of information about the game. Put more charitably, the game and information are treated as interchangeable (1953:67). In one sense, this is a minor conceptual embarrassment. Von Neumann and Morgenstern's mathematical results are not in jeopardy and, one may argue, that is what really matters. Yet these results become useful, or misleading, to social scientists only under an interpretation. And von Neumann and Morgenstern's specific informational approach, which is used to implement their psychological interpretation, forces them into a clear error.

If P^* is a game's actual course of play, what is $\{P^*\}$? Following the von Neumann and Morgenstern reading of their axiomatization, it is the information that P^* is the play, "*the umpire's actual information*" (1953:75). But this is incorrect; '$\{P^*\}$' is nothing more or less than the class whose single member is P^*. Von Neumann and Morgenstern have violated the distinction between use and mention. When one writes (uses) '$\{P^*\}$', one is talking about (mentioning) a class $\{P^*\}$. In contrast, when one notes that '$\{P^*\}$' asserts that, or is the information that, P^* has some particular property, one is immediately talking about the *expression* or typographical mark '$\{P^*\}$'. $\{P^*\}$ is a thing; it does not denote information about a thing. In using the same typographical mark to represent both the class whose single element is the actual course of play and the information that P^* is the actual course of play, von Neumann and Morgenstern ignore this use-mention distinction. Carelessness about this distinction induces bizarre twists of reason (see Quine 1951:23–26 for some classic examples).

The von Neumann–Morgenstern axiomatization is a pioneering effort, and one may well ask whether its infirmities are relevant today. In fact, these infirmities have become increasingly relevant as game theorists have begun to explore the role of information in an increasingly sophisticated fashion. Aumann (1987) is a good example, since he is unusually articulate about issues of interpretation.

Aumann is interested in modeling games in which players use information rationally—technically, they operate as Bayesians (see DeGroot 1970)—and in which the probabilities generating strategies for the different players need not be independent but can be correlated. What is interesting about Aumann's model, for our purposes, is that what he gives with one hand—greater recognition of the incompleteness of player information about the course of play—he takes with the other in the form of strong assumptions about common knowledge (again, he refers to Lewis 1969). The following technical digression will clarify how the initial attempt to simulate the playing of a game through the concept of information deeply affects contemporary theory.[12]

As modeled by von Neumann and Morgenstern, the way an actual play of a game turns out is, in general, understood only by the outside observer or umpire. The limitations of the players are reflected in what are called information partitions. An information partition for a player spells out which possible states of the world (basically, those relating to possible plays of the game) are indistinguishable to him. A poker player, for example, may not know whether he is raising against a full house or a pair. In Aumann's (1987) model, players have common knowledge of each player's information partition.[13]

This common knowledge, Aumann argues, is not so much an assumption as a "theorem" or tautology within the model (1987:9). For suppose, he reasons, player 1 is uncertain about player 2's partition. Player 2's actual partition is still a fact about each possible state of the world or situation involving the game. And these possible states of the world compose the elements sorted out by player 1's partition. Since one cannot represent a player's uncertainty without representing what the player is uncertain about, player 1's partition must include player 2's true partition as one aspect of each of the possible states of the world it covers. Thus, there is no room for player 1 to be uncertain about the partition of others so long as the range of possibilities is restricted, as it is, to possible plays of the particular game in question.

I have no complaints about Aumann's reasoning, given a model in which the relation between the structure of the game and information about it is so intimate. Yet the problem with this model becomes evident when he explains why his conclusions are not themselves formalized or justified in a formal way. "The answer is that the assertions have no formal content" (1987:10). As Aumann notes, within his model knowledge is about events. These events are sets of states of the world (specifically possible plays of the game). Knowing a particular event relative to a particular state of the world, therefore, requires that the appropriate set of states includes the element of one's partition containing that state of the world. "But neither a partition nor a prior [an initial belief about probabilities] is an event; formally speaking, the concepts of knowledge and common knowledge do not apply to them" (1987:10). This is because the partition as such does not occur as an event. The structure of partitions, Aumann writes, "simply represents different methods of classification" (1987:9). Although interpretations involving common knowledge informally "aid us in understanding the model, they do not affect the conclusions."

The problem with this explanation is its failure to motivate the unequal treatment of events and other components of the game. Knowledge of events evidently matters because events occur in the game, whereas knowledge of the partitions of others does not matter because they do not occur as such. His point is well taken. There is a difference between what actually happens and somebody's classification of what happens. Note, however, Aumann's earlier ruling that such classifications are aspects of a full description of each state of the world and, therefore, of each event. They do occur in the sense that the occurrence of any state of the world implies the existence of the partition in question. Indeed, not only is Aumann's earlier defense of the common knowledge assumption at stake. As we have seen, von Neumann and Morgenstern's information-based interpretation of game theory could not long survive if classification were relegated to a second-rate status.

Aumann, in short, must insist on the common knowledge "theorem" since without it the very interpretation of the game in terms of information is undermined: in his analysis, a play of a game must carry with it all the information reflected in the game's outcome. The reason, rooted in von Neumann and Morgenstern, is simple. A play of the game, in their formulation, *is* the information that this particular game has been played in some particular way.

On the other hand, Aumann must deny the operational importance of the common knowledge assumption since, as he recognizes, games involve sequences of actual behavior, not just "external" ways of classifying behavior. An interpretation of a game, in other words, ought to be just that, an interpretation of something existing independently. Insofar as the game is properly defined by a set of behavioral events, the common knowledge assumption jumps the operational bounds of the model and, accordingly, is denied formal content. Small wonder that Aumann (1987:11) responds to this dilemma by questioning the importance of the distinction between exogenous and endogenous.

It is worth mentioning that Aumann has deepened the subjective dimension of game theory in order *inter alia* to establish a notion of equilibrium that he believes is better motivated than the theory's premier solution concept, the Nash equilibrium. A Nash equilibrium arises when each player has selected her best response to the choices of the other players. One problem is that this solution is usually determined in such a way that, given what everyone else is doing, each player is indifferent between her equilibrium response and others. So she no longer has an immediate motivation to maintain the equilibrium. Yet if it is not maintained, some other player's current strategy may no longer be a best response.

By embedding common knowledge assumptions and Bayesian calculation into the game theoretic setup, Aumann hopes to demonstrate the rational appropriateness of the game's equilibria. Yet this increased internalization of game theory threatens to sever it from a theory of rational choice that was originally rooted in behavioral choices over externally defined alternatives. In reaction, some game theorists are trying to reclaim the theory's ostensible concern with "observable events, consequences, and action" (Nau and McCardle 1990:443).[14]

In sum, rational choice theory is at once more conventionalist and less conventionalist than standard sociology. It is more conventionalist insofar as the "double contingency" supposedly tamed by norms and values continues to pervade game theoretic relationships. Purely social interdependencies are never binding on rational agents. It is less conventionalist insofar as it treats rules not as conceptual creations but as physical facts of life.[15] The informational interpretation, finally, attempts to negotiate between the physical facts of the game—the rules and actual behavior—and the conceptualization of the game by players. Information keeps conventionalist hopes alive.

2.

Standard game theory abstracts from social interdependencies. A natural, and naturalistic, way for it to explore the role of institutions, therefore, is to abstract from the existence of institutions as well. The task then becomes to determine what game theoretic problems institutions would solve for a collection of individuals who, lacking them, exist in a state of nature. Representing the physical facts of life for socially unorganized agents, this state of nature is routinely modeled as a prisoners' dilemma, whose "rules" in this case are indeed just a "physical background." What makes the state of nature a prisoners' dilemma is, among other things, each individual's incentive to take the accumulated possessions of others (choices A_2 and B_2 from the earlier game matrix), whether or not those other players reciprocate. The resulting anarchy need not produce a life that is "nasty, brutish, and short," but the Hobbesian problem of order is real enough, since participants outsmart themselves into a suboptimal outcome.[16]

Within the limits of the static prisoners' dilemma game there seems to be no way to avoid this outcome, since suboptimality is the direct product of fully rational behavior. Yet in good conventionalist style, residents of the state of nature can create social alternatives not inscribed in the original game. They either can agree to a set of binding rules (a constitution) prescribing behavior leading to the better outcome (A_1, B_1) or simply recognize a third party who will directly enforce it. One way or the other, this social contract removes the incentive for a rational individual to act antisocially (Buchanan 1975).

The physical background defining the original prisoners' dilemma does not disappear, of course. Rather, through the contractual innovations of the players, the original dilemma is embedded in a wider game as one (default) outcome. The threat of returning to the state of nature, in fact, helps maintain the original agreement. Stated crudely, institutional order emerges because rational agents prefer it over anarchy. This preference for institutional order is an induced preference reflecting each agent's underlying interest in the outcomes that are more likely to occur within institutions. As created objects, institutions are simply instruments for achieving these results.

Thus, social contract theory still views institutional order as a product of participant choices even when the coordination equilibria associated with true conventions are absent. Contract theory simply substitutes an explicit plebiscite for Parsons's tacit acclamation. Contemplating a mental "bazaar of constitutions," to appropriate Plato's phrase, actors construct the social order they wish to inhabit. In the one case, they are guided solely by instrumentally rational goals; in the other case, by legitimating norms and values. In either case, a created social order blunts the natural impact of preferences.

By relying on an explicit plebiscite, social contract theory is more obviously conventionalist than sociology. Correspondingly, its problems are more exposed. For one thing, removing the internalized social guidance offered by values and norms highlights the creative aspects of constitutional choice, making it less easy to rationalize institutional constraint within an austere game theoretic setup. For another thing, this plebiscitary state of nature typically occurs only once in a society's history, which makes social contract theory less relevant in the case of ongoing institutions. Perhaps, rational actors who escape the state of nature escape the jurisdiction of social contract theory as well. In the remainder of this section, I shall explore the attempt of social contract theory to grapple with these two related sets of problems.[17]

How can participants within the prisoners' dilemma contemplate alternatives strictly external to the dilemma? It is not enough to say that the institutions they envision are legitimately external since they are simply contemplated possibilities. Alternative outcomes within the dilemma are also contemplated possibilities. It is difficult to see a principled difference: if social contracts are available at the beginning as possibilities, then they should be included in the original game theoretic description as alternatives.

If social contract theory is correct, the prisoners' dilemma is a misspecified model of the state of nature. The participants do not spontaneously restructure the existing game to include outcomes outside the state of nature. Rather, the prisoners' dilemma is transcended when the game is first encountered.[18] Ostrom (1990:7) nicely captures the conventionalist intuition behind this transcending: "The prisoners in the famous dilemma cannot change the constraints imposed on them by the district attorney; they are in jail. Not all users of natural resources are similarly incapable of changing their constraints."

The implied expansion of the game seems to take some of the creative, conventionalist steam out of social contract analysis. Actors in the state of nature are now understood to operate within a game whose possible outcomes include "social" and "natural" states of affairs in equal standing. In this sense, the game theoretic status quo ante is as much social as not. Or to put the point more methodologically, this blending of the constructed and the natural weakens the contrast drawn by James Buchanan and Gordon Tullock (1962:326), in their classic social contract analysis, between game theory, which in their view takes the rules of the game as given, and social contract theory, which in their view investigates the choice of the rules themselves. This contrast becomes weaker still once the state of nature is left behind.

Social contract theorists might respond in the following way. The criticism just broached, like so many of the ill-informed but routine criticisms of our theory, mistakes the state of nature for a real place. It is, rather, an analytic device designed to capture the frankly artificial nature of institutional arrangements. It is true that when natural base and conventional superstructure lose their distinct identities, the state of nature becomes hard to distinguish from social settings. But this is a plus, since social settings become equally hard to distinguish from the state of nature. Specifically, we can exploit this similarity by parlaying social contract theory into an account of how existing institutions persist. This allows us to generalize our conclusions by showing, in effect, that the overarching calculus associated with social contract theory is used even when choices are made within established institutions: "We think of the individual as engaging continuously both in everyday operational decisions within the confines of established organizational rules and in choices concerned with changes in the rules themselves" (Buchanan and Tullock 1962:261). Institutional as well as extrainstitutional alternatives are always in the individual's choice set, both within the state of nature and without.

Long after the primordial state of nature has faded from view, agents still treat the institutional regularities they face as mere evidence to be used in deciding whether to reproduce the institution or descend into anarchy. In this conventionalist account, then, institutions are never full-fledged background conditions of choice. Rather, they are created and re-created in a constant, usually implicit process of recontracting (Buchanan and Tullock 1962:260–62).

The dynamic process maintaining constitutions implies the continuing relevance of the contract approach, which otherwise would be consigned to history texts. As we have just seen, however, this relevance is secured by severely weakening the ordinary association between social contract theory and the state of nature. Though choice within institutions is much like choice within the state of nature, choice within the state of nature is much like choice within institutions.[19] History aside, the state of nature no longer plays a distinguished role.

In practice, Buchanan and Tullock try to preserve the continuing influence of the pure state of nature by insisting that any constitutional choice be made by unanimous consent. This holds when a constitution is first established or when it is being scrapped. Clearly, a unanimous consent requirement imposes a special burden on the formation of a polity; and even when institutions exist, it apparently restores the state of nature as the default option, since proposed institutions are always subject to each participant's veto, which ultimately includes a threat to revert to a preinstitutional state. As Buchanan (1975:79) puts it, these decisions "may be based on imagined shifts in the natural distribution in anarchistic equilibrium [the state of nature] which always exists 'underneath' the observed social realities."[20]

Buchanan and Tullock seem to justify the reasonableness of this restriction by denying that any decision rule requiring less than unanimity can adequately explain constitutional choice. Such a rule, they suggest, presumes the existence of a political relation of domination between those who agree and those who do not. To use the rule to explain or legitimate politics in the deepest sense would, therefore, be circular.[21]

The conventionalist thus insists on a certain kind of asymmetry between the state of nature and institutional order. Although, analytically speaking, institutional arrangements can revert to the state of nature, and vice versa, Buchanan still sees the state of nature as the analytic base, the ground "underneath" individuals when they decide inside and outside of institutions. You can take the agent out of the state of nature, but you can't take the state of nature out of the agent.

This asymmetry, however, conflates two distinct ideas. One is that preferences concerning alternative institutions are independent of the institutional status quo in which agents happen to find themselves. If they prefer some existing institution this is because the institution is good for them, not because it happens to exist. Yet insofar as this is true, preferences are also independent of any subterranean state of nature.[22] Insistence on the unanimous consent rule must be justified separately.

The other is the idea that the members' decision to preserve or dissolve their institutional framework is, in the end, analytically independent of the institutional circumstances under which the decision is expressed. Supposedly, these members, tagged with institutionally influenced roles and powers, nonetheless compare the institution to an imagined state of nature. But this choice is largely meaningless since the state of nature is no longer an automatic default option. No individual typically has the wherewithal to create anarchy unilaterally, and the collective decision now occurs outside a state-of-nature setting. The individuals making the collective decision, in short, may have rights, powers, and preferences different from those they would have had in the state of nature.

So Buchanan and Tullock's argument fails with respect to either of two interpretations of the state of nature. If state-of-nature relations are the "real" base for intrainstitutional decisions because institutions originally emerged from them, Buchanan and Tullock face the ancient question about earlier generations binding later ones. If the state of nature is analytic, which is the intended interpretation, then the state of nature fails to play its original role within an existing institution. The decision to revert to the state of nature is institutionally structured or certainly institutionally influenced.

In fact, were agents in a position to choose between an existing institution and a noninstitutional state of nature, the institution would have no particular power. The institution would be irrelevant or function solely as a convention in the strict sense defined by Lewis (1969). It therefore is understandable why Buchanan and Tullock insist that proper departures from an institutional status quo require unanimous consent. That is to say, individuals within institutions "must choose rule changes on which all players can agree if the game is to continue.

. . . The implicit rule for securing the adopting of changes . . . in the structure of the social contract must be that of unanimity" (1962:261). This makes existing institutions powerful indeed.

Unanimous consent arguably is needed within a state of nature to explain the emergence of politics in a fundamental way. Within a politics that has already emerged, however, existing institutional arrangements help explain their own persistence. Under these circumstances, requiring unanimity allows individuals to secure not their extrapolitical position as private individuals but rather their intrapolitical position defined as a set of rights, powers, or institutional guarantees. These fully dressed individuals are the ones who veto changes. They are no longer clones of those who decide de novo about institutions, and therefore they are no longer automatically entitled to their prerogatives.

Buchanan and Tullock, for their part, downplay the conservative implications of applying the unanimous consent rule within institutional settings. The rule, they claim, does not improperly bias decisions toward the status quo since "the idea of *status quo* in terms of established organizational rules is hazy at best" (1962:261). Organizational rules are not independent, observable facts but are parasitic on the private decisions of the participants.

Yet as Charles Plott (1972) points out, the notion of a free-floating constitutional decision completely divorced from a constitutional context is at least as hazy. In order for individuals to estimate the net gains and losses they expect from alternative constitutional arrangements, they must have a relatively clear idea of how their existing rights and possessions will be affected. This clarity is impossible when decision makers exile themselves from the very context in which these rights and possessions are defined. The decision context, in short, determines the baseline against which proposed institutional arrangements are judged. An institutional decision context, in particular, determines the baseline for making decisions about changes in the institution. And though the unanimous consent rule in the state of nature may be a useful analytic device for exploring the emergence of politics, there is no getting around the fact that institutions are a different ballgame.

One obvious difference concerns the case when individuals depart existing institutions in numbers short of unanimity. This creates complicated inter- and intrainstitutional relations involving two states of nature, one between the deviants and the institution and the other among all individuals in a noninstitutional setting. This intermediate case, moreover, is crucial to conventionalists since the interdependencies of institutional life can never be allowed to overrule the independent, bottom-line judgments that reside within each and every individual. An individual, with or without allies, must always be in a position "to reject the 'contract' entirely; he may revert to the state of nature" (Buchanan and Tullock 1962:262). This reversion, of course, is the reversion of an outlaw, which may represent a negligible loss for the institution.

Morally the two states of nature may be equivalent; theoretically there is supposed to be a world of difference between unanimous consent cases and all others. So Buchanan and Tullock's approach to institutional interdependencies—interpreted as a "contract"—spells trouble for the special status of the unanimous consent rule. Since variable numbers of individuals can make the decision to reject the contract, there should, in this respect, be no qualitative difference (in the social contract view) between an individual's solitary decision to desert an institution and an individual's solitary decision to enter the state of nature: "In this, as in other aspects of our construction of the constitutional implications of a consistent individualistic philosophy, the shifts in the fraction of the population approving or disapproving certain changes are not of central importance" (1962:262).

The implied demotion of the particular fraction known as unanimous consent is incompatible with Buchanan and Tullock's previously noted elevation of it.[23] By insisting on its importance, they attempt to preserve the conventionalist foundation of institutional life while at the same time granting institutional constraints operational importance. In an institutional setting, in other words, the unanimous consent rule captures the effect of institutional constraints insofar as that requirement makes institutions difficult to leave. But Buchanan and Tullock's conventionalism cannot, in the end, abide this operationalization of constraint. It makes the very decision to depart from an institution a collective rather than an individual matter. Conventionally understood, an institutional "constraint" simply reflects the percentage of the population that chooses to conform to the identified institutional regularity.

We are now in a position to summarize the problems of social contract theory. When a specific decision rule for getting out of the state of nature is not itself part of the original state of nature, constitutional decisions are ill-defined. When this decision rule is recognized as part of the status quo, on the other hand, the state of nature loses its special position and the decision rule no longer seems to be an object of choice; thus, thoroughgoing conventionalism is stymied. Indeed, as Plott (1972) notes, if every rule for organizing a polity is chosen according to some rule, decision makers face an infinite regress.

Plott, I should add, has no illusions about the specific case of unanimous consent. It is no less a political decision rule than the alternatives Buchanan and Tullock reject. Hence, the assumption of unanimous consent, applied either inside or outside the state of nature, does not avoid the circularity of invoking a political mechanism to explain political arrangements. This circularity, Plott concludes, presents Buchanan and Tullock with the problem of infinite regress just noted. And the circularity will continue to plague any brand of conventionalism that insists on explaining institutions as the product of an explicit collective choice: "All rules are nested in another set of rules that define how the first set of rules can be changed" (Ostrom 1990:51). At any rate, the state-of-nature construct fails to block the circularity.

Plott's own solution is to demonstrate how all the background conditions of choice—including the rules for making decisions and the status quo as status quo—can be formalized as *objects* of individual decision. The infinite regress is broken without ignoring any special role the status quo plays. As Plott (1972:97) summarizes his own position, the question of institution creation is to be answered "by an application of the theory of games *after* a satisfactory theory of individual preference for rules has been developed." Thus, games can become the products as well as the conditions of individual and collective choice.

Although Plott's reformulation saves the social contract format, it puts the entire conventionalist approach in a precarious position. For one thing, his particular brand of conventionalism only deepens Buchanan and Tullock's already strong assumptions about the mental paraphernalia agents bring to the decision-making situation. Not only does each agent supposedly survey a selection of complete constitutional alternatives; each agent also comes equipped with full ex ante preferences concerning political decision rules.[24] Certainly, Plott, like Buchanan and Tullock, imputes substantial political content to the agent's psychology before there is supposed to be politics. The result is not so much an explanation of politics as a change of venue, moving politics from the public arena to the mind. It is unclear how an explanation of political institutions appealing to preformed representations in the mind can avoid triviality, not to mention empirically rooted skepticism about the assumed psychology.[25]

An ex ante preference for rules, moreover, does not itself determine the game that individuals will be playing when in fact they make their collective choices. The mere stipulation that they will be in a state of nature hardly solves anything. Defining the specific rule-bound game that will be a focal point for subsequent calculations and decision making represents a coordination problem—a larger game of incomplete information—that is very complex (Calvert 1991).

An explanation of institutions, finally, is not the same as an account of them once created. In time, they become the status quo and represent new constraints and conditions of choice. Just because each individual has a full psychological representation of these institutional frameworks does not mean they are somehow dissolved. My point is not just that Plott's version of social contract theory shows that choices made within institutions are different from choices about institutions made from the vantage point of an abiding state of nature. Rather, in the absence of an abiding state of nature, rational choice theory cannot avoid considering the impact of the institution as the framework in which preferences are expressed. For even if the application of game theory depends on a theory of individual preference for rules, the institutional game is still the context in which these preferences are revealed.

In Buchanan and Tullock's original contract theory, of course, the state of nature is always lurking in the background. This condition just intensifies the problem. It leaves institutions extremely vulnerable to the kind of rational considerations that first spawned them, for only the very powerful or the very gullible will approve of every outcome emerging from an institution. Indeed, Buchanan and Tullock (1962) carefully distinguish between unanimous support for an institution as a whole and the less than unanimous support required for each authoritative decision. When calculating their support for proposed institutions, members of the state of nature recognize that they will be on the losing side of some decisions.

Those who support the agreement ex ante will, therefore, often have good reasons to dodge or renegotiate the agreement ex post, even though institutions are designed to deflect this opportunism (e.g., Williamson 1985). On the other side of the equation, those who ostensibly enforce the agreement face considerable incentives to violate or exploit it. The general difficulties that principals have controlling their agents (e.g., Pratt and Zeckhauser 1985) are only exacerbated when the constitutional system itself, including the law, is the subject of the contract among the parties. Institutional machinery, once established, also represents a significant lure to subjects seeking the rents available to rulers and their partners (Coleman 1988:266–76; Brennan and Buchanan 1985; Vanberg and Buchanan 1989:54–6).

All these problems are not just signs of the inevitable weakness of institutions. They are symptomatic of the inability of social contract theory to make sense of institutional constraint, with a concomitant inability to explain why institutions are created in the first place. In social contract theory, the individual's capacity to assess the state of nature and find it wanting in light of better alternatives is of a piece with the capacity to scrutinize and transcend the resulting institutional arrangements (Buchanan 1975). The power to leave the wilderness is also the power to return. When institutions are understood in the manner of social contract theory, they exist on the sufferance of the participants. So long as institutions are continuing objects of choice, the choosers, in the end, will not be the objects of institutions.

3.

In the last ten years or so, rational choice theorists have begun to address the problems of social contract theory with considerable resourcefulness. Attempting to avoid the synoptic psychology of the social contract approach, Andrew Schotter's (1981) model of the genesis of institutions offers a good illustration of the achievements and continuing difficulties associated with this new development, known as the new institutionalism.

The initial state of nature, according to Schotter, is best modeled as a prisoners' dilemma supergame, an infinite sequence of ordinary (that is, static) prisoners' dilemma games. Cognizant of this sequence, agents do not confront supergames one iteration at a time. They adopt policies about how they should choose contingent on the previous choices of the other participants. As a result, Schotter demonstrates, tacit behavioral norms can develop that lead rational players to produce the superior outcome (A_1, B_1), believing with near certainty that unilateral deviation from it will be disadvantageous. Though defined as a set of norms, an institution is also a solution to supergame problems rooted in the state of nature (Schotter 1981:155).

Schotter demonstrates that so long as residents of the state of nature condition their behavior on their developing expectations concerning the behavior of others, a stable system of behavioral regularities—an institution—can emerge. Tacit behavioral norms evolve that perform essentially the same function as political authorities, constitutions, or Leviathans perform in more standard contract theory: the norms indicate the punishments or adverse behavioral reactions participants can expect if they fail to conform to the institution. As each individual's expectations about the behavior of others converge with their actual behavior, the emerging behavioral regularity becomes stable.

Since the following comments will be critical of Schotter's solution, I first want to emphasize the extent to which he avoids many of the problems plaguing the social contract approach. He does not invoke unanimous consent or any other decision rule in his explanation of institutional arrangements. True, all individuals ultimately do decide to conform to the institution, and that is what assures its stability. Yet individuals do not conform because they unanimously agree on a decision rule. Each finds conformity best given her information about existing patterns of behavior, the punishments awaiting nonconformity, and the preferences of others. Participants are not expected to enter the game equipped with full-blown political plans or intentions. There is not a single act of creation.

Institutions, rather, arise as a by-product of individually rational adaptations to new information about the behavior of others. This information about past behavior encourages mutual trust for the future. Schotter thus brings the explanation of political institutions much closer to what Nozick (1974) calls an "invisible-hand explanation." They are shown to be "the result of human action, but not the execution of any human design" (Ferguson 1980:122).

Since institutions develop organically, Schotter's scheme is much more "local" and evolutionary than Buchanan and Tullock's. At the same time, this evolutionary process does not reach the level of disaggregation described by Buchanan as an "uncontrolled and uncontrollable process of historical development" (Buchanan and Tullock 1962:318). Schotter's organic process is situated somewhere between the two extremes, reflecting the importance of rational choice in a social environment over which the individual has only a partial influence.

This simulation of social contract outcomes seems to achieve for its players a kind of organization associated with institutions, yet apparently without social contract theory's implausible psychological machinery. The more accurate reading, however, is that although the full machinery is not required initially, the relevant psychological paraphernalia of the social contract is in place by the time the evolutionary process reaches equilibrium. At equilibrium, specifically, players are required to have accurate expectations about everyone's behavior, which Schotter expressly equates with universal knowledge of the institutional norms (that is, the rules or regularities of behavior). They must also know that all others conform to the norms, that everyone knows that they all know, and conform to, the institutional norms, and so on. Ultimately, the full psychological machinery must be in place in order for institutions to exist. Social contract theory delayed, it turns out, is not social contract theory denied.

In a word, the core of the scheme is conventionalist. Schotter, in fact, explicitly draws on Lewis (1969) for his definition of institutions, adopting all the features of his proposal save its self-policing quality. What polices institutions, according to Schotter, is the anticipation of adverse behavioral reactions, not a direct unconditional preference for universal conformity. But agents are expected to conform knowingly to the institutionalized regularities of behavior and to know that everyone else conforms. Thus, a critical step in the existence of an institution is the formation of correct expectations concerning these regularities, which otherwise would not be stable.

What makes Schotter's approach conventionalist is its requirement that all behavioral regularities associated with the institution must eventually be the intended expression of correct participant expectations. The latter are the real source of the regularities, which merely verify individual expectations and choices. Institutions, accordingly, act in the intended way. Conversely, institutions disappear by definition the moment those intentions and complete, accurate expectations about behavioral regularities disappear.[26] In the final analysis, institutions are defined to be what their participants think of them and intentionally reproduce. In preceding chapters we saw how artificial and limiting this definition is.

To be clear, my complaint is not that Schotter treats the rational choice diptych of preference and belief as the proximate cause of institutional regularities. It *is* the proximate cause. Nor do I believe that institutions, as Schotter defines them, cannot arise in the real world. But the requirement that there be a "correspondence" between the diptych and the institutional regularities deactivates institutions by definition. It precludes the possibility of their doing something independently of either the knowledge or the intentions of the participants. Institutions merely confirm the accuracy of the real forces, beliefs, and preferences.

There is, it is fair to say, a formal sense in which institutions are not passive in Schotter's setup: the behavioral regularities expressing participant expectations also lead participants to reproduce those regularities. Participants act on the information that their expectations have been fulfilled. Yet in that sense, as I observed in chapter 1, a deer shot by hunters plays an active role insofar as the hunters act on the information that their expectations have been fulfilled. In the same sense, when voters find their hands on the intended lever in a voting booth, they are encouraged to follow through. The hunter and the voters remain fully responsible, as do the participants in Schotter's institutions. An institution merely serves to complete a feedback loop whose sole driving force is the rational agent. Any additional role for the institution is automatically discounted since the corresponding beliefs and preferences take up all the explanatory slack.

My point, in short, is that Schotter's overly strong psychological assumptions allow him to fudge the potentially active role of institutions conceived as the by-product of individual decisions. Conventionalism is hard to give up, so Schotter precludes these problematic institutional effects by packing all the institutional details, the regularities of behavior variously called norms or rules, into the heads of the participants. Acting on this knowledge, participants continually reinvent the institution, reproducing the behavioral patterns associated with it.[27]

The attraction of defining institutions in terms of rules is that rules can be ambiguously understood either as abstract entities—universals—capable of being apprehended by one or more people or as the internalized counterparts of those entities. In the former case, institutions take on the character of objects external to the participants and provide one possible port for a new institutionalism adrift on a sea of subjectivity. As I previously noted, the problem with this interpretation, which is not strictly conventionalist, is that there is no satisfactory account of human interactions with these abstract entities. Alternatively, rules and regularities can be understood as internal pieces of an individual's psychological machinery. In that case, Schotter can no longer assume that what the observer describes as an institution corresponds to what the participant knowingly and intentionally reproduces based on these internal constraints.[28]

Ambiguity, nonetheless, is a clever policy. Asked to explain what institutions are, rational choice theorists can talk about public rules to which people conform. Asked to explain why the rules are effective, they can talk about their psychological efficacy, normative or prudential. The efficacy of institutions is still explained in individualistic, psychological terms.

In the specific case I have been considering, the correspondence between psychology and institutional object disguises the need to choose between the two alternatives and to show how each can be cashed out in ontological terms. Given the correspondence, Schotter's theory can "externalize" rules and regularities when institutional effects are at issue and "internalize" them when trying to account for those effects. His theory thus attempts to appropriate the benefits of positing external institutional objects by internalizing the costs in the form of strong psychological assumptions. Without these assumptions, the crucial distinction between the external institutional object and its internal representation would be more apparent.

To anticipate the results of the fuller analysis I undertake in chapter 4, institutional realism would reaffirm this distinction as follows. An agent's decision is not simply a force acting from without on an institutional regularity of behavior reflecting all agents' decisions. Rather, the institution in which agents are embedded establishes certain constraints on their behavior regardless of whether they are understood as such. The institution exerts this influence by restricting the set of feasible alternatives. Specifically, in institutional settings there are limits to the agent's freedom of movement, if this freedom is defined in the usual way as the possibility of selecting different alternatives, holding all other agents' choices constant. When this is understood by rational agents, they may incorporate these limits by making their own choices according to what is called evidential decision theory. But the limits obtain regardless.

4.

So far, I have portrayed strong psychological assumptions as ad hoc devices for solving problems posed by the conventionalist demands of standard rational choice theory. These assumptions can be given a firmer foundation. Rational expectations theory assumes that information, like other commodities, is costly and therefore is used optimally. This means that rational participants, efficiently processing all available information, can detect any emerging patterns of behavior they witness and, accordingly, can choose whether to maintain them. Agents will behave as if they are able to predict the resulting behavioral regularities using the model their information best supports.

Schotter (1981:78–79) notes that the resulting rational expectations equilibria have the useful self-fulfilling quality associated with his institutional equilibria. Robert Lucas, a leading rational expectations theorist, implicitly concurs by suggesting that there really is no alternative approach to the study of social arrangements: "conventions and institutions do not simply come out of the blue, arbitrarily imposing themselves on individual agents" (1981:4). Lucas, in effect, frames a terse appeal to conventionalist intuitions: if institutions were not chosen, their existence would be miraculous.

The influential rational expectations literature notwithstanding, it still is important to distinguish between internal representations of macro-level processes, however rationally used, and the macro-level processes themselves. The relevant distinction in the rational expectations case is between the internal model that agents employ and the external model, as defined by the theorist, that they are trying to specify. As it turns out, the identity of the two models is by no means assured even when the external model is made "true" by the behavior of agents who develop their internal models in a fully rational way.

A gap between the internal and external models is particularly likely to open up insofar as there are interdependencies among the agents within an institution or economy (Frydman and Phelps 1983). For one thing, agents with the same information will not necessarily infer the same model, as any empirical researcher is well aware. Even fully rational agents can infer different models or arrive at different estimates of a model's parameters. Second, agents may have insufficient information to estimate their models, a task interdependency complicates. Third, there is no guarantee that optimizing individuals produce forecasts consistent with equilibrium, even when they are using the correct model of the economy. Rational expectations theory accordingly must take additional steps to connect rationality and equilibrium behavior.

Within some models, for example, a necessary condition for the existence of a rational expectations equilibrium is the initial or eventual homogeneity of perceived and actual participant beliefs (see Phelps 1983; Frydman 1982).[29] Or, in the somewhat more dramatic formulation of a noted economist, "Expectations of natural events cause no problem. But expectations of a higher order—expectations of others' expectations—force economics away from this traditional safe haven. Where such expectations are important to an area of study, we shall find ourselves—God forbid!—in the same barrel with sociology and political science" (Cagan 1983:45).

In light of this, Roman Frydman and Edmund Phelps (1983:11) suggest that institutions can make up the shortfall between individual rationality and rational expectations equilibria by ensuring the necessary homogeneity. Thus, in claiming that agents are rationally induced to form models of their environment, Frydman and Phelps argue the rational expectations approach "points toward a macrotheoretical foundation for microeconomics and therefore macroeconomic behavior" (1983:28).

Rational expectations equilibria may require homogeneous beliefs. Homogeneous beliefs, in turn, may require social norms or institutions. But in Schotter's work, as in all works of standard rational choice theory, the institutionalization of behavior is tantamount to the homogenization of beliefs concerning the norms or rules of behavior. Apparently, rational expectations are no substitute for institutional analysis.

To be fair, Schotter (1981:109–39) thinks institutional norms reduce the information requirements for rational behavior and thus induce equilibria when coordination would otherwise be difficult or impossible. Agents need not know the history of the game they are playing but can rely instead on the norms developed within the game and passed on to them. These norms embody all the information that agents could get from that history. For some situations, then, Schotter's account tells us how players can get their information. Yet it does not guarantee a solution to the problems with rational expectations theory described above. With respect to the knowledge requirements imposed on rational agents, Schotter has made a significant advance. In crucial respects, however, he presents an evolutionary version of Buchanan and Tullock.

5.

Standard rational choice theory is forced to stretch the required psychological ambit of institutional participants who, by the very definition of an institution, must internalize institutional regularities. Accordingly, rational choice theory does not, in the end, recognize the extent to which participants may have unintended, partial or incompletely understood behavioral relations with institutions—or at least with any institutions that matter (see note 9).

By the same token, Schotter's theory of institutional norms allows him to distinguish the conditions agents face prior to the formation of an institution and the conditions they face during and after. This contrasts with Buchanan and Tullock's (1962) approach, where the original state of nature plays a role even within the most highly developed political institution. Although Schotter continues to burden institutional theory with unjustified psychological assumptions, perhaps his kind of approach solves contract theory's other problem: making sense of institutional constraint.

An important claim to this effect is made by Kenneth Shepsle (1986; 1989:137–38, 144), who suggests that a fundamental temporal asymmetry—institutions are first created and only then have their effects—serves to weaken the impact of social contract theory's homogeneous treatment of institutional and state-of-nature settings. Once created, Shepsle notes, institutions become the background for any decision to dissolve them. And just as the framework of the prisoners' dilemma encourages the formation of institutions, so does the institutional framework discourage its own dissolution. Specifically, institutional conditions influence players in two ways. One, Schotter's, is the certainty of adverse behavioral reactions to any deviation from the institutionalized regularity. The other, Shepsle's, operates through the uncertainties surrounding any attempt to initiate nonconformity.

As Shepsle observes, existing institutions represent a familiar, settled pattern of behavior. The much greater uncertainty attached to deviation induces risk-averse players into continued conformity. Those attempting to structure a new institutional arrangement, moreover, confront serious transaction costs.[30] Innovative bargaining is onerous and alternative agreements are opportunistically broken. In sum, deviation from the institutional regime is fraught with relatively high uncertainty and low expected utility. Social contract theory, by contrast, underestimates these frictions insofar as it treats institutional outcomes as "preference-driven" (Shepsle 1989:136).

The upshot of Shepsle's proposed solution is this: "Like relationships, institutions may be thought of as part of what embeds people in social situations. They are the social glue missing from the behavioralist's more atomistic account" (1989:134). I think Shepsle is right about the significance of institutions. On those very grounds, I doubt whether his account of institutions is complete.

In his account, institutions are still rooted in participant preferences for feasible outcomes, just as the conventionalist insists. He simply amends this claim by recognizing that actors have not only preferences but also expectations concerning the actions and preferences of others. What the institutionalization of behavior means, in other words, is that agents are better able to anticipate their fellow members' behavior. This translates institutional constraints into the tightening of beliefs.

Yet as Schotter makes clear, these beliefs are inferences based on previous behavior, which agents treat as a form of nonverbal communication or signaling concerning the emerging institution.[31] Thus, what distinguishes existing institutions is not so much their current constraint but rather the likelihood that the regularities associated with them will again be chosen by their free-thinking participants. This way of embedding people in social situations is not qualitatively different from that of the atomized theory.

The original social contract analysis recognized that since each agent's results depend on the choices of others, all must reason strategically in light of everyone's preferences and alternatives. Supplementing this game theoretic insight, the new institutionalism insists that these agents are also entitled to factor in their uncertainties about the likelihood of alternative outcomes and the costs of obtaining them. By this interpretation, individuals face a game whose payoffs reflect the agents' fully calculated opportunity costs, the expected utility of the alternatives forgone. This seems less a radical departure from atomized contract theory than an intelligent modification. If the original theory is preference-driven, Shepsle's, still atomized, is preference-plus-belief-driven. Institutions are not the glue joining agents so much as handcuffs to which all parties have keys. What institutions per se do remains unclear.

Institutions, it appears, do not have any distinct constraining role but merely summarize the fact that participants see no advantage in changing their situation, which therefore reflects their choices. Victor Goldberg (1985) has effectively argued that the transaction costs standing in the way of institutional change are, in this sense, just like other costs that individual actors face. An appeal to them, therefore, does not in and of itself make an ostensibly institutional analysis any more an analysis of institutional constraint.

Nor would it necessarily help to refine this appeal by insisting on a possibility Goldberg in fact notes, that these transaction costs are distinctive by somehow being institution-specific. As it stands, this suggestion is too vague. According to the new institutionalism, for example, all this means is that owing to differences in risk, the transaction costs of deviating from institutional regularities are, in general, substantially higher than the transaction costs of departing from other social situations.

Note, again, that this diagnosis does not use the concept of institutions to explain social order but rather treats it as a catchphrase for the existence of social order. Institutions become one fairly arbitrary end segment of a continuum measuring uncertainty concerning the expected behavior of others.[32] Indeed, if the equilibrium that makes the consequences of conformity more predictable were in fact the noncooperative equilibrium of the prisoners' dilemma, or its super-game, then presumably we would find ourselves talking of agents being embedded in the social glue of anarchy.

New institutionalists still insist that the institutions they define are able to constrain. Institutional constraints are demonstrably effective, Shepsle and Weingast (1981) suggest, since the same set of individual preferences leads to different outcomes in different institutional settings or structures. The congressional committee system, for instance, precludes the infinite cycle of outcomes that would otherwise occur if Congress directly aggregated the preferences of its members. The emergence of these structurally induced equilibria shows that institutional constraints are data for agents rather than mere correlates or products of their expectations.

Does this influential work secure a place for institutions within rational choice theory? The claim that different institutional arrangements can lead to different outcomes is relatively uncontroversial. As many defenders of the standard theory quickly concede, an unstructured preference aggregation model of institutions is neither accurate nor particularly promising as an explanation of stable outcomes (e.g., McKelvey and Ordeshook 1984:182–83). What they are unwilling to concede is that this notion of institutional constraint represents a genuine addition to the rational choice apparatus. Their reasoning is as follows. The appeal to structure-induced equilibria is an unsatisfactory or at least incomplete substitute for a full explanation of institutional phenomena, for the appeal to structure invokes institutional forces that are themselves in desperate need of explanation. Yet when this explanation is unpacked, the old theory of institutional choice emerges:

> Structures induce equilibria because individuals select structures within which preferred equilibria appear. We are saying . . . that since institutions and rules are the products of human choice, we should assume that like other choices, they are designed to attain some preferred set of outcomes. And when such outcomes cannot be attained under them and when some set of persons possesses the appropriate means, those institutions will either be modified or bypassed. (McKelvey and Ordeshook 1984:201; see also Riker 1980)

Note the tacit assumption that appropriate means do not include the existence of appropriate institutions, and that the products of human choice are intended objects refashioned as intentions and information are revised. The result is Buchanan and Tullock minus the explicit state-of-nature setting.

It is not difficult to see the conventionalist presuppositions lurking behind this fundamental challenge to Shepsle and Weingast's apparently more substantial understanding of institutions. But their response to this challenge, though important, does not dispute these presuppositions (Shepsle and Weingast 1984:219). Rather, after conceding their truth, they invoke the preference-plus-belief-driven model discussed above. Once again, rational choice theory solves the problem of institutional constraint by requiring rational agents to internalize the operative features of the whole institution. In the next chapter, we will begin to see why the idea of structurally induced equilibria, which I have already used to illustrate institutional constraint, can be defended without the conventionalist addendum.

4.

The Return of Institutions

According to conventionalists, institutions do not simply come out of the blue. Yet although institutions do not come out of the blue, they do not necessarily come out of agents' heads à la social contract theory. Institutions arise by evolution as well as revolution. In response to this challenge, the new institutionalists have developed a fall-back position. "The whole of Roman law may not have sprung fully formed from any one person's forehead, but its bits and pieces, much like the bits and pieces of a European cathedral built over many centuries, were surely the result of human agency" (Shepsle 1989:145). Institutional realism asks, Why not go further? People do not have to intend even the institutional bits and pieces as such, and a fortiori their calculations may not even encompass the aggregate institution as a single entity. Nor must individuals understand its effects as institutional. And even if they do, their institutional context may constrain the ways they can act on this knowledge.

To go further is to appreciate that an institution, unlike a convention, need not be an object per se of agent decision making, either by definition or by requirement of theory (though I by no means exclude this empirical possibility). Considered as an aggregate of human beings, an institution is an arrangement of both their behavior and behavioral dispositions leading them to reproduce the arrangement in question. In the process, institutions typically relieve individuals of the full obligations of supervision and forecasting. The choice posed by conventionalism, then, between institutions that arbitrarily impose themselves on individual agents and institutions that agents knowingly impose on themselves is too stark.

An institutional game, in particular, imposes constraints on its participants that at any given time constitute a brute fact of life for them. These constraints are not self-selected; they nonetheless are social structural—institutional—rather than "only" physical. In other words, each agent's status as a physical component of a physical aggregate coincides with his status as an institutionally defined component—a player—of the institutional game. The existence of interlocking institutional roles can cue the agent into the institutionally determined dependencies that connect one agent's free choices with those of the other players.

Thus, rational actors working within these institutional constraints may be more successful when they understand them, even if they cannot control them. The unavoidable physical fact of behavioral connection permits one player to recognize and exploit the fuller institutional significance of his decisions. Paradoxically, institutions can constrain and enhance the agent's prospects. By contrast, the standard approach sees agents' decisions not only as physically distinct but, in the end, as socially independent.

One impediment to taking institutional constraint seriously, or even allowing it as a theoretical possibility, has been the perception that the institution-as-creation theme is inescapable if institutions are to be explained at all. For if institutions are not creations, they must be granted a distinct ontological status, and this, conventionalists feel, is no solution at all. True, the basic rules of the institutional game— the structure of physical possibilities—already enjoy an independent status. They are constituted by the facts and laws of nature, so their independence is unproblematic (except to a philosopher of science). To count institutions as distinct entities, on the other hand, is apparently to embrace some atavistic form of holism.

The solution I propose is not to define institutions as unintended or incompletely understood. That is an empirical issue. My point, derived from the preceding chapter, is just the opposite: for extraneous and unconvincing reasons, rational choice theorists have defined institutions in a way that sets serious, a priori limits on these empirical possibilities.

As shown in chapter 1, it is possible to understand institutions as distinct entities having empirically contingent relations with their participants. The trick, again, is to interpret them as physical aggregates of their membership, limited to the time these members happen to be doing whatever is institutionally relevant. By this interpretation, the institution is not necessarily the object participants conceive it to be, yet it is not supernatural either. Its existence, in fact, is no more or less problematic than that of the participants themselves.

An institution in this sense is influential as a context—the aggregate of institutional participants facing any agent—even when this is not perceived or expected accurately. The piece of the institution an agent encounters can still encourage her to reproduce, however unknowingly, the local conditions that eventually elicit reproduction of the whole. For one thing, the institution is composed of real people who are prepared to behave in ways that physically affect the agent, whether or not she sees the whole picture, whether or not she can give a rational choice account of these obstacles, or even whether or not her account describes the constraining behavior in the same way as the actor who intentionally produces it.

Conventionalism has tended to assume that because a rational act takes place under some intentional description (agent *A* chose *x* over *y*), the constraint it represents should appear under the same description. This assumption helps coordinate the actions of different actors in such a way that they can be understood to produce the same institution. Institutional realism, on the other hand, can recognize that the constraining features of an action may be unknown, incidental, or accidental to the agent producing it—indeed, may be comprehensible only as a description relating different and relatively isolated producers. In more familiar language, the constraint may be structural, as when members of a tribe do not find the option of starting a corporation available to them.

As I have noted, a second and more subtle reason for the impact of institutional constraints is the possibility that agents can make use of the fact that all agents are similarly constrained. Insofar as the institutionally defined roles of players are connected to form a game, players may be in a position to recognize the larger institutional significance of their actions. Since all players are institutionally constrained, what one player does may provide him with valuable information about the actions of others. When players use their behavior diagnostically, they again violate the standard conventionalist assumption that they are, in a fundamental sense, socially independent.

Ultimately, institutional constraint in the absence of full participant understanding is of a piece with the diagnostic use of constraint just discussed. That is to say, constraints that can operate behind the backs of agents are precisely the kinds of constraints that, once understood, can still be effective and therefore exploited. Of course, the idea that constraints on an agent can operate without being filtered through a set of accurate expectations about them is hardly unknown in rational choice theory. As Gary Becker (1976:153–68) shows, the central propositions of demand theory can be fulfilled in the absence of rational agents or even stable preferences. Budget constraints exert their pressure regardless. Yet these constraints are largely explicable as direct physical constraints on time and resources.[1] This is not generally true for institutions, new institutionalist talk of transaction costs notwithstanding. That rational choice theorists are tempted to reduce institutional constraints to psychology is understandable.

Conventionalists see institutions as collective solutions to game theoretic problems, not as the structures within which these problems are solved. Institutional realists, by contrast, hold that nothing, especially no institution, is a collective choice *simpliciter*. Individual decisions are collected or aggregated and acquire social meaning only within a certain format, which is typically institutional. Tip O'Neill's maxim—all politics is local politics—is mistaken because, aside from any ordinary empirical doubts about it, the content of politics and its effect on individual participants may transcend the particular institutional parts they confront in their decision making. What political actors collectively decide may go beyond, or contradict, what as individuals they intentionally decide. More important, even a proper interpretation of what they intentionally decide must get its bearings from the institutional context.

Nor would an individual's or a society's carefully developed political intentions and understanding automatically translate into control. People can comprehend the institutional facts that their behavior collectively reproduces without deluding themselves into thinking that mere comprehension necessarily makes these facts any less potent or any more subject to their dictates. Institutional embeddedness still matters so long as individuals, acting on this comprehension, must act within the very institutional constraints they may fully understand.[2]

According to this interpretation, existing institutions are not at the mercy of time travelers whose baseline for judgment is an ancient state of nature. The baseline for judgment within institutions is nothing other than the institutional status quo. Institutions are the framework in which agents make decisions concerning the inventory of possible acts, alternative collective arrangements, and opportunities for leaving or reforming the social order in light of who, as participants, they are. Although these institutions may not be there at the end of the day's calculations, they are unavoidably there at the beginning.

In this chapter, I begin to develop this claim in a more positive fashion by exploring in detail the precise connection, broached in chapter 3, between the structure of a game and its players. This analysis shows not only how institutional realism can interpret game theory but also how the issue of realism is delicately entwined with the most basic details of game theoretic research. In the end, conversely, even heroic psychological assumptions cannot rescue the conventionalist reasoning that supports some well-known solutions to specific games.

Institutional realism should not be viewed as establishing merely a gestalt-like choice in which the same behavioral arrangements can be viewed institutionally or conventionally depending on one's deeper philosophical predilections or attitudes toward robust psychology. I want to show that institutional realism is needed, not merely possible. For that, one must sort out the formal details of the conventionalist approach to rational choice and institutional modeling in addition to the more substantive theoretical issues revolving around social contract theory and the new institutionalism. To this end, I shall explore both sides of the institutional coin: the institution as an aggregate of rational decision makers and the individual decision maker as one of its parts. The remainder of this chapter pays somewhat greater attention to the first side; the next chapter pays somewhat greater attention to the second.

1.

I have likened institutions to the games studied by game theorists. It is time to develop this idea more fully. Think of an institution as a game in extensive form.[3] Roughly, the extensive form characterizes the full sequence of possible moves players can make and the payoffs to each player for each possible outcome.[4] At every stage of this game, a particular player faces a specific set of alternatives from which to choose. The persisting institution includes the particular way the entire collection of players chooses from among these alternatives, move by move. To the institutional realist, the alternatives at any move are determined by the aggregate of behavioral dispositions facing each of the players. I mean *determined* in a technical sense. Corresponding to each aggregate of behavioral dispositions is an institutional game described in extensive form. Conversely, this description cannot change without some change in the aggregate.[5]

Each player is in effect assigned a role in the game. Players fulfill their roles if they behave appropriately when the opportunity to move arises, whatever the ruminations. The game then proceeds smoothly. In the aggregate, of course, the dispositions of players and not just their actual behavior matter, since outcomes in games are contingent on choices in a systematic way. Sometimes this institutional contribution is disguised: when players have perfect information—when they always know exactly where they stand—there is no discrepancy between a player's information about what she is doing and what is actually occurring.[6] This situation, needless to say, is bound to encourage conventionalists.

Games of imperfect information, which are more common, are also less encouraging. Here players do not know exactly which of several possible plays of the game they are actually setting in motion. The poker player bets in ignorance of other hands, the voter votes in ignorance of the choices made by the rest of the electorate. Each player's possible choices, nevertheless, helps determine the alternatives for other players who may have to operate under imperfect information as well. Whatever the level of ignorance, when the game terminates there is still a determinate outcome assigning payoffs to each of the players. Players may never know which outcome actually did occur.

In games involving imperfect information, players may be fully conscious of what they are doing but they fail to understand the full significance of their actions. This gap between information and fact is awkward for conventionalists since it attributes important aspects of the game mechanism to features beyond individual knowledge. As we saw in chapter 3, the conventionalist solution is to assume the existence of some nonplayer, the umpire, whose omniscience maintains the game's psychological interpretation, or at least the illusion of one. Institutional realism, by contrast, is comfortable with the gap between information and fact since a gap signals the institution's contribution.

Fortunately, information can be incorporated into a realist analysis of institutions without seriously disrupting the formal structure of game theory. Understood as a game, an institution defines possible courses of action. These alternatives are not themselves chosen within the institution; they are discovered. In this interpretation, information partitions characterize the way the game structure gets physically expressed—through dealing cards face down, drawing the curtains on voting machines, or decomposing each team of bridge players into two separate partners who have separate memories.

Information, in turn, summarizes how the physical process by which the game plays out impinges on these participants, determining what players do or do not witness. The resulting patterns of information associated with a game thus reflect the systematic relation between player and institution rather than the mental state of the individuals involved. Although information and its partition are certainly crucial to predicting what will happen within the game, they do not, in contrast to von Neumann and Morgenstern (1953), define the game.

This institutional interpretation is able to ground Aumann's (1987) earlier-noted distinction between events and classifications. In the institutional view, the actual course of the game is always an element of some element of the partition, not because of player or umpire knowledge, but because it is the actual course of play for all players whether they know it or not. When a partition, in other words, represents the state of information in the system, one is not entitled to assume that actual, flesh-and-blood institutional participants always have this information. Rather, predictions concerning an arbitrary play of an institutional game cannot distinguish among outcomes that the pattern of information does not itself distinguish: predictions are only to within the partition. Put less impersonally, even perfectly rational participants can do no better, on average, than the partition suggests. The partition, in sum, is defined behaviorally.

2.

An institution, then, is an entity about which its participants may or may not have opinions. Whatever their opinions, participants combine them with their preferences to produce behavioral dispositions and behavior constituting the institution itself. These dispositions and behavior, in turn, acquire a social identity by virtue of their place in the larger institution. As a result, contextual facts about the institutional game persistently intrude when theorists assess and predict the supposedly private calculations of the individual. This means that rational agents do not necessarily execute particular internal, machine-like programs. Their rationality can depend on their situation. Conventional game theory, we shall see, only masks this dependence through its common-knowledge assumptions or other postulates designed either to cap the hierarchy of beliefs about beliefs or to incorporate irrational or shaky behavior into game solutions.

This is not to make the definition of rationality the distinguishing feature of institutions. Institutions differ from conventions to the extent that they can exist independently of the will of participants and influence them in turn. The assumed role of rationality, rather, distinguishes institutions from social structures by presupposing a greater degree of choice on the part of the members of an institution. Though institutions matter, institutional participants need not passively internalize society's instructions or fail to take advantage of opportunities to affect the social organization of their lives. Institutional realism reconciles these ostensibly opposing considerations.

This reconciliation hinges on the distinct ontological identity of institutions. As distinct objects, they can be known, influenced, or even destroyed. They are not just the background of people's lives, like race or gender, but are circumstances they can face as active agents. Yet each individual is a component of these circumstances. An individual who is aware of the institution's influence and wishes not to reproduce it is still, at any given moment, an integral part of it. The sheer existence of the institution confronting participants means each preference, each belief, and therefore each choice is a time slice of the very entity they wish to control. As a result, even rational agents may not have the leverage to rise above their conditions of social interdependence, which intrude even in their rational decision making.

A critic may well respond to this proposed reconciliation as follows: "No individual, I will concede, has complete information about his circumstances. Nor can an individual completely control them. Yet your own distinction between institutions and social structure suggests that you have chosen a bad example to make this point against conventionalism. Institutions are precisely the circumstances of people's lives that tend to be possible objects of choice for them, whether as objects of approval or disapproval. All you have shown so far is that, conceptually speaking, institutions are not *required* to satisfy ordinary assumptions about information and control. What you conveniently ignore is that these more realistic "as if" assumptions can be incorporated in a theory of institutions modeled as games of incomplete information. To spell it out for you, you have not shown that institutional realism makes any predictions about behavior that differ systematically from those of standard rational choice theory. So let us say, in the spirit of compromise, that your theoretical point is well taken. Now let us move on to doing positive social science." That is what I begin to do in the remainder of this chapter.

I do not concede, of course, that the critic's concessions are in any way minor. If the scope of the participants' understanding and control in *institutional* settings is now acknowledged to be an open, empirical question, the critic concedes a new understanding of the nature of social order generally. No longer does social order necessarily depend on recognition from social actors.[7] Yet the critic is right: it is time to show how institutional realism can address what I have only recognized in the abstract, namely, the embeddedness of individuals and their rationality within the institution.

The way I propose to translate this insight into a particular model of institutions is to retrace the progression of the preceding two chapters from rationality to game theory within a framework more congenial to institutional realism. This framework is only one possible solution to the problem of institutional embeddedness. Though consistent with institutional realism, it is not strictly implied by it, not least because the general conception of institutions developed in chapter 1 does not entail rationality on the part of institutional actors. To simplify terminology, however, I shall continue to refer to this refined version as institutional realism.

Although there are considerable theoretical advantages to formulating the analysis in rational choice terms, this is precisely the approach least likely to accommodate impersonal, institutional influences. If institutionally relevant behavior is explained by reflex and habit, idiosyncratic motivations, and decision routines, then the idea that behavior has an unrecognized social content is perhaps easier to swallow. Rational individuals, by contrast, are less likely to have anything going on behind their backs. In that respect, rational choice theory represents not only an opportunity but also a particular challenge to institutional realism.

Before introducing a spate of fairly technical distinctions between institutional and conventional games in general, I think it may be helpful to focus once again on the particular case of the prisoners' dilemma, the launching pad for institutions. In this case, as we have seen in chapter 3, joint cooperation (A_1,B_1) is better than joint non-cooperation (A_2,B_2), but apparently it is rational not to cooperate. "External solutions" (Taylor 1987) to this dilemma, as with Buchanan and Tullock (1962), are unsatisfactory because they are exogenous to the original game and require psychological assumptions that are both conceptually and empirically unsatisfying. "Internal solutions," as with Schotter (1981), are similarly burdened by their assumptions.

Taking a page from Shepsle, let us assume that the process leading players out of the dilemma is not a template for the process subsequent to the initial solution. In particular, let us suppose, following a style of argument framed by Hechter (1987) and Taylor (1988), that a solution to the continuing problem of institutional stability is piggybacked on more local solutions. The latter involve relatively small numbers of people linked by kinship or at least capable of monitoring the behavior of other players and thereby providing selective incentives for cooperation. These local solutions can be arranged in more elaborate hierarchies of control, including formal sanctioning mechanisms, that provide genuinely public goods under circumstances where non-exclusion is truly a problem.

Now, says the conventionalist, suppose that an agent faces this institutionalized hierarchy as a game theoretic fact of life; and in deference to institutional realism's fastidiousness about psychological assumptions, assume that the agent comprehends all this only as a game of incomplete information (that is, up to a probability distribution over possible games). Is there still a problem?

Yes there is, so long as we still want to understand a hierarchy as a constraint on each of its human members—a constraint, that is, by virtue of the hierarchy's status as a social structure. If we are to capture that notion of hierarchy, the institution cannot be completely resolved into an observer's *description* of a chain of behavioral consequences with the chain itself failing to constrain anyone. When the sanctions are applied locally or by other more formally empowered guardians of the status quo, the constraint is purely individual to individual, with the constrainers acting in a purely purposeful way. Rather, following Shepsle's (1989) own desideratum, the hierarchy may determine a situation in which the fact of institutional embeddedness—the institution as social glue—also matters.

Under what circumstances, then, does the constraining role of the game theoretic structure, understood as a social structure, transcend the conventionalist's boundaries? The conventionalist tries to accommodate the idea of hierarchical constraint by imagining that each agent compares it with the possibility of repairing to the state of nature, where a new hierarchy might be forged. Of course, this makes the hierarchy less a constraint than a vulnerable artifact. In any case, what supposedly prevents the larger game in which the hierarchy is embedded from becoming a wholesale prisoners' dilemma is the sanctions controlled within the hierarchy and the transaction costs and uncertainty associated with the alternatives.

This picture, I assert, cannot capture two related developments. On the one hand, the mass institution that is remote from its original and local organizational components may no longer be able to rely on individual sanctions to maintain the high expected utility of continued conformity. On the other hand, an agent's place in the institutional structure may provide a kind of glue that substitutes for the more primitive glue of local arrangements. The fact that the individual is institutionally embedded means that her behavior reflects or is institutionally connected to the behavior of others, and vice versa. These connections can be recognized by participants and assimilated into their rational decision making. Operationally, by virtue of the institutional structure, embeddedness establishes an expected utility "cliff" between actions within the institution and actions outside its defined alternatives: participants are much better off remaining within the institution.

Consider a soldier in a war who is serving some relatively isolated role such as guard duty. The military certainly maintains an organizational hierarchy that may provide some of the constraints on this soldier envisioned by the conventionalist story told above. Yet an individual's guard duty can be a lonely and unsupervised task with relatively small expected benefits and relatively high immediate costs. Well short of deserting the post, the soldier can shirk his duty or seek less visibility in subtle ways that would be hard to detect in part because they are strategies within institutional bounds. Some uncertainty may be involved with shirking, but considerable uncertainty may be involved with being an exposed sentry. Is there some additional institutional constraint on this soldier?

To the conventionalist, the soldier is still, analytically speaking, an outsider in the institution to which he belongs. If, by contrast, we think of him as embedded in an institutional structure assigning various roles to various players, then the fact of institutional membership means being embedded in—being a time slice of—the institution itself. If so, the larger prisoners' dilemma game has been transformed. When players are institutionally embedded, stochastic dependence among their actions by virtue of sharing particular membership roles as players can increase the expected utility of intrainstitutional actions, whereas the absence of dependence may decrease the expected utility of extrainstitutional actions. The prospective deviant, therefore, is relatively isolated.

The individual soldier who shirks may rationally perceive broader implications in this shirking if he understands his own intrainstitutional behavior as predicting the behavior of all whose behavior and existence are similarly categorized by the institutional structure, that is, all who occupy the same or similar institutional roles. When the soldier conforms to institutional requirements, his behavior's stochastic connection to the behavior of other, similarly situated role occupants raises its conditional expected utility. When, by contrast, he deviates, this dependence no longer follows him, and behavioral isolation is the outcome. Any institution defines its particular form of deviance; as they say for legal institutions, *nullem crimen sine lege*. The deviation has no identity, no social or institutional links, other than that provided by the victim institution itself.[8]

The latter result echoes Shepsle's (1986; 1989). Yet recall that according to his approach, the institutional backdrop for this assessment amounts to little more than the fact that deviance is riskier than conformity: institutions are defined by the existence of highly predictable responses to particular choices and unpredictable responses to the others. Institutions, in other words, do not determine these risk differentials; they *are* the risk differentials.

The approach proposed here interprets institutional embeddedness in terms of role expectations mediated by the role structure of the institution. Agents may in time understand their institutional environment, even perhaps increasing their information about the consequences of deviance as well as conformity. Yet they do not necessarily become better equipped to master this environment, reforming or revolutionizing it if they are so inclined. Rather, stochastic dependencies embodied in role expectations survive this more comprehensive understanding and may continue to encourage the persistence of the institution.

By the same token, the existence of stabilizing stochastic dependencies within existing institutions should not disguise one other empirical advantage of institutional realism: its ability to get by without demanding of the agents any wider appreciation of wholesale institutional alternatives, even if only to within some probability distribution. One additional example may suffice to drive the point home.

Why do tribal natives in Papua New Guinea not have a stock market? After all, we have it on the authority of Adam Smith that people are universally prone to truck and barter. Insisting that existing tribal arrangements do not come out of the blue, would conventionalist rational choice theorists say that these natives prefer tribal conditions to stock markets?

A realist answer along the lines I have just outlined would appeal to the structurally induced advantages of intrainstitutional action. For this particular case, an answer even more deeply rooted in institutional realism is better. Given the institutions of Papua New Guinean society, and absent exogenous influences, a stock market simply is not an alternative. Tribal members work within their institutions and not on them because to step outside the institutional structure is to step into a social void.[9] This claim, I might add, is consistent with the notion of rational peasants or political entrepreneurs who take advantage of the opportunities for change afforded by existing arrangements.

My suspicion, of course, is that theoretical models aside, conventionalists would more likely argue in practice that tribal members do not have a complete mental inventory because information costs preclude developing and storing a full set of psychological alternatives. Natives satisfice, seeking satisfactory rather than optimal results. One might dismiss this appeal to psychological costs and benefits as a fancy way of saying, "I don't know," in a manner that is not conspicuously inconsistent with the model. Another response might focus on certain conceptual problems one encounters when trying to fit the satisficing idea into the standard (that is, psychologically rooted) theory of rational choice: to find the optimum inventory restriction relative to the costs of developing it further requires an exploration of inventory possibilities and costs beyond the restriction (see Winter 1964; Elster 1984).

Yet a response more in keeping with my present concerns would reject the entire issue as an artifact of conventionalism. Conventionalists are trying to make sense of a world in which thinking about institutions is analytically prior to the institutions themselves. It is no wonder that the resulting models spin their wheels when asked to consider institutional alternatives that lack even a plausible public referent. To the institutional realist, the content of the imputed thoughts is ultimately anchored in the existing social world through the behavioral alternatives available to the natives. Some might take this as a methodological caveat; as noted in chapter 1, I consider it to be much more substantively significant.

3.

In one sense, the association of game theoretic roles with institutionalized expectations bears the familiar mark of sociology. Yet from a rational choice perspective, as we have seen, traditional sociology understands roles in terms of normative expectations linking agents who in fact are no longer free to pursue their interests rationally: agents execute normative programs rather than effectively choose (Bourdieu 1976). Nor would rational choice theory be comfortable postulating norms as brute facts of social life. By the same token, the standard rational choice theory of institutions does not fully confront the phenomenon of institutional constraint. There is, I suggest, a way to escape social contract theory's frying pan without jumping into the sociological fire.

I propose reinterpreting institutionalized normative expectations as purely cognitive ones. What socially links agents occupying institutional roles, in this view, is their recognition that by virtue of being thus embedded in an institution, each individual's behavior provides useful information about the behavior of other occupants. What one agent does as an occupant of a particular role is a guide to what similarly situated occupants will do or have done. In the place of shared norms guiding the behavior of different role occupants, then, are unavoidable stochastic dependencies among the choices of those occupants.

In contrast to the sociological view, agents are still assumed to be optimizing relative to their beliefs and preferences. In contrast to the standard rational choice view, agents are not free to decide whether to conform to these role dependencies and thereby "accept" the institutionalized links they have found. Agents, for example, cannot exploit this particular information about other role occupants by free-riding on the expected behavior of others. Registered voters, to take the case I will develop in chapter 6, cannot decide to abstain on the belief that others will live up to their role expectations and vote. The agent's decision to vote or abstain gives unavoidable information about the comparable behavior of other voters, information that will affect the agent's calculation of conditional expected utility. Likewise, the physically isolated soldier cannot free-ride on the defensive energies of his colleagues; his own behavior has crucial implications for their behavior.[10]

Thus, what defines institutional embeddedness for rational agents is that the content of this information—and therefore the expected utility conditional on the agent's choice—changes with changes in the agent's decision. What makes this institutionalization a fact to be accommodated, in other words, is the participant's sense, by virtue of occupying an institutional role, that her behavior is a good index of the behavior of other participants. This belief need not be based on a knowledge of biographies or sociodemographic data, since knowledge about the ultimate source of behavioral dispositions is neither here nor there. To the extent that institutionalization matters, each participant's beliefs reflect a contextual fact about those in institutional roles, a fact determined by a myriad of forces of concern only to social scientists and busybodies. The behavioral result is what counts: each participant sees her actions as linked, as a matter of institutionalized fact, with the actions of others. Whether or not they understand the original source of these links, participants at any given time confront them as facts of their institutional life.

Technically, we can say that an agent i is institutionally connected to other occupants of the role with respect to an action A associated with the role to the extent that, for any other arbitrarily chosen occupant j, $prob\,(A_j|A_i\ \&\ I_i) - prob\,(A_j|\neg A_i\ \&\ I_i) > 0$, where the subscript on action A indicates which actor is performing it and I is i's information. Obviously, other factors will influence these probabilities aside from the sheer fact of role similarity. So there may be substantial variation in the expression as it ranges over the various j's. Barring the simplifying assumption of uniformity, this more serious concern would have to be addressed. One possibility is that role dependence for agent i can be defined as: $min_j[prob(A_j|A_i\ \&\ I_i) - prob\,(A_j|\neg A_i\ \&\ I_i)]$ for all j in the role (cf. Hirshleifer's 1987 explanation of public goods provision in terms of a "weakest-link social composition function"). This gives us some sense of the role's core influence.

Still, since there are negative as well as positive influences on the dependence, one might ask whether even this formulation gets at the role's specific contribution. My answer has both a substantive and methodological dimension. Substantively speaking, insofar as the players are relatively anonymous, role occupancy is the relevant information for those decisions that lie within the institution. While it is true that the institutional context is only one factor determining appropriate expectations, it is also true that not all the institutionally relevant influences on the players are contemporaneous. Indeed, it is the aggregate effect of these influences, expressed as current preferences and beliefs, that constitutes the institution. Thus, the idea of stripping away a player's entire history prior to institutional participation is not even useful as an ideal. We are, as noted in chapter 1, dealing with whole people, while what counts within the institution and becomes socially identified there is behavior, not its full etiology.

Methodologically speaking, the decision theory I will impute to these institutional participants—evidential decision theory—does not require them to sort out the obscure causal influences on their behavior. Contemporaneous stochastic dependencies are what matters to these agents. This theory will be taken up in the next section.

Institutional participants may discern, then, an unavoidable stochastic relation between their behavior and that of others within the institution (unavoidable, again, does not mean inexplicable). If this relation were merely a matter of social convention, the participants could mentally step outside their roles in order to decide whether it was best to act with or against them. But this is an institution. Their very ruminations contrasting inside and outside—indeed, the contrast between inside and outside itself—are institutionally defined. The stochastic dependencies shadow them, appearing each time they calculate the conditional expected utility of possible actions. *Stochastic dependence is the social glue of institutions.*

"If the leaders of a country's economic policy are determined to embark on a program of disinflation, then they ought . . . to devise a way to convey the idea that expectation of disinflation should be presumed, that it should be taken to be a fact. . . . In any case, there seems to be a need for a symbol, a catalyst, that will precipitate the expectation on the part of all persons that a certain desired expectation has become general, shared" (Phelps 1983:40). Much as the new institutionalism has learned to substitute supergame equilibria for the Leviathans of social contract theory, institutional realism would substitute institutions for the signals from authorities whom Phelps invokes to homogenize beliefs. Occupying an institutional role can itself be a signal about expectations.

4.

The interpretation of signals and information just proposed serves to shift game theory from the study of psychology, however behaviorally oriented, to the study of the aggregate institutional behavior. This change in focus pays practical dividends. It clarifies, in particular, issues in game theoretic analysis that arise when the course of actual play intrudes into what is usually modeled as a closed information system. As we shall see in the next chapter, this has a bearing on the solutions and predictions of game theory for those situations. For the present, I want to examine more systematically how what might be called rational role expectations might be integrated into rational choice theory. For this we will need to look at game theory a little more carefully.

Standard rational choice theory understands the relation between individuals and their environment in an initially plausible way. Circumstances impinge on decision makers in the guise of information; decision makers use that information to form beliefs about the consequences of their actions; and in light of those beliefs, decision makers act on the basis of their preferences concerning those alternative consequences. A game theoretic situation arises when the environment includes other rational decision makers.

Stated more accurately, it arises when each decision maker correctly believes that there are other decision makers. Their social situation, in an external or public sense, is just a physical collection of human beings. The real game, so to speak, takes place in the minds of the individuals involved. "One might almost say that what game theory is *about* is the . . . process (via 'if I think that you think . . .' arguments) by means of which beliefs are constructed" (Binmore 1987:211–12).

There are certain parts of this story I do not question. First, there is its account of the way choices physically come about. Although the actors in question may be parts of institutions, they certainly remain physically discrete parts. Hence their choices must emerge via an internal process transforming informational input into behavioral output. In no sense can institutions circumvent this individual-level mediation. Second, I am more than willing to abide by von Neumann and Morgenstern's (1953) hardheaded verdict that games—specifically, the rules that players confront—ultimately are part of nature. The realist ontology, in other words, applies not only to the institution as a whole but also to whatever remains of the institution when any particular individual's physical contribution is subtracted. Institutional realism, as a reminder, refuses to traffic in emergent properties.

To see where institutional realism diverges from this account, it will be helpful to note what might first seem to be a minor semantic quibble. When von Neumann and Morgenstern (1953:41–43) describe a game, we have seen, they characterize its rules as the physical *background* into which each player decides to inject a behavior. This places the choosing individual on one side, the physical background on another. As I have just indicated, this is unexceptionable from the standpoint of an ontological accountant. Difficulties ensue, however, as soon as one tries to place an explanatory overlay on the game theoretic entity called an institution. In the latter case, according to the approach I have suggested, the institution will play a role in the very identification of its individual components. The conventionalist, by contrast, wants the overlay to be structured in such a way that the central terms of the explanation—rationality, belief, and preference—can be confined to the individual's side of the divide. The gist of chapter 3 was to raise doubts about the ability of rational choice theory to achieve this aim.[11]

Institutional realists, then, join von Neumann and Morgenstern in acknowledging that the institutional game that individuals confront is part of nature. But they refuse to file individuals on the one side, nature on the other. For if individuals are components of the institution, then they are equally part of nature. So rather than assimilating what is social about the external world to the individual (and, more precisely, to the individual's psychology), institutional realism is inclined to assimilate what is social about the individual to the external world. Individual choices, as I put it earlier, have a social identity by virtue of their social context. The separation of individuals as physical entities should not be allowed to obscure this.

There is a variant of rational choice theory capable of attending to the natural interweaving of individual and institution. Richard Jeffrey proposes a decision theory in which the standard division between individual and nature is discarded:

> A state of nature would then specify what act the agent performs,
> along with everything else one usually takes it to specify. . . . For
> the most part, [alternative] prospects would be outside the agent's
> power to affect, for example, he might prefer fine weather to rain
> tomorrow, even though there are no acts he can perform to realize
> either prospect. But among the prospects there would be certain
> propositions which he can make true or false as he pleases, and
> such propositions do duty as acts, for example, the act of taking
> his umbrella as he leaves the house in the morning would be
> represented by the set of states in which he does just that. Re-
> member: the agent is part of nature and his acts are ingredients in
> states of nature. [In contrast to the more conventional represen-
> tation] I prefer to think of acts as ingredients in states *ab initio*.
> (Jeffrey 1974:75–76)

Institutional realism, of course, translates *nature* as institution and
states of nature as states of the institution and ultimately as structural
descriptions of the collections of individuals composing it. In this
translation, Jeffrey's theory respects the institutional interdependence
of the participants.

I do want to introduce one qualification concerning Jeffrey's discussion. Actors, he suggests, can make certain propositions true or
false as they please. There is a perfectly reputable sense in which the
institutional realist must agree.[12] If an actor can freely choose between
bringing about one event instead of another, then this actor can make
the corresponding propositions true or false. The proximate cause of
the behavior is the actor. On the other hand, the institutional character
of that behavior, the fact that it counts as this or that choice, is not
something the actor controls within the institution. Given an inventory
of institutionally defined alternatives, an actor perceiving them can
choose which to make true. It does not follow that the actor thereby
controls the original inventory. As noted in chapter 1, causing an event
is not the same as causing the event to have such and such a character.

Rationality, belief, and preference can be correctly ascribed to an
institution's members without detracting from the claim that these
descriptions apply, in part, by virtue of the institutional context; that
is, this temporally extended object encompasses the current behavioral
dispositions and behavior of the institution's members. Accordingly,
when a particular choice makes a proposition true, one can ascribe to
the chooser a causal influence without necessarily assuming the actor
intended the proposition to come true, controlled the catalog of propositions he could make true, or would even recognize or understand
the proposition he did make true.

Since this issue of causal influence will come up again, perhaps a
little more detail is in order. I am adopting Donald Davidson's (1980)

analysis of causation as a singular relation between events (denominated *cause* and *effect*), albeit events understood as four-dimensional objects (see chapter 1, note 14). In the present setting, this means four things. First, in the absence of causal *properties,* there is a certain arbitrariness to distinguishing this or that four-dimensional object as a cause or effect (Quine 1960; 1985). Ontological egalitarianism thus tends to encourage a degree of Humean skepticism about objective causation.[13] Second, causes and their consequences can be described in alternate ways, including ways that do not make the causal relation apparent. The institutional character of an event need not correspond to any natural causal characterization. Third, only in an epistemic sense does choice or action cause an indeterminate future to be resolved into one of several possible worlds or events. In a four-dimensional ontology, the future is as fixed and determinate as the past or present.[14] Fourth, in deference to the causal norms regulating scientific theory, one can disallow backward causation, although I happily leave this question to physics.

Obviously, causation under ontological egalitarianism is a complicated matter, and the specific case of institutions shows why. Considered as separate pieces of the institution, actors help make propositions about the institution true. Individuals within institutions, in other words, cause whatever they cause. Yet understood as a proper *part* of the institution, an actor *cum* behavior is literally of a piece with the very institution she influences. This complicates the identification of the causal relation, assuming that there technically is one, since neither causes nor effects are easily associated with the actor considered in isolation. This is not because actors or actions are particularly difficult to distinguish on ontological grounds, but because the identity of the actor as the source of this or that social act is complicated.

Consider the effects produced by the individual as causal agent within an institution. Identifying what the actor causes in any particular case might seem to require nothing more than a steady focus on a physical chain of events. Such and such a voter pulled the voting lever, which caused the machine to register a vote for John Smith, which caused . . . But the causal narrative used here has a contextual dimension. That is, the singular relation between the behavior and some perhaps far-flung physical effect is only useful insofar as it falls under the more general institutional description associated with the overall pattern of rational choice.

Note, for example, all the institutional baggage that comes with the phrase, "Register a vote for John Smith." Physical behavior is as it is; but voting, dissenting, signaling, and the like do not acquire their institutional identities automatically. To qualify, they must fit into an existing arrangement of institutionally related individuals. Therefore, when the effect of an action is to be specified in institutionally loaded terms, determining whether it satisfies the specification has an institutional dimension, which in turn is related to the ongoing dispositions of the actors involved. After the specification, one might declare that the causal effect of a particular rational action is a certain physical behavior or other physical consequence. But this view is retrospective. Independent of institutional context, the effect will not be distinguishable as such. *Pace* Weber, we cannot rely on actors to infuse their behaviors with appropriate identities.

Likewise, there is even a contextual dimension to identifying the actors themselves as the causes of their own behavior. For it is one thing to say that each behavior is produced by some psychological process or state internal to the actor. It is quite another to say there is some specifiable mechanism causing the rational choice one finds in an institutional game, or to say there is some distinguishable psychological event standing out from the continuous four-dimensional stream constituting the actor's life.[15]

In a sense, rational choice theorists already signal the distinction between a causal mechanism and the sheer physical production of behavior when they profess indifference to the realism of their psychological assumptions (Friedman 1953). The mechanism specified by rational choice theory can be entirely unlike the actual psychological process used by rational agents. How can standard rational choice theory justify such seemingly odd permissiveness about empirical controls? Its proponents typically appeal to a strongly instrumentalist philosophy of science, one interested in accurate predictions rather than the truth of theoretical propositions. I now suggest that the indifference to psychological realism has more substantive significance: the very notion of rational choice is surprisingly indifferent to the internal processes of the participants.

Jeffrey's analysis is an ideal vehicle for confronting these myriad complications. By treating individuals and their actions as "ingredients" of an encompassing state of nature, Jeffrey neatly sidesteps the traditional problem of separating actors from their environment. The propositions that individual actions make true encompass the whole messy arrangement of what in our example is the individual and the institution. Appropriately, Jeffrey's definition of rationality is openly indifferent to causal considerations, which depend on the distinctions and somewhat artificial separations described above. An act is rational, according to Jeffrey (1983), if the agent's expected utility given that action is higher than the agent's expected utility given any other action. A causal connection between act and valued outcome is not required.

The soldier on duty or the dissatisfied New Guinean, then, contemplates extrainstitutional behavior by calculating its conditional expected utility. Given the separation of the deviant act from institutional structure, its social significance will be relatively small. Accordingly, it carries little information about the behavior of others. Intrainstitutional behavior, by contrast, can have relatively high conditional expected utility insofar as the institutional structure defining the role of player provides considerable information about the similar behavior of others. These role expectations, in turn, influence rational behavior favoring the persistence of the institution.

The crucial consideration, again, is that the agent is not modeled as an outsider acting *on* the institution. In more technical terms, the notion of expectation is deliberately homogeneous, showing no special regard for expectations that reflect the causal consequences of an act. This feature has generated a considerable amount of controversy, which needs to be addressed if rational role expectations are to be assigned any role in explaining institutions. The next section offers, in some detail, a more general case for the legitimacy of the underlying theory of rational choice, which has been called evidential decision theory.

5.

Causal decision theory, which was discussed in chapter 3, probably has the support of most specialists; it grounds the standard interpretation of game theory. I wish to defend a version of evidential theory, however, as an empirical tool. Although in many cases the division between these two camps has no practical impact, there are important cases where their recommendations diverge. Empirical research concerning such cases seems to favor evidential theory, as we shall see later.

A rational action, according to evidential decision theory, is one yielding the actor the highest conditional expected utility. When a choice is rational, making it is welcome news to the decision maker. Although I am only interested in empirical applications of this definition, I recognize that its scientific standing may depend, in part, on its normative legitimacy. Evolutionary biological and social pressures may favor normatively rational strategies for survival. On a more prosaic level, not just any deductive theory counts as rational choice theory. It must describe "truly" rational behavior.

The obvious complaint against the normative validity of Jeffrey's general approach is that it mistakenly focuses on the evidential value of behavior. As a result, the complaint goes, its followers are fooled by irrelevant statistical relations between their possible actions and the outcomes of interest. Rational individuals should go to a doctor when they are sick, even though there is a positive statistical relation between going to the doctor and being terminally ill. They should be concerned only with relations reflecting the causal efficacy of their actions, not with administering "probabilistic placebos" (Jeffrey

1981:478). This criticism, which is associated with causal decision theorists, holds that a rational decision maker chooses an action on the basis of its capacity to cause favorable outcomes.

In his widely discussed defense of evidential theory, Ellery Eells (1982) observes that agents who understand the underlying causal connection will not view the fear of serious illness as a deterrent to seeing the doctor. They will "screen off" the negative evidential value of that action by recognizing their *reasons* for seeing the doctor as the genuinely bad news. When evidential theory is properly understood, Eells claims, irrelevant statistics are ignored and the medical recommendations of the two theories agree.[16]

Although this convergence for the doctor case is reassuring, Eells's defense, unfortunately, is problematic. For one thing, since actors must recognize their urge to visit the doctor as part of their initial preferences, this kind of screening off, as Eells (1982) notes, assumes that the entire causal chain leading to an action is funneled through the actor's beliefs and desires, which corporately constitute the complete proximate cause of the decision maker's behavior. It will become clearer in chapter 5 that this is an iffy or at least unclear proposition: definitions of rationality arguably must include the possibility of being subject to unforeseeable influences affecting behavior. At minimum, there will be peripheral *ceteris paribus* clauses lurking around Eells's ostensibly self-contained analysis.

Even if the belief-desire matrix acted as a perfect funnel, a rational agent meeting Eells's requirements would still not be home free. In order for screening off to work, the decision maker not only must act according to the matrix of beliefs and preferences, but also must know what they are. Thus, in the doctor case, prospective patients have to recognize their reasons for seeking medical attention. This self-knowledge is often unavailable, making screening futile, and, regardless, may not eliminate biases built into the calculation of conditional probabilities (Horwich 1985; see also Eells 1985a:181–82).[17]

Suppose, for example, one does not yet know what action rationally follows from one's beliefs and desires. Under those circumstances, knowledge of one's causal influences (for example, an illness) may easily lead one to believe, incorrectly, that the apparently rational choice to see the doctor reflects the causal condition in question. The action rationally chosen then becomes evidence for the causal condition, and screening off fails. As a result, one may mistakenly choose not to see the doctor on the assumption that giving in to the urge is related to the medical condition.

Since agents cannot be assumed to enter into the decision with full knowledge of their beliefs and preferences, perhaps they can develop that knowledge through a formalized process of introspection (Eells 1985a). What they must do, in effect, is ponder their initial choices made without full self-knowledge and use those contemplated choices as information about their beliefs or preferences. The process is supposed to go something like this. First, agents approach the decision problem with subjective conditional probabilities establishing their expected utilities for alternative actions. Second, agents make an initial choice. Third, before agents jump the gun, they reconsider the negative newsworthiness of the choices they have not made. Fourth, when agents factor in the information that develops in light of their tentative choices, the negative newsworthiness of the proper one can be appropriately discounted.

Thus, agents learn from their inclination to see the doctor that they are indeed motivated to seek medical help, a fact statistically related to having a fatal disease. Once they understand this inclination, therefore, it prompts them to stay away. When agents realize their initial choice, however, the actual decision to see the doctor will appear to be superior since it gives them no *additional* negative evidence about their condition and, therefore, is "safe." Through a dynamic process of introspection, rational agents in effect construct the knowledge conditions that Eells (1982) requires them to satisfy.[18]

There are two sets of problems with this general defense of evidential theory. First, agents face daunting technical complications in trying to monitor their own deliberations as required (Harper 1985). Second, if institutional realism is correct, there is something amiss with the whole strategy of defining rationality in terms of deeper and more systematic introspection. A concern with the actual dynamics of decision making is simply out of place, particularly when it depends on self-analysis. For present purposes, the latter is a conventionalist impulse that must be restrained here as well. Although the realist message to "externalize" rationality comes out most clearly in the case of game theory, it is still applicable in the case of isolated decision making.

My own view is that screening off should be applied when agents approach the decision problem or not at all: if screening off is possible, it must take place when agents initially establish their expected utilities for alternative actions. Or to put the point somewhat differently, it is entirely unclear why, after making a choice, agents are able to block influences on their actions when this is an ability they previously lacked. Decision makers engaged in dynamic introspection are expected to step outside themselves by treating their choices as additional data for their ruminations. Yet why do the troubling statistical relations remain locked in with this data instead of haunting their further calculations? Must a fatal disease have its awkward impact only on initial inclinations and not on any subsequent preferences and decisions? Nor is it clear why decision makers still regard decisions not acted upon as significant—as *theirs*.

It is not only hopeless but also misguided to expect rational decision makers to dodge questionable statistical relations by intercepting their own thinking processes in order to contravene their choices before acting, or in order to become conscious of their original preferences and beliefs. I do not assert that agents should therefore be satisfied with their initial estimates of conditional probabilities, thereby treating the calculation of expected utilities as obvious or automatic.[19] Just the opposite: it is Eells's introspective agent who apparently treats the beginning probability estimates as obvious, adjusting them only when necessary. The agent should have hesitated, so to speak, not before choosing but before initially assigning probabilities.

As I said earlier, I have come to praise evidential decision theory, not to bury it. I believe that insisting on a careful determination of initial probabilities is the saving caveat. The original probability estimates that seem to present such a stumbling block for the theory may simply be the wrong ones for a rational decision maker to assume. At the very least, the correct baseline estimates cannot always be read off from the wording of the decision problem (Levi 1975 gives an early intimation of this point).

What I have described as screening off is, in this sense, better understood as a process determining the appropriate subjective probabilities (see Price 1986). Before going to the doctor because I am sick, I determine that the act itself does not present any additional evidence of my being ill. Correctly understood, the probability of being ill conditional on seeing the doctor is judged equal *in this particular case* to its probability conditional on not going. Contrary probability estimates do not have to be screened off. Like other errors, they simply should be avoided.

Evidential theory, in this interpretation, does not depend on standard screening off and therefore does not require agents to have conscious knowledge of their beliefs and desires, or to engage in sequences of feigned decisions. Rather, what is usually seen as a process by which agents adjust their subjective probabilities becomes a process by which agents determine their *initial* conditional probabilities on the basis of all the available evidence.[20] In requiring agents to use their best estimates of their conditional probabilities, evidential theory puts no special burden on its practitioners (cf. Skyrms 1980:131, 136). Agents who are rational according to causal decision theory also need to determine the probabilistic consequences of their beliefs about causation, a task that can be quite complex.[21]

Kip Viscusi (1989) examines an analogous process of adjustment. Subjects involved in psychological experiments are often presented with decision problems in which probabilities are already stipulated. If subjects behave in line with the introspective defense I first considered, they would accept these figures as the basis for their subsequent calculations. Only deep introspection would lead them to revise these original estimates. Yet these subjects, Viscusi points out, bring their own beliefs to the decision problem. The subjective probabilities they use to make decisions, therefore, will reflect a process of updating in which the newly presented probabilities are integrated with prior beliefs. Since decision makers are not empty-headed, they will not take the probabilities presented to them at face value.[22]

The only difference in the doctor case is that the misleading probabilities presented at the time of decision are not formally introduced by experimenters. They are, at best, assumed to be self-generated estimates that leap out when the need to make a decision first arises. As with the experimental subjects, nevertheless, prospective patients do not have to take these first inklings as definitive. If, as the present defense of evidential decision theory suggests, these inklings are mistaken, it would be strange indeed to assume rational decision makers adopt them as their working hypotheses. So even supposing these inklings exist, one must grant agents the right to assess them in light of their prior and wider beliefs about their circumstances. The dynamics of this assessment do not involve monitoring tentative choices or preferences but require opinion formation using standard inductive techniques.[23]

6.

Although evidential decision theory seemed to give incorrect instructions, I have rationalized the right choice in the doctor case, and in its numerous counterparts in the literature, without demanding any problematic introspection from decision makers.[24] Causal decision theory, however, does not need all these mental gymnastics to get the same result. Since in this view one's decision to see a doctor has no causal impact on whether one has a disease at that moment, the troubling statistical relation between the two never enters one's mind, or at least one's calculations. Evidential decision theory holds true, then, only because it succeeds in duplicating the results of causal decision theory.

Philosophical scruples about causation aside, why work to mimic causal theory when one can have the original? The answer is that there are situations in which the recommendations of evidential decision theory and causal theory do diverge. In these situations, there is a serious choice to be made. Some supporters of evidential theory, like Eells (1982) and Jeffrey (1983), believe that these cases of divergence count against evidential theory. They have dragged in the dynamics of introspection precisely to bring the two theories in line. For reasons already indicated, I prefer to stick with the nonintrospective version, arguing instead that this divergence does not discredit evidential theory. The cases generating divergence, moreover, turn out to be precisely the important ones for exploiting the notion of rational role expectations. So by defending the full legitimacy of evidential theory, I am also assuring its wider empirical application.[25]

Let us return to the prisoners' dilemma. In chapter 3 I considered the possibility that each agent believes both players will do the same thing. Suppose that as a player you believe there is a strong likelihood that your opponent will do exactly what you do. Your own decision provides evidence concerning your opponent's decision, their causal independence notwithstanding. Although you cannot affect the other player's choice, your own choice to cooperate may make the conditional probability of the preferred outcome very high.

Evidential theory, accordingly, will recommend cooperation under some circumstances in the prisoners' dilemma.[26] The key issue for evidential theory is whether that choice yields higher conditional expected utility than defection (I am assuming, of course, that in contrast to the doctor case, it is impossible to eliminate the statistical relation between choice and outcome). The causal camp, on the other hand, continues to make the opposite recommendation. Your cooperative action will not change the behavior of your counterpart, so ignore the fact that your decision is an unavoidably excellent predictor of your fellow prisoner's behavior.

The causal theory analysis has considerable appeal. Causal theorists do not engage in what is apparently wishful thinking about the evidential value of behavior but raise a seemingly much more straightforward issue: What do the alternative behaviors produce? One way that evidential theorists have tried to provide an equally strong motivation for their view is to suppose that each prisoner believes her behavior to be a perfect predictor of the other's.[27] Prisoner B, let us say, is a perfect clone of A, and both have had exactly the same relevant experiences. No biologist, psychologist, social scientist, or friend is able to detect any difference between them, aside from their being physically discrete. B's actions given A's, and A's actions given B's, are certain: $prob(B_1|A_1) = prob(B_2|A_2) = prob(A_1|B_1) = prob(A_2|B_2) = 1$. Under these circumstances, each prisoner believes that on the basis of the usual assumptions about the game setup, $prob(B_2|A_1) = prob(B_1|A_2) = prob(A_2|B_1) = prob(A_1|B_2) = 0$.

As each sees the situation, the effective choice is between mutual cooperation and mutual noncooperation, which means cooperative behavior is preferable.[28] Causal decision theory, however, continues to recommend against cooperation. A rational agent should ignore even a perfect statistical relation between the two prisoners' actions since there is still no causal relation. Note, incidentally, the resemblance between this case and the game theoretic assumption, sometimes used in defense of backward induction arguments, that each player *knows* that the other players are rational despite facing a situation in the game that rational players would not have produced (see chapter 5). In both cases, the causal decision theorist would insist on the distinction between epistemic certainty and causation.

To evidential decision theorists, their causal theory counterparts are asking the prisoners to ignore what they perceive to be a basic, unavoidable truth about their joint behavior. Though not characterizing a causal relation, this truth, as the prisoners see it, involves more than the mere coincidence of their two actions. They do not just believe that $prob[(A_1 \ \& \ B_1) \ or \ (A_2 \ \& \ B_2)] = 1$. Rather, their beliefs concern the behavior of others conditional on their own.[29] These prisoners, in particular, do not believe that reasoning via subjunctive conditionals allows them to leave our world— a world in which each prisoner's behavior is certain conditional on the other's—for a possible world in which they can take advantage of this certainty by being sure that the other party would cooperate were they to change their minds.[30]

Every attempt by the prisoners to discard these statistical relations and, as a result, either take advantage of the cooperation of others or avoid becoming victims themselves, will be thwarted by the statistical relation between these attempts and the behavior of those others. It is as though the prisoners were trying to play a pursuit-evasion game with their own shadows.

The pursuit-evasion simile notwithstanding, evidential theory does not pretend one agent's decisions cause the statistically related actions of the other agent. The theory is not delusional. Unlike causal theory, on the other hand, it does recognize that although rational prisoners have free choice, their actions inevitably represent the free choices of people who have some unalterable characteristics. When those characteristics are similarly true of others, all can expect to do better for themselves if they acknowledge this social fact as they would any physical fact.

I do not deny the possibility that the prisoners can act out of character, deviate from role expectations, and foil the statistical relation. By the same token, acting out of character cannot be their expected, rational behavior. Consider the prisoner who, knowing that prisoners of his type will probably choose X, therefore chooses Y. This switch also provides him with evidence that prisoners of his type will likewise switch to Y. Maybe the prisoner is successful in changing type. Yet a change of type is not something one simply wills through an exercise of modal logic. Proof of change can only be delivered over time, as the prisoner's behavior in fact diverges from the behavior of other prisoners.[31]

Yet assuming statistical dependence in fact exists, one can still ask why sane prisoners would believe themselves to be trapped by it. There are two reasons why an unavoidable dependence might be credible. One, the dependence may be perceived as a brute fact not literally deducible from any causal factors. This possibility might be justifiably dismissed as whistling in the dark were it not for the persistent view among physicists that some physical relations involve "action at a distance." Under certain conditions, the spin measurements of two subatomic particles will be related even though there is no physical connection between them. Moreover, there seem to be strong arguments to the effect that any theory attempting to supply a cause, or so-called hidden variable, will make systematically incorrect predictions about the particles (Skyrms 1980:122–27).

This example, needless to say, does not entitle us to assimilate the crudities of the prisoners' dilemma to the intricacies of quantum mechanics. Rather, I simply note the possibility that reasonably rational and intelligent thinkers may buy into a scheme in which the absence of causation does not preclude a scientifically meaningful relation among objects. The inability of physicists to provide a causal explanation of the particular truth considered here has not undermined its scientific standing. I hope we can grant the prisoners this much.

There is another reason why the prisoners might believe they face an unavoidable dependence. Suppose, in contrast to the physics case, that a common cause or set of causes does affect the dispositions of the two prisoners. In the science fiction example involving prisoners who are clones this is obvious, but a more realistic story might have them experiencing common socialization patterns, schooling, and so forth. One's first inclination is to assume that this is precisely the sort of case in which screening off is appropriate: the prisoners should recognize the source of their dispositions and, on that basis, act contrary to expectations. This thinking assumes, however, that rational agents, having recognized the dependence, can avoid it.

A belief in the power of self-knowledge seems to have sustained both classical rationalism and the credibility of psychoanalysis. If, by contrast, rationality is seen as a particular arrangement of preferences, beliefs, and actions, there is no reason to think that rumination about the arrangement, even rational rumination, possesses some overarching power. Does this mean that the agent is helpless? Not at all. A person justly feels most free, Weber (1949) argued, when she is rational and, accordingly, she is then most entitled to say that *she* did such and such. If, however, the rationality of an act is considered to be a matter of decision rather than "good news," this anthropomorphizes not only the decision makers, which of course is appropriate, but also their relations to the world, which is much more questionable.

In the case at hand, I am in effect entertaining the possibility that the statistical relation is between the prisoners' behavioral dispositions rather than between their preferences or beliefs. In this form, the relation shadows the prisoners through their entire process of deliberation, whether as a brute, unexplained fact or as one attributable to clear, common, institutionally mediated causes.

Would-be defenders of freedom of choice may argue that this interpretation short-circuits any serious process of rational deliberation, since the upshot is that the dynamics of deliberation cannot help the prisoners evade the relevant statistical relation. To the extent that statistical dependence holds no matter what the prisoners decide, Eells (1985a:183–84) in particular argues, there is no sense to the idea of rational deliberation anyway.[32] Why this is so, however, is not entirely clear.

As Eells understands the case of unavoidable dependence, a common cause affects the prisoners like a tidal wave brooking no resistance. I agree that under these circumstances, it is pointless to impute a process of deliberation to the prisoners since there is nothing for them to deliberate about. Yet common causes can work in much more subtle ways consistent with individual freedom. Suppose, in particular, that the freedom associated with rational deliberation is a variety of causal process rather than something antithetical to it (Smart 1963; Nozick 1981:291–362). So long as the common cause has its effect through this rational process—so long as it does not operate unconditionally—then fully predictable rational actors can also be externally caused.[33] One can be caused to be rational, caused to have one's particular reasons and beliefs, and even caused to have intuitions favoring evidential decision theory over its causal rival.

7.

I have been arguing for social truths about human behavior that rational choice can exploit but cannot surmount. In the present case, the social truth is an unavoidable stochastic dependence in the behavior of agents facing the prisoners' dilemma. If this dependence is due to kinship, ethnic identity, or a similar group-based criterion, it might suggest one way that players can extricate themselves from the state of nature.

More important, my message is that this dependence can be rooted in the institutional structures that emerge out of the state of nature; and the denial of my message is part of what I have labeled conventionalism. In relation to the prisoners' dilemma, the denial proceeds by relegating social truths to epistemic ones and treating the other truths, represented by the physical rules of the game, as objective. Agents, in this view, have the freedom to ignore what is epistemically certain. They are free to envision counterfactual possibilities, because certainty, unlike the facts, can be foiled. The institutional realist, by contrast, takes social facts more seriously.

Does evidential decision theory "solve" the prisoners' dilemma

	B_1	B_2
A_1	1,1	0,x
A_2	x,0	y,y

Figure 3. Expected Prisoners' Dilemma

when the appropriate statistical relations obtain? In one sense, it does not. The normal form of the prisoners' dilemma (the form presented in chapter 3) simply assumes the objective independence of the players as part of its rules. Players cannot ignore off-diagonal outcomes even when their behavior is statistically dependent, because player A maintains unilateral control over vertical movements in the matrix and player B unilaterally controls horizontal movements (see Harper 1985).

So rather than confuse the terminology, one can think of the existence of unavoidable statistical relations, when determined by the appropriate conditional probabilities, as transforming the original game. The transformation, of course, does not occur because the players have conceived of new alternatives but rather because their factual circumstances have changed. Earlier in this chapter, I informally raised the possibility of this kind of transformation. It is now time to put it in more explicitly game theoretic terms.

In contrast to the standard prisoners' dilemma, the replacement takes cognizance of conditional probabilities. Suppose, for instance, that the conditional probability of identical behavior is high and the conditional probability of different behavior is correspondingly low. In this expected prisoners' dilemma, the new normalized expected utilities might be the ones characterized in figure 3, where $0 < x < y < 1$. What I have done, in other words, is to combine the utility and probability matrices to produce the expected utility for each outcome. When each player finds a sufficiently high conditional probability for (A_1,B_1), its conditional expected utility exceeds that of (A_2,B_2), which in turn exceeds the off-diagonal expected utilities whose initially high values are subject to heavy discounting.

Following an idea of John Harsanyi (1967–68), we can think of each player A in this revised game as facing a player B drawn from a pool of alternates, some percentage of which are exact clones of A, who will decide to do B_k whenever A chooses A_k ($k = 1,2$), and some percentage of which will do B_j ($j \neq k$) whenever A chooses A_k. Thus A can anticipate whether B has clone-like or anticlone-like attributes only up to a probability distribution.[34]

Under these circumstances, (A_1,B_1) can be an equilibrium outcome for agents maximizing conditional expected utility. When it represents the cooperative outcome in a state of nature, the off-diagonal outcomes are discounted on exactly the same grounds as the probability of diagonal outcomes is increased, namely, high conditional expected utility for identical strategy choices. In fact, when there is perfect statistical dependence, residents of the state of nature can even "eliminate" the off-diagonal outcomes, much as a player in the standard theory can eliminate dominated strategies (strategies that are no better, and sometimes worse, than some other).[35]

When (A_1, B_1) arises within an existing institutional setting, on the other hand, it alone can be assigned an unequivocally high conditional expected utility owing to rational role expectations. With regard to the off-diagonal outcomes, player A presumably will evaluate $prob(B_1|A_2)$ as high to the extent that he expects continued role conformity by B, but player B might estimate $prob(A_2|B_1)$ to be low on the same grounds. If so, the probability of (A_2, B_2) will be correspondingly low. Note that the possible variations in conditional probabilities for the same outcome imply no inconsistency on the part of players; their own actions on which they condition beliefs simply provide private information to them.

This initial indeterminacy does not mean that the problem of factoring in rational role expectations when one party considers leaving the institution is unsolvable.[36] Complications arise in the preceding case from trying to model a world containing institutions as one would the state of nature. Here again, I think Shepsle's analysis of costs provides a fully appropriate justification for heavy discounting on all extrainstitutional outcomes. Within an institution, institutional realism suggests high conditional expected utility. Outside the institution, social isolation suggests that the prisoners' dilemma is broken because the expected rewards of unilateral noncooperation are not there. The result is the matrix given in figure 3.

The contrast between the straightforward results of conditional expected utility in the state of nature and the more complex results in the institutional case suggests a continuing role for group identification even within the institutional context. Rational role expectations, by definition, focus on intrainstitutional alternatives. They lose their distinct grip when the occupant leaves the role. Group identity, whether ethnic, familial, or religious, follows the agent out of the institution. This can decrease the expectation of social isolation given deviant behavior. In any event, institutional realism does not suppose that institutional role expectations obliterate all other ties that particular individuals might have.

Before leaving this topic, I should also mention another standard way of incorporating probabilities in games, namely, through mixed strategies. Although they are not used in the particular substitute for the prisoners' dilemma I have considered (or in the prisoners' dilemma itself), they do raise an interesting problem for conceptualizing stochastic dependence. Agents adopt a mixed strategy by using a randomizing device to select the pure (that is, nonstochastic) strategies they will play. In such cases, would a rational actor take seriously any residual dependence between the chosen strategy and the strategies of others? Is not the very purpose of mixing to prevent the exploitation of such relationships?

If a player is not able or willing to be committed irrevocably to the outcome of a random process for choosing strategies, then the dependence among *pure* strategy choices retains its importance. If, alternatively, full commitment to a mixed strategy is possible, then "such a commitment should itself be considered an action" (Aumann 1987:11). As Guillermo Owen (1982:13) puts it, the random choice of a pure strategy is irrational; what can be rational is the choice of a randomization scheme. If so, the decision to use the specific mixed strategy under the circumstances prompting this choice can itself be subject to unavoidable statistical relations.[37]

8.

Clearly, an interpretation of games consistent with institutional realism requires a particular understanding of the freedom of agents and their influence on outcomes. This understanding is so crucial, in fact, that it is worth pursuing a little further, even at the cost of having to introduce a new puzzle from decision theory, called Newcomb's problem. As the puzzle is usually posed (see Nozick 1969), you are presented with two boxes and a choice between the contents of the first box or the contents of both. In the second box, there is a thousand dollars. As for the first, which is opaque, some being has put a million dollars in it if the being predicted that you would choose only the first box; it deposited nothing if it predicted that you would choose both boxes. The being is a spectacular predictor with a nearly perfect record in past trials. Although your decision can have no causal impact on the contents of the first box, the probability of your getting the million, conditional on the choice of one box, is much higher than the probability conditional on the choice of both boxes.

So what is your choice, two boxes or one? For those tempted to answer this question with another—What is the relevance outside of science fiction?—notice that this problem is structurally like the prisoners' dilemma (see Lewis 1979), though for better or worse, the decision theory literature has favored the former example as a test case.

Causal decision theory suggests choosing two boxes. Since your choice cannot causally affect the contents of the first box, the choice of both boxes, yielding either $1,000 or $1,001,000, dominates the choice of one box, yielding by comparison $0 or $1,000,000. Evidential decision theory, on the other hand, suggests one box, since you prefer not to think yourself out of a fortune. Causal decision theory, in other words, banks on your freedom to choose independently of the prediction. Evidential theory banks on the strong statistical dependence between choice and outcome.

In assessing the prisoners' dilemma, I argued that the issue between the two theories is not the existence of freedom but rather the interpretation of freedom in relation to social facts. Although prisoner B has no causal affect on prisoner A, A still cannot transcend the fact that both are embedded in a particular social situation that their individual decisions will reflect. Although A and B make their own decisions, they cannot assume the stance of outside observers, let alone designers, of their own decision processes. Newcomb's problem isolates this dimension of freedom much more cleanly, as an extended exchange between Isaac Levi (1982; 1983; 1985) and defenders of causal decision theory makes clear.

Levi wants to show that causal decision theory pays a price for writing off crucial conditional probabilities solely because they are epistemic. He sets up a pseudo–Newcomb's problem in which there are two opaque boxes, one of which has a high probability of containing a million dollars and the other a low probability of containing that sum. Decision makers can choose the first opaque box by itself or choose the second opaque box along with one containing a thousand dollars. Levi maintains that if the principle of causal independence recommends two boxes in the original Newcomb's problem, it recommends the two-box solution here as well. His argument is relatively simple. Whether either of the opaque boxes has the money is causally independent of the decision makers. So choosing two boxes again wins out over choosing one in a case where everyone would agree with the one-box choice.

Taking up the cause of causal decision theory, David Lewis (1983) argues that Levi has confused two claims about independence. The correct claim is that decision makers do not have control over the contents of the box they choose. It either has the million or it does not. But decision makers do influence whether they choose a box with a million in it, since they choose between the high-probability and low-probability boxes. So the causal theory does not recommend the two-box solution in the pseudo–Newcomb's problem.

Levi replies as follows. When decision makers choose both boxes in the original Newcomb case, they choose, with high probability, an empty opaque box. Although they do not cause the opaque box to be empty, they do in fact choose an empty one, and this choice constitutes an element of the causal chain leading to that outcome—indeed, an outcome they can expect. Their causing themselves to receive a box that turns out to be empty is of course descriptively different from their causing themselves to receive an empty box; but in each trial of Newcomb's problem the identical events are described by these different formulations (see the earlier discussion of causation in section 4).[38]

The decision maker, I am assuming, has no causal influence on the contents of the box, which were settled beforehand. Backward causation of this kind would make sense of Levi's argument, but it is too high a price to pay. A better explication of Levi's point would be to interpret causal influence as a matter of initiating or doing something having certain causal consequences rather than the more legal notion of knowingly initiating actions having those consequences. Apparently, this is what insulates Levi's argument against Lewis's distinction between the two types of causal influence.

Still, Levi will concede, he is ascribing causal powers to the decision maker's choice, and there are certainly some causal processes involving the decision maker that mock this notion. So I need to show why the distinction between choice and actual behavior, which was also crucial for introspective defenses of evidential decision theory, does not undermine Levi's broad-based criticism of the causal approach.

The key to saving Levi's argument, I suggest, is taking a strong line on free choice. Although choice is an intervening element in an extended causal chain and free choice a more specific kind of element, neither renders the future less determinate than it ultimately turns out to be. The nature of the causal process is not changed. When the decision maker contemplates the choice of one box, this choice does not become a substitute link in a causal chain that now may lead to a different outcome. Until the decision is made, the causal chain does not remain suspended in midair; the chain either exists or it does not. More to the point, it either produces a big payoff or it does not. Decision makers cannot dodge causal responsibility by troubling themselves over shadow worlds concerning chains that might have been.

Decision makers facing either Newcomb's problem or the pseudo-version have freedom of choice: they can choose an action that will probably bring them a million dollars or one that will bring them a lot less. Their actions, which they choose, lead to the outcome in question. Surely, neither their eventual success nor their eventual failure is a precondition for having a causal role. In either case, their chosen actions are links in a causal chain leading to the outcome that occurs. And just as surely, their ex post realization that a mistake was made does not in itself impugn the freedom of the ex ante choice.[39]

From the "inside," of course, decision makers facing an uncertain future may well divide the world between things under their influence (that is, their choices), and things not under their influence (that is, the contents of a particular opaque box). This inside view is apparent in Lewis's (1983) distinction between causal influence over whether the box you choose in the pseudo-Newcomb's problem has a million dollars and causal influence over whether you choose a box having a million dollars. Yet the choice of the decision maker, whatever it turns out to be, does get made and constitutes simply another link in the causal chain leading to great wealth or something considerably less. From the "outside," one can see that the choice made did produce the results expected ex ante with high probability.

Thus, it turns out that the abstract debates of chapter 1 return to haunt more specific debates over the proper formulation of the concept of rationality for Newcomb's problem and its terrestrial variant, the prisoners' dilemma. The spatiotemporal ontology of events and causes undermines certain attempts to bestow on free choice an ontological status it does not have, namely, the resolution of either an objectively indeterminate future or an undefined causal chain leading to it. Realism's deflated view of free choice thus supports evidential decision theory.

9.

Before returning to the connection between institutional realism and evidential decision theory, I want to consider relevant ways in which this theory may help explain some experimental findings concerning behavior in the prisoners' dilemma and related situations. A theory with such a title, after all, ought to be reasonably consistent with the evidence.

A considerable experimental literature suggests that under some circumstances a surprising degree of cooperation is obtained in one-shot prisoners' dilemma games and its variants, or in iterated versions of the game with a defined point of termination (e.g., Rapoport and Chammah 1965; Marwell and Ames 1981). Clearly, evidential decision theory has a better chance of rationalizing the one-shot case and, issues surrounding backward induction aside, a better chance in the finite case as well.

Isolation of the players, moreover, breeds defection, whereas communication has a positive effect on cooperation (e.g., Dawes, Mc-Tavish, and Shaklee 1977). Stated in terms of evidential decision theory, communication reduces or eliminates the anonymity of the other players and therefore can build stochastic dependencies that increase cooperation. Cooperators, it turns out, are also more optimistic than noncooperators about the amount of cooperation they expect.[40] These higher expectations, furthermore, depend to some extent on the individual's actual decision to cooperate (Dawes, McTavish, and Shaklee

1977; Quattrone and Tversky 1986; 1988). There is an obvious explanation in term of evidential theory: individuals are using their actions diagnostically.[41]

Another interesting experimental finding is that cooperation in multiple runs of the prisoners' dilemma often peaks on the first trial and declines thereafter (e.g., Isaac, McCue, and Plott 1985). Dawes and Thaler (1988:191–92) suggest cooperators are learning that their fellow participants are taking advantage of them. Along the same lines, the evidential theorist might suggest that a rate of cooperation below expectation provokes downward adjustment of the conditional probabilities ascribed to the cooperative outcomes. Although subjects are initially willing to bet that their own cooperation is evidence of cooperation on the part of others, evidence of less than expected cooperation on the nth trial induces them to discount the subjective probability of cooperation on the $n + 1$ trial.

Increasingly, explanations of the experimental findings for prisoners' dilemma and related games appeal to altruism or a participant sense of ethics (Dawes and Thaler 1988:192–95). The former appears to involve some sense of identification with the larger group (Margolis 1984), while the latter often reflects a simple sense of fairness (Orbell, Schwartz-Shea, and Simmons 1984). Without wishing to deny the existence of altruism or ethics, I believe advocates of these revisionist explanations should be cautious about confusing altruism or ethics proper with group identification.[42]

For example, evidential decision theory can incorporate a sense of group identity, in the form of stochastic dependence among members of a group, without implying the special concern for the group usually associated with altruism (though the two are by no means incompatible). If evidential decision theory is correct, cooperation can emerge even in the absence of strict altruism.

A similar distinction between facts about the decision calculus and its motivation applies to ethics. The idea of judging one's conduct by seeing how it generalizes as a universal command has been a major theme in moral philosophy. Kant's categorical imperative is but one example. Yet we have seen ordinary rational agents generalize in an analogous way. An evidential decision maker who believes cooperation has high conditional expected utility asks, in effect, What if everyone did that (or would be more likely to do that)? and behaves accordingly. This actor's attempt to generalize is consistent with completely self-interested behavior.

The evidential decision maker's sense of self-interested solidarity with others can, in theory, take two distinct forms. One form arises because individuals have a mutual stake in cooperation. It is fueled by the agents' appreciation of their parallel preferences and shared beliefs. Under these circumstances, perhaps, A and B can agree on the best way to achieve their preferred result. Yet this form of solidarity may still be subject to the kinds of calculation that eliminate cooperative strategies in the prisoners' dilemma.

A second, more tenacious form of solidarity arises when how A acts suggests how B will act. This provokes a sense of mutual identity in which A and B see themselves as representative persons. Here, actions speak louder than calculations in ways evidential decision theory is prepared to recognize. This sense of identity is not necessarily ethical or altruistic. Of course, it may well be interpreted that way by observers, or by participants acting as their own observers.

There is a final consideration in favor of the empirical utility of evidential theory, namely, mountains of evidence on the core phenomenon known as the consensus effect. (See, for example, Fiske and Taylor 1984:82–83; for a somewhat different attempt to rationalize this consensus effect, see Dawes 1990.)

10.

If evidential decision theory is correct, it is possible for rational actors to leave the state of nature, even one likely to be characterized as a prisoners' dilemma. The prisoners in question rely on their belief in the stochastic dependence of their actions, perhaps a belief encouraged by their common situation, similar behavioral dispositions under biologically extreme conditions, and so on. Their descendants, who live in the midst of institutions they partly created and partly found, are removed from the state of nature. In general, they are also removed from the physical circumstances that made the original stochastic dependence salient or even likely. Ironically, institutions may undermine the conditions motivating the very cooperation sustaining them.[43]

Although institutions mitigate the circumstances encouraging their arrival, they are not without resources that evidential decision theory can characterize. An institution is often a game of incomplete information. Players typically enter not knowing all details of its structure, its history, or the preferences and beliefs of other agents. Yet each may know that he has a distinct role to play. This role is defined, in part, by what others who occupy roles within the institution do or are prepared to do. Evidential decision theory, I have argued, is capable of attending to these institutional statistics. If one sees the conformity of others to especially productive institutional regularities of behavior as stochastically dependent on one's own decision to conform, then the rational incentive to deviate, free-ride, or otherwise take advantage of the existence of the institution is reduced. In a stable institutional setting, the principle of maximizing conditional expected utility creates, as I put it earlier, an expected utility cliff between conforming and nonconforming behavior.

Generally speaking, then, if there is institutionalized dependence, stochastic relations among the acts of distinct agents are unavoidable and can be properly factored in when the agent determines what is rational. Those who would object to this approach presuppose a radical freedom from social connections. Even knowing that a particular outcome will occur for certain is not supposed to limit the agent's freedom to choose another outcome, because this conventionalist view of social order is prepared to distinguish strictly between (1) the agent's choices and their consequences, which are subject to the agent's free intervention, and (2) everything else in the world, which is fixed and determined. The conventionalist's insistence on humanity's self-aware causal influence over social events may seem hardheaded, but the metaphysics lurking in the background is quite delicate.

The standard, conventionalist view of rational choice, I grant, has the weight of intellectual history on its side: the history of game theory, its legacy as reflected in social contract theory, and the continued role of state-of-nature theory in the new institutionalism. If, however, we are ready to surrender the sharp distinction between forces of nature and individual agents, and between both of these and the forces or facts of society, we shall find ourselves with a more coherent conception of rational choice and institutions, not to mention one more likely to fit the behavior observed in real social settings and in experimental simulations of prisoners' dilemmas.

In contrast to the standard alternative, agents using evidential theory can comprehend the institutional facts that their behavior helps reproduce without deluding themselves into thinking that mere comprehension necessarily makes these facts any less potent or any more subject to their personal whims. Institutional embeddedness matters because individuals must still act within institutional constraints that they now understand in the guise of conditional probabilities.

5.

Rationality in Institutions

To say that agents embedded in a particular institutional role structure behave differently than those outside is, for all its reasonableness, to come perilously close to committing a serious faux pas. For after berating others over their failure to clarify what an institutional structure might be, and berating Marxists precisely because of their answer, the preceding chapter is embarrassingly mute on the topic. I have said that my references to structure should always be translated into talk of structural descriptions. It is time to make sense of this admonition in the context of game theory, where the relevant components of structure are the rules of the game.

Moreover, by centering the definition of institutions around the notion of stable regularities of behavior and behavioral dispositions, whether fully understood by participants or not, I have deliberately slighted the distinction between institutions in the tradition of social contract theory, where institutions are defined by an explicit set of accepted rules, and institutions in an organic theory like Andrew Schotter's (1981). A better understanding of rules is needed in order to subsume the two historical scenarios under institutional realism.

In this chapter I offer first an interpretation of rules consistent with realism by distinguishing the physical aggregate constituting the institution from the rules that characterize it. Next, I take up the related problem of integrating ideology into rational choice theory. Although the conventionalist approach to institutions can be criticized for taking the human power of description too seriously, the institutional realist account of rules must still show how alternative rule-like descriptions of the institution could play a role in a rational agent's decision making. I address this question in a manner relevant to social science by asking whether ideological conceptualizations can play a significant role in rational choice.

Last, I bring these two parts of the chapter together by considering the role of rationality itself within an institutionally interpreted game theory. With respect to the institution's physical status, of course, the issue is one of analyzing how an individual's behavioral dispositions fit into an aggregate of individuals having institutionally relevant behavioral dispositions. But with respect to the institution's social status, this issue has a conceptually trickier counterpart: analyzing how, from the standpoint of institutional realism, rationality fits into a game structure.

1.

Obviously, institutional realism cannot accept the idea of rules as an undefined and unreduced term. Its nominalism does not abide abstract entities looming over the players. It is in no position, on the other hand, to ignore rules. On all accounts, rules are part of the structure of the game, describing the way the game must be played. If they are used by the participants, institutional realism must come to terms with them.

There is also a pragmatic reason why rules should not be neglected. When in chapter 1 I defined an institution as a human aggregate, I rebutted the objection that this definition includes too much— namely, all the nonsocial characteristics of people in social situations. We can now confront the opposite complaint, that the definition includes too little. Where are norms, values, rules, organizational hierarchies, and other ingredients of institutional life? Although I cannot address all these terms individually, the notion of rules is representative of those elements of institutional organization operating at the interface of individual and institution. They occupy the gray zone between the psychology and game structure.

In the preceding chapter, I examined another inhabitant of this gray zone, information partitions. Information partitions are not psychological. They characterize the limits on rational play structurally imposed on all players. By the same token, these partitions are not purely structural in the sense of defining mere classifications. They reflect the way the game is physically played. Like partitions, rules, in my account, will describe the game. Yet they will also be understood as concrete utterances or inscriptions serving a particular function in organizing the game.

Consider the descriptive dimension of a game. An institutional aggregate consists of players who have a psychology appropriate to people who are competent to play. With this in mind, we can begin with the flatfooted view that the rules, as stated by the observer, characterize the relevant social relations among those who exhibit this institutionally appropriate psychology: if so and so does *x*, then some other so and so does one of *w, y,* or *z.* A rule, in this sense, just describes, with varying degrees of accuracy, how the game is played when it is played. It fails insofar as players deviate from it.

Yet a rule-oriented characterization of institutional structure is also quasi-normative. It provides a standard to judge the adequacy of any particular individual's conformity to institutional requirements: if so and so does *x,* then some other so and so must do *w, y,* or *z.* Conversely, when people play badly, this is evidence they have not understood the rules of the game. In this respect, a rule-oriented description tests the individual rather than the other way around. It shows how the behavior of the individual must be organized in order for the game to continue.

To see how these two aspects can be reconciled, it will be helpful to consider the parallel case of grammar. Many linguists view the rules of syntax or grammar as constitutive of linguistic behavior and understanding, much as many game theorists view rules as constitutive of games. But the rules of grammar can also be understood in the grammar-school sense, as rules awkwardly imposed on verbal behavior, here summarizing, there standardizing the common pattern. I suggest that we understand game rules in a like fashion.

This kind of grammar rule, of course, perfectly describes only those who already speak properly. Such people need not already know—indeed may find it inconvenient to learn—the explicit rules. In such a case, the rules merely summarize rather than generate the individual's linguistic behavior. Unfortunately, not everyone is an A student. A rule of grammar, in the grammar school sense, also provides a normative standard for these less fortunate speakers and, one hopes, a useful guide for their improvement.

Ideally, a grammar's normative power derives from its utility. When speech deviates from the rules, it violates the competent language user's expectations about linguistic behavior and makes assimilation of its message harder. For less competent users of language, moreover, explicit rules may be a key to learning what for them is a second language or at least a modified first. As a guide to behavior, it can also be a key to gaining access to more complex, subtle, and smoother patterns of communication conveying higher status to their users. (Though controversial, see Bernstein 1964 on this point.)

The idea of a language user's expectations, of course, seems to imply an internal grammar: so-called bad grammar violates the language user's expectations because it is compared to her internal grammar. The grammar standard I have in mind is much more modest. The standard arises, I shall assume, when a discrepancy between actual behavior and the hearer's expectation, however it is motivated, leads to problems in communication. Or better, it arises when there is a general correlation between conformity to external rules and the ability of participants to assimilate information. The explanation for this fact, if there is one, may be idiosyncratic, reflecting a mixture of psychological factors unique to each individual.[1]

Rules of grammar, in this view, do not directly constrain speech or guide every detail of its production. Indeed, these rules may succeed in conveying usable information precisely because their users are not picky about full compliance. Grammars need not accurately describe the thought processes even of expert grammarians, nor must they make sense of all exceptions to the rules accepted by competent speakers. Hard cases, it must be recognized, make for bad policy and bad grammars. At any rate, the rules of the institutional game provide information about institutional structure just as grammar texts provide useful rules of thumb for proper speaking and writing. Although an agent is not required to have a complete understanding of these rules, they clearly can play a role in teaching him how to participate.[2]

If a rule were an abstract entity, the failure of players to conform—the inevitable divergence between behavior and rule—would not endanger it. The rule would exist in its abstract way but not be realized. By contrast, the flexibility of the dual approach, which uses rules to describe and judge people, looks quite suspicious. How much divergence from an institutional rule can there be before one decides that it does not in fact describe the institution?

This question, fortunately, is not as subversive as it may first appear. For the realism of institutional realism gives it a certain breathing room: since the existence of an institution does not hinge on any particular observer's rule-bound description of it, institutional realists can afford to be indiscreetly pragmatic about their interpretation of rules.

Suppose, for instance, that there is a rule-oriented description of an institution that applies to most, but not all, of the individuals interacting within it. Most of its bureaucrats follow the institution's procedure, for instance, but inevitably some do not. These ostensibly deviant bureaucrats may follow what conventionalist observers would likely categorize as informal rules. The notion of informal rule is a nice device to preserve the conventionalist idea that organizations are constituted by the rules people choose in order to govern themselves. The institutional realist, on the other hand, would simply note that in this case the formal rules are only partly accurate.

When there is not enough accuracy, the outcomes associated with the bureaucratic institution will not materialize and the institutional description should be dropped. The descriptions that are still accurate remain so; they are just not used. When there is enough accuracy, on the other hand, the accurate descriptions remain useful and nonconformity can be analyzed in terms of those who conform. The institution and its definition of alternative actions still confront those who do not conform, defining their failures, their inabilities, their perversity, or the point of their protest.

Insofar as the institutional description applies, the institution-related predictions about behavioral outcomes hold; insofar as it does not apply, the predictions do not hold. What matters is whether the array of possibilities each agent faces is stable owing to the interactions of the players themselves. The institutional description of the behavioral aggregate becomes useful only insofar as ordinary deviations from the regularity, which can be expected, do not short-circuit the reproduction of the institution.

As another example, suppose a voter in an election votes inappropriately, perhaps by incorrectly marking a ballot. Any number of things can happen as a result. The election may be called off, in which case the electoral institution survives if proper behavior is restored for the next election. The institution, of course, does not survive if elections cease. (One may wonder whether an arrangement so sensitive to disturbances of this sort should be called an institution in the first place.) More likely, elections continue with an n-person game becoming an $(n - 1)$ -person game.

The continuation of the institution introduces two subcases. In one, the strategic situation for the remaining players is basically unchanged. The sensible response is to regard the institution too as unchanged, much as a human body is generally understood to be unchanged when individual cells die and are replaced.[3] In the other subcase, the strategic situation is changed. Here the natural reaction is to recognize a change in the institution even when important similarities remain.

2.

Although I have distinguished the notion of rules associated with institutional realism from the notion standardly associated with game theory, I have not given any specific reasons why the former view is better. The purpose of this section is to remedy that deficiency by showing how the status of rules parallels that of information. Information, I have argued, does not define the structure of the game, however well it might reflect it. Rather, it lies in the gray area between the institutional mechanism and the individual. Rules, I suggest, also lie in this gray area. The problem is that they are closer to being part of the mechanism than is information. Perhaps, one might think, this difference makes a difference. If it does, the analogy between rules and information is misleading.

By analyzing a problem known to logicians as the hangman's

paradox, I shall argue that rules, like information, cannot be identified with institutional mechanisms but are summary descriptions of them. Rules, in other words, depict rather than materially generate institutional behavior. A version of the hangman's paradox, I should mention, may also menace attempts to ground game theory, and the Nash equilibrium in particular, using Bayesian decision theory (see Brandenburger and Dekel 1989:49). Here, the discussion of the paradox shall be retraced in essential respects by my subsequent analysis of an important game theoretic technique called backward induction.

Adapted to present purposes, the hangman's paradox runs as follows. Suppose a particular country has two rules regarding the death penalty. First, punishment should be swift, meaning hanging within ten days of sentencing. Second, punishment should not be cruel, meaning the condemned should not know on which day the sentence shall be carried out until noon of the execution day. One condemned prisoner, K, claims that these rules are contradictory. For suppose in a given case that noon of the ninth day passes without a hanging. Then the condemned person in question would know that the hanging is to be on the tenth day, which violates the rules. So the hanging cannot be on the tenth day. But then the condemned person would know by noon of the eighth day that the hanging must be on the ninth, the tenth having been eliminated. This knowledge also violates the rules. Following this reasoning, K successively eliminates hanging days, proving the sentence cannot be properly carried out.

This paradox has provoked some to complex reflections on the nature of knowledge. In this case, luckily, there is a much more straightforward resolution. K has mistakenly identified the actual behavioral process with the rules. For this reason, he thinks logical manipulation of the rules in effect manipulates the legal process. Yet the institution of law is one thing, rule-bound descriptions of it another. Which means, say goodbye to K.

Although descriptions of institutions can be contradictory, an institution cannot be. So at best all K can demonstrate is that the rules, considered as descriptions, are contradictory or inaccurate. The institution is as it is. But K's actual proof relies on precisely this conflation of rules and institutions, missing the point that the accuracy of the description depends on how the institutional processes play out, not the other way around. If, in other words, institutional processes proceed without violating the rules, no formal proof can show otherwise. K learns this when he is surprised to find the hangman appear on noon of the fifth day.

Quine (1976:20) makes an analogous point about K's reasoning. He notes that although K's reductio ad absurdum technique allows him to hypothesize the truth of certain assumptions about the rules, it cannot make these assumptions true: "It is notable that K acquiesces in the conclusion . . . that the decree will not be fulfilled. If this is a conclusion that he is prepared to accept (though wrongly) in the end as a certainty, it is an alternative which he should have been prepared to take into consideration from the beginning as a possibility." When K protests that the rules are contradictory, he is not impugning the institution so much as his own understanding of it.[4]

In one sense, of course, K is entitled to discount the possibility of hanging with knowledge in advance because, by assumption, the rules fit the facts and convey adequate information about them. The real culprit in his reductio ad absurdum is the further assumption that a logical analysis of rules is equivalent to a social scientific analysis of the institutional mechanisms corresponding to them. Under this traditional positivist view, ably represented by Hart (1961), rules and social mechanisms are mirror images, which entitles K to rejoice in finding a contradiction. Only an analysis of the mechanisms, however, really entitles K to the belief he so hopes is correct. The fact of the noon hanging, showing that there is no contradiction, undermines this belief, along with its underlying assumption that the actual legal institution is constituted by rules: "The judge tells K on Sunday afternoon that he, K, will be hanged the following noon and will remain ignorant of the fact till the intervening morning. It would be like K to protest at this point that the judge is contradicting himself. And it would be like the hangman to intrude upon K's complacency at 11:55 next morning, thus showing that the judge had said nothing more contradictory than the simple truth" (Quine 1976:21). Institutional rules, as Hart has emphasized, are not merely inside people's heads; but they should not for that reason be identified with external social practices (see Dworkin 1977). The hangman's paradox suggests that they fall between these two extremes by helping establish the relation between institutions and their participants. Rules do not constitute these mechanisms but provide information about them.[5] Rules as objects are, once again, inscriptions or statements. They themselves do not constrain in any direct sense, though they certainly may provide information relevant to a player's behavior.

3.

This analysis of rules raises another complication for an institutionally relevant interpretation of rational choice. In the physical world of the state of nature, individuals distinguish and react to objects in their environment using their inherited mechanisms for classifying things as same and different. Color classifications, for example, are clearly important ways to sort things, and these classifications, though hardly fundamental for modern physics, continue to matter in social settings as well. Rule descriptions similarly sort the behavior associated with the institution.

Yet unlike colors, institutions have no obvious natural identity. As I have stressed in the name of ontological egalitarianism, they comprise a fairly arbitrary collection of objects from any physical or biological point of view. This is not meant to denigrate them as objects, but it does force us to ask how egalitarianism meshes with the alleged ability of actors to distinguish particular collections of objects as institutions and, more important, to identify particular roles or groups within them. How does a rational agent apply the notions of same and different when alternative classifications seem arbitrary? How specifically does the idea of rationality cohere with that of alternative, relatively arbitrary categorizations?

The question, in effect, asks how rational actors choose among alternative conceptual schemes, though for present purposes a more natural substitute for *conceptual scheme* is *ideology*.[6] Ideology, in this sense, provides the format in which evidence about the social world, including its institutions, is assessed and even recognized as such. An ideology need not be codified into a well-articulated set of general principles but can be the "lived relation" (Althusser and Balibar 1970) between people and their world, a relation often resulting in distinctive and even competing understandings (e.g., Mannheim 1936).

Suppose, then, we think of an ideology in the following simplified terms. One, it is a set of categories partitioning (some portion of) an individual's perceived world. Two, it is a set of beliefs or propositions constructed with those categories. Three, it includes a preference function and probability distribution defined over these propositions.[7] The first two criteria suggest a definition very much like Douglass North's: "By ideology I mean the subjective perceptions (models, theories) all people possess to explain the world around them" (1990:23). Yet while North associates these perceptions with the limited cognitive capacities of people, I maintain that ideologies are perfectly consistent with full rationality.

In any case, rational choice theorists have tended to shun this kind of definition. Kau and Rubin (1982) define ideology as a conception of both the good society and the means to bring it about, but clearly their emphasis is on ideology as a source of, or other name for, political preferences that lead a legislator not to concentrate solely on reelection. Elster (1984) and Roemer (1985) suggest that one consequence of having an ideology is a restriction on the actions or strategies an agent is willing to consider; but Roemer's own analysis shows that in some circumstances ideological restrictions on strategies can be rationalized.

In the seminal statement of the rational choice approach to ideology, Downs (1957) emphasizes the role of ideology in reducing the cost to voters of acquiring information about political candidates and their policies. Similarly, Enelow and Hinich (1984) treat Downs's conceptualization of ideology as a predictive guide used by voters who face residual uncertainty about the policies that candidates will adopt. Voters need not personally identify with these ideological labels. In sum, ideology in this account is not a way to conceptualize or process information but is a substitute for information, albeit a substitute rationally selected by the voter.

For all its influence, there are two related problems with the economy-of-information approach, which has dominated the formal theory of voting. First, it ignores the traditional association of ideology with conceptual schemes. This dimension of ideology is in fact the one emphasized by Mannheim (1936), whom Downs cites in support of his more instrumental position. Second, independent of the cost of acquiring information is the issue of how agents use the information they have. Those we call ideologues seem to be, if not immune to new evidence, then inclined to assimilate it in nonobvious ways. The popular association between ideology and fanaticism, I suspect, is not attributable solely to the extreme preferences of particular ideologues.

Hannah Arendt's (1963) study of the "banality of evil," for example, suggests that apparent ideological fanaticism can be coolly cognitive as well as emotional. To put her point in more traditional social science terms, ideologues seem particularly adept at reducing cognitive dissonance. The trouble for rational choice theory, of course, is that this skill does not seem to be the monopoly of fanatics (Festinger 1957). In any case, an ideology in this sense helps process the information that is cheap enough to acquire.

Why is this broader understanding of ideology downplayed in rational choice theory? The possibility most relevant here is that the broader view is perceived to be antithetical to the theory. For if ideologies are distinct and irreducible ways of conceptualizing the very experience from which rational agents learn, then apparently *rational learning* would be a misnomer for the tendency of individuals to make self-fulfilling deductions from assumptions that are relatively immune to disconfirmation. In this spirit, Sartori (1969) contrasts the ideologue's "deductive" style of reasoning with the pragmatist's "inductive" style.

Bayesians have usually tried to circumvent this problem of persistent bias by emphasizing the extent to which rational agents with different priors (that is, initial beliefs expressed as probabilities) will nonetheless reach the same conclusions when given enough information.[8] But the role of conceptualization goes deeper than this: it influences the very categories within which priors and evidence are formulated. When these lose their objective or shared character, convergence between ideologically different agents is much less credible. In short, ideology in the broad sense seems to threaten the rational choice assumption that there is one common and optimal way to update beliefs.

Insofar as it ignores the more inclusive and historic notion of ideology, rational choice theory confirms the judgment of its critics, who suggest that recognizing conceptual influences on information processing is tantamount to embracing an alternative conception of political assessment and belief revision (Conover and Feldman 1984; Miller, Wattenberg, and Malanchuk 1986; Peffley, Feldman, and Sigelman 1987). Similarly, the persistent finding that an agent's choice is influenced by the way a given decision problem is characterized—the so-called framing effect—is also seen as posing a strong challenge to rational choice theory (Tversky and Kahneman 1987).

A reconciliation of rationality and ideology, on the other hand, not only offers a potentially useful supplement to the standard theory but also allows institutional realism to make sense of ideological thinking about institutions and thereby refine the hypothesized link between individuals and their institutional environment. I intend to show there is a theoretical basis for this reconciliation. Although ideology, as a conceptual framework, is not neutral with respect to decisions, it is not a substitute for, but an integral component of, rational decision making.

4.

A rational person learns from experience, changing her beliefs as she acquires new information. Yet to someone whose conceptualizations help define this information, the evidence it represents is no longer independent of belief. Agents having different ideologies, in particular, can be exposed to the same substantial body of evidence yet come to radically different conclusions. One agent might view exchanges in the labor market as providing increasing evidence that capitalism leads to increasing levels of individual satisfaction, whereas another agent will see the same exchanges as steadily putting capitalism in greater jeopardy. At first sight, the Marxist prediction of revolution, if sincere, must rely on an ideologically tainted reading of the evidence. Yet both these ideologues, I contend, can be rational, even though, for them, believing is seeing.

Following Goodman (1983), I shall argue for this contention using a standard partition of evidence into *green* and *not green*—an apolitical example designed to minimize the impact of preconceptions and maximize continuity with the existing philosophical literature. According to the usual view of rational learning, a succession of green emeralds should inductively strengthen any rational agent's belief that "all emeralds are green." Goodman, however, asks us to consider a different "ideology," one partitioning evidence into *grue* and *not grue,* where *grue* means "observed before time t (say $t = 10^{100}$ A.D.) and green or not so observed and blue." Each of these partitions can be considered the basis for an alternative ideological scheme.

As one might suspect, these ideologies lead to different generalizations from the evidence. To the user of *green,* the emeralds that are observed strengthen the hypothesis, "All emeralds are green." To the user of *grue,* however, the appropriate generalization is the bizarre hypothesis, "All emeralds are grue." In the latter case, a succession of green emeralds strengthens the *grue* user's belief that emeralds will suddenly be blue at some particular time $t,$ just as generally positive economic data apparently strengthen the Marxist ideologue's conviction that the revolution is coming in the foreseeable future. Yet bizarre or not, Goodman argues, these generalizations are, formally speaking, impeccable. Pure considerations of inductive rationality do not justify a preference for the *green* hypothesis over the *grue,* or for the capitalist's over the Marxist's. Relative to its conceptual scheme, each hypothesis is increasingly confirmed.

In making this argument, Goodman's concern is to show that formal considerations will never suffice to distinguish justified from unjustified inductive practices. The relevance of his claim for institutional realism is somewhat different: by holding formal inductive rationality constant, we see the irreducible role of conceptualization or ideology. For ideologies not only categorize and thereby color evidence, in this case almost literally. Equally important, Goodman shows that this influence on the ideologue's inductive generalizations is entirely consistent with the ideologue's rationality. Variable conceptualizations go hand in hand with adherence to the strictest inductive rules.

Formally speaking, ideologies oriented by *grue* and by *green* converge to their respective conclusions in exactly the same inductively rational way. Nonetheless, rationality does not prevent their adherents from converging toward different beliefs prior to time $t.$ If so, the idea that more and more evidence should bring rational agents ever closer to the same posterior beliefs—that ideology should diminish in importance—represents wishful thinking. By the same reasoning, there is no basis for expecting convergence to some best, "nonideological" system of categories. There is no end of ideology.

Since my analysis of ideology rests on Goodman's claim, it might be useful to forestall two of the more obvious objections to his argument.[9] The first, which Goodman anticipates, focuses on the gross way that *grue* differs from *green:* since *grue* explicitly refers to time, the complaint goes, it lacks the homogeneous quality of legitimate, nonpositional predicates.

Goodman, in response, accuses this complaint of begging the question. The apparent lack of homogeneity found in *grue* actually presupposes the appropriateness of *green*. To see this, let us give the *grue* ideologue an additional category, *bleen,* defined as 'observed before *t* and blue or not so observed and green.' Now the shoe is on the other foot. To the adherent of the *grue-bleen* ideology, it is the supporter of *green* who uses a positional predicate: she categorizes emeralds as *grue* until *t* and unaccountably switches to *bleen* thereafter.

The second objection to Goodman's position is similar to the first, yet more directly Bayesian—the standard form of induction in rational choice theory—and therefore best able to clarify the way institutional realism integrates rationality and ideology. Roger Rosenkrantz (1982) proposes treating the hypothesis, "All emeralds are grue," as the conjunction of two hypotheses:

H: All emeralds examined before *t* are green

and

K: All emeralds unexamined before *t* are blue.

The hypothesis that all emeralds are green is similarly the conjunction of *H* and

K': All emeralds unexamined before *t* are green.

Defining the degree of confirmation of hypothesis *H* by evidence *E*, $dc(E,H)$, as $p(H|E) - p(H)$, Rosenkrantz utilizes the following proposition (the proof is simple but illustrates the process of Bayesian induction; see appendix 1):

$$\text{If } H \text{ implies } E, \text{ then } dc(E,H\&K) = p(K|H)\, dc(E,H) \qquad (1)$$

Now let *E* stand for the evidence of green emeralds before *t*. *E* is a consequence of *H&K* and therefore confirms it. According to (1), however, the dc for *H&K* is a fraction of the dc for *H* alone, whereas the discounting probability $p(K|H)$ for the grue hypothesis *H&K* is, Rosenkrantz claims, much smaller than the discounting probability $p(K'|H)$ for the green hypothesis *H&K'*. In a limited sense, then, Goodman is right: *E* helps confirm the grue hypothesis. However, Rosenkrantz concludes, *E* provides much greater confirmation for the green hypothesis. The suspicious logical consequence of *H&K, K,* is on the whole less believable after a more complete Bayesian analysis (see the similar discussion in Eells 1982).

I have described Rosenkrantz's technical argument in some detail because it illustrates the proper role of inductive rationality according to institutional realism. Its proper role, first of all, is not to overcome all vestiges of ideological thinking or to replace ideology with rationally warranted beliefs. Rosenkrantz's attempt to accomplish this appeals to our background knowledge that emeralds are color-constant, which is his translation of $p(K|H) < p(K'|H)$.[10] The problem is that grue users would translate this same background knowledge differently, since to them emeralds have been as grue-constant as they have green-constant. The only difference is that until these ideologues had a spokesperson in Goodman, no one had noticed.[11]

The proper role of Bayesian induction is to operate within an ideological scheme. Within an ideology, learning—the modification of beliefs—can continue to take place. Specifically, (1) shows that relative to an ideology Bayesian induction can still make the crucial factual distinctions, allowing both *green* and *grue* ideologues to comprehend and distinguish their alternative conceptualizations. In this case, for example, at least one of the two schemes must in time fail. So there are, in principle, factual grounds for choosing between ideologies on the basis of their ability to explain or predict events. By the same token, a rational user of *green* need not see the world the way a user of *grue* does.

In short, Bayesian updating remains valid relative to an ideology.[12] Put in a more positive way, although ideology is not an unbiased framework for understanding reality, and although there is not even a single ideology toward which all rational decision makers necessarily converge, having an ideology is entirely consistent with rational decision making. *Even if there is an objective standard of rationality to which everyone conforms and they have the same underlying preferences, they may still be ideologically and therefore behaviorally diverse.*[13] The only mistake the Bayesian approach makes is in treating the ideological framework as a constant rather than as a variable.

Notice, by the way, the implications of this approach to ideology for rational expectations theory. In chapter 3 I suggested that some of the standard methodological complaints against this approach—the need for homogeneity of expectations, the difficulties of converging to the same model let alone the correct one—say as much about the irreducible interdependencies of rational actors facing social situations as they do about rational expectations assumptions. We now see another problem about convergence: actors hoping to learn the correct model may operate using different ideologies (cf. Blume and Easley 1982). More generally, the idea that agents will converge to a homogeneous understanding of institutions, equally recognize unintended consequences, draw uniform conclusions from them, and increase their mastery over the institution is much less secure when agents have ideologies.

In practice, agents must choose an appropriate ideology, and the behavior rationalized by it, using ideologically ambiguous information. Without going into somewhat tangential details, I suggest that the choice can be understood along the following lines. Relative to each possible ideological interpretation the agent considers, information about future goods and policies or other objects of uncertainty is incorporated in the standard Bayesian way, namely, through Bayes' rule or other procedures derived from it (see DeGroot 1970). In fact, by putting further restrictions on the operational definition of ideology, this notion of ideology can be introduced into Enelow and Hinich's (1984) spatial model of voting.

Yet a given piece of information will support inferences in more than one ideological framework. Thus, while the agent may have alternative ideological interpretations for any piece of evidence, there is no overarching framework for conceptualizing what may amount to the joint realization of evidence in all the agent's potential ideologies.[14] The impact of ambiguous information is distributed among the possible ideologies according to Jeffrey conditionalization, a generalization of Bayesian updating suitable for unclear evidence (Jeffrey 1983). Presumably, the agent will decide to believe in the ideology that makes best statistical sense of the world.

One distinctive feature of Jeffrey conditionalization is that the order in which information is received can affect the agent's inferences. When it does, newer opinions will dominate older ones since agents revise their opinions by reconsidering not only their larger beliefs but even their earlier observations. This revision, which cannot occur under ordinary conditionalization, has a useful ideological interpretation. Agents who revise their ideological beliefs this way will reinterpret the very data on which their previous ideological beliefs were based. As far as these agents are concerned, they did not simply suffer from a shortage of information; they misinterpreted the information they had.[15] My impression is that this retrospection is indeed characteristic of ideological converts. To ex-communists who came to write for the *National Review,* for example, the evidence originally seen as supporting the Soviet Union underwent an ex post facto reinterpretation.[16]

In principle, the number of ideologies resident in a society can equal the size of the population involved. Worse, there no a priori limit on the number of possible ideologies in each citizen's personal inventory, though her comparisons are constrained by search, development, and processing costs as well as the institutional environment that gives even prospective ideologies much of their content. Even so, these abstract considerations should not lead one to expect an ideological Tower of Babel. Agents have a clear incentive to adopt the frameworks of those with whom they most often interact. The fateful time *t* facing the *grue* ideology may never arise in the social case insofar as the social reality constituted by ideologically informed agents may be doing the adapting rather than vice versa. Put another way, socialization no longer becomes a matter of simple inculcation since those who are its targets may have a rational incentive to learn the prevailing ideology. They will choose to be inculcated.

Nor is the neophyte the only one interested in conversion. Functioning members of society will also find that the useful categories are widespread and the widespread categories are useful.[17] Public goods and externality problems aside, these members presumably will not leave the development of ideologies to chance. They will inculcate particular ideologies through a process Talcott Parsons has aptly called pattern maintenance. The patterns of interest, in this case, are associated with institutions, which can be viewed as particular categorizations of the social whole.

The possibility of inculcation opens up an important role for agenda setters, or what we might now call institutional structure setters. In times of political uncertainty, their ideological cues can help define the public's understanding of its institutions (see chapter 7). For a rational individual interested in predicting the future will want to anticipate these patterns even when they are not unequivocally supported by the evidence or anchored by properties and other supposedly reality-induced classifications. Thus, when this process of adaptation is aided by ideological leaders, the result is similar to the process Riker (1990) describes as heresthetics.

5.

Having fitted rational agents with an institutional grammar useful for describing institutional structures, and with an ideology for making that grammar operational, I can set about making institutional realist sense of rationality itself. The conventionalist, of course, is interested in a rationality that is self-contained and independent of the institution. The institution must be kept distinct if it is to reflect rational choices. Yet this creates a problem: insofar as the institution and the rational choices of agents mirror one another, there is little room for institutionally relevant behavior that does not correspond to the postulated rational choice foundation. Recall that a conventionalist institution is really an anticipated equilibrium rooted in preferences and beliefs, not actual behaving individuals. An institution subsists in people's minds. Can irrationality as a behavioral fact play any role in this scheme? Or to put it bluntly, if an institution is a construct out of rational choices, where do real-life mistakes fit in?

The classic framework for the conventionalist analysis of institutions in rational choice theory is, once again, the prisoners' dilemma. I have already examined two extreme forms of the dilemma, the one-shot game and the supergame consisting of infinite iterations of it. In the first case, rational players outsmart themselves to produce a collectively inferior outcome, whereas in the second case it is possible for the players to behave more satisfactorily. To examine the notion of rationality, I now take up an intermediate case involving a finite number of iterations.

Until recently, it was agreed that this intermediate case produces the same inferior outcome, iteration after iteration, as the one-shot game. The reasoning depends on a backward induction argument.[18] At the final—let us say nth—iteration, it is better for both players, A and B, to play their dominant strategies, A_2 and B_2 respectively, for the same reasons that it is better in the original one-shot game (see chapter 3). Since this is the last iteration, their decisions can have no negative consequences for future play. This means, however, that at the $n - 1$ iteration both A and B know that each, as a rational agent, plans to defect (play the dominant strategy) at the final iteration. At the $n - 1$ iteration, therefore, neither has a reason to hold off. By the same logic, both players will decide to defect at the $n - 2$ iteration. Identical reasoning holds for all iterations back to the first play of the game. Cooperation, the argument concludes, is never rational.

This conclusion, it is fair to say, strikes many as counterintuitive, particularly when n is large. One response is to redefine the strategic situation of the players in ways I shall discuss shortly. Another response is to challenge the backward induction argument directly. Both the problem and the responses reflect the conventionalist foundation of game theory and suggest why institutional realism is a better alternative. (For another approach to the same conclusion, see the earlier discussion of the hangman's paradox).

The challenge to the induction argument is fairly straightforward (see Pettit and Sugden 1989). When players initially contemplate the looming n iterations of the prisoners' dilemma, they presumably are entitled to assume that all participants are rational and understand the rules of the game. If the induction argument is correct, this means that certain situations will never arise, namely, those in which one of the players has cooperated at a preceding stage of the game. For no rational player would cooperate at any stage.

Suppose, however, that these expectations prove incorrect: as a matter of fact, A does cooperate at some iteration prior to n. At that point, B may well conclude that A is not behaving rationally. But if this is a conclusion B is prepared to reach at a subsequent iteration, it should be a conclusion B entertains before the game begins. The backward induction argument hinges on B's incorrect initial assumption that at each iteration players will believe their counterparts to be rational. Backward induction, ironically enough, depends on the unwillingness of the players to make appropriate inductions.

According to one interpretation, Philip Pettit and Robert Sugden (1989) merely defeat a popular argument for persistent noncooperation in the finitely iterated prisoners' dilemma. In a more positive light, they have enriched the strategic possibilities open to the players. When, for example, A deviates from "rationality" in the manner described above, this may suggest to B the utility of responding with what would otherwise be an irrational strategy of cooperation. Indeed, the resulting string of cooperative iterations may be better for both players. Apparently, players like A can circumvent the very prescriptions their own rationality demands by acting "irrationally" to alter the beliefs of the other players. This, in turn, can induce better outcomes—cooperation in the iterated prisoners' dilemma—than would otherwise obtain. In general, consistent noncooperation is no longer the unique prediction. Numerous outcomes are possible depending on the inferences that players draw from each other's behavior.[19]

What is happening under this more positive interpretation, I suggest, is that conventionalist game theory is looking in the mirror. Its guiding assumption, remember, is that the beliefs and preferences of players define the game they are playing. Different beliefs, and different beliefs about beliefs, would redefine their situation. Understood this way, the hierarchy of beliefs about beliefs about beliefs about the other player's rationality seems to allow alternative ways of structuring the game. An observer might attempt to stabilize the situation by inserting a claim as to where the hierarchy ends or as to how players behave as a simple matter of fact. But these claims look ad hoc from a conventionalist standpoint.

Backward induction, then, does not allow players to come to grips with the actual behavior in the game when the behavior was unanticipated owing to its apparent irrationality. Like conventionalism generally, the backward induction argument is oriented toward psychology rather than behavior. Yet the criticism of it similarly insists on an infinite range of iterated beliefs, revisions of iterated beliefs, and inducements of iterated beliefs held by others, whenever individuals are fully rational. Actual behavior in the particular interdependent context of the game is never allowed to preempt all this by defining the content of rational thought. As a result, when the conventionalist picture of game theory is taken seriously, one of its important tools, the backward induction argument, forfeits many of its most prized applications. The result is indeterminacy—more indeterminacy, however, than an institutional realist needs to stomach.

So where does institutional realism stand in this debate? It stands full-square in the middle. Both the backward induction argument and the criticism of it share a crucial conventionalist assumption: the a priori status of rationality independent of institutional context. Rather than assuming that shifting configurations of belief, playing cat and mouse with one another, define and redefine the game, institutional realists are inclined to accept the game and the behavioral interdependence it represents as brute facts facing the players. According to institutional realism, no player, however rational, can expect to avoid this interdependence by exploiting it from some imagined position external to the game. In chapter 4 I developed a specific proposal for recognizing the sense in which rational players must accept their interdependence; the best way to appreciate the strength of this alternative is first to trace the debate over backward induction a little further.

Fans of the backward induction argument have at least two important replies to Pettit and Sugden (1989). Common beliefs, to proceed with the first reply, are particularly important to conventionalist game theory because without them there would not be one particular game all players were playing.[20] The idea of common beliefs, say proponents of backward induction, can rescue it from indeterminacy.

Suppose that among their common beliefs, players believe each other to be rational and believe each is capable of duplicating the other's reasoning process. Given these common beliefs, neither party is capable of outguessing the other. If so, A has no business trying to induce otherwise irrational behavior by encouraging B to have false beliefs about A that A obviously does not share. Each player, therefore, should stick to the original strategies recommended by the backward induction argument. The entire case against the induction argument, the first reply concludes, represents a massive diversion for A & B leading them full circle.

If this reply is correct, A cannot credibly induce B to infer A's irrationality so long as A has no personal doubts about it. Pettit and Sugden (1989:179) have a ready counter: "Suppose that A believes Z [in this case, Z = both A and B are rational]. The claim that therefore B must believe that A believes Z depends on the additional premise that B is rational, for if B were irrational there would be no grounds for expecting him to be capable of replicating whatever reasoning led A to his belief." This additional premise is unjustified, they conclude, since the assumption of rationality need not hold up as play proceeds.

Notice how Pettit and Sugden's response, like the defense of backward induction, follows conventionalism in taking the internal specification of rationality seriously. Evidently, game theory, like the players it studies, is supposed to capture the reasoning process each player goes or went through before behaving. But surely one way to view rationality in game theory—the way usually held to justify its unrealistic empirical assumptions—is not as an internal reasoning process that brings forth a game. Rather, it can be seen as a relation between imputed beliefs and preferences on the one hand and actions on the other.

So while I certainly agree with Pettit and Sugden's insistence that A's assumptions about B should be falsifiable, their response hinges on a conventionalist view of the priority of rationality, as a process internal to the agent, over the behavior it "produces." An entirely rational B, however, need only *behave* as if her reasoning process replicated A's. Conversely, B may even consciously replicate A's reasoning and simply fail to behave accordingly, which makes B irrational. Whether B is judged rational seems to hinge, for Pettit and Sugden, on whether B succeeds in replicating A's reasoning, but in fact B's supposed reasoning is rational only in the case when A's reasoning is itself judged to be rational. Unfortunately, judgments about A's rationality are also contingent on B's reasoning.

Cristina Bicchieri's (1989) similar quarrel with the backward induction argument is instructive in this regard. Suppose again that A plays "irrationally" at some stage, leading to a position that B could not have reached were A rational and a believer in B's rationality. Assuming common knowledge of beliefs, B evidently cannot conclude, says Bicchieri in her version of backward induction, that it is not the case that A believes that B believes A to be rational. (In Bicchieri's useful notation, B's prohibited conclusion is $\neg B_A B_B R_A$, where the regular B and R stand for "believes" and "is rational" respectively and the subscript letters denote who is being described.) Nor can B deny A's belief in B's rationality (that is, B's prohibited conclusion is $\neg B_A R_B$). The only legitimate conclusion, according to backward induction, is $\neg R_A$. So on the supposition that A's preceding irrationality suggests future irrationality, B is now entitled to play irrationally as well.

Like Pettit and Sugden, Bicchieri objects to the conclusion that $\neg R_A$. Although ostensibly B can know that $B_A R_A$ without R_A being true, A is assumed by game theory to know what rationality is. Since "there is no such thing as unconscious rationality" (Bicchieri 1989:77–78; she makes the same claim for irrationality), A cannot falsely believe R_A. So if $B_A R_A$, then R_A, contrary to the conclusion of the backward induction argument.

My response, again, is not to defend the backward induction argument but rather to show that the argument and the response to it share certain conventionalist assumptions. Whereas Bicchieri treats rationality as a distinct thought process, I have said that it is better seen as a behavioral disposition. If so, A's and B's arguably private information about their own rationality arises only because A and B presumably have been more frequent witnesses to their own previous behavior. Knowing the process going on in one's own mind—and I am not convinced about privileging even this—does not necessarily entitle one to privileged judgments about the *content* of that internal process. The arguments against backward induction make clear that an assessment of rationality is a highly contextual matter.

I am not saying that rational people must do what objectively turns out best for them. Rather, rationality in this case concerns (1) a relation between beliefs and preferences on the one hand and behavior on the other, and (2) an interdependency in the calculations of A and B concerning their behavioral dispositions. Condition 1 means A cannot will rationality into the thinking process alone. Condition 2 means that just as one cannot say whether A is rational by looking at A's beliefs in isolation from A's choices, so too is there no way for A to have a specially guaranteed sense—to *know* in advance—that his reasoning, considered in isolation, is rational in this game theoretic situation. There is no property of A's actual reasoning process that is sufficient unto itself to make A rational. A crucial factor is the behavior that A actually produces in the context of the behavior that B is believed to be disposed to produce.

To the institutional realist, then, rationality is not a determinate mental state lodged in A but rather a behavioral disposition whose rationality depends on the institutional context in which it is behaviorally displayed. To that extent, it is misleading to assess A's rationality by examining A in isolation.

6.

I turn now to the second possible reply to Pettit and Sugden's critique of the backward induction argument. Suppose that there is common knowledge not just of everyone's beliefs but also of their rationality.[21] If so, then inferences about A's or B's irrationality based on actual behavior in the game are strictly precluded. Beliefs about rationality are irreversible and, therefore, backward induction survives.

While conceding the validity of this argument, Pettit and Sugden assert that it undermines the whole idea of strategic thinking that motivates game theory. For under the common knowledge assumption, neither A nor B is entitled to contemplate in any strategic way the possibility of deviation from rationality. Since they know each will inevitably make the rational choice, there is no point to wondering what would happen otherwise.

There is something correct both in this second possible reply and in Pettit and Sugden's reaction to it. Since the world is as it is (to summarize a large chunk of chapter 1), the institutional realist must be sympathetic to any insight into the pointlessness of changing it through mere contemplation. Thinking hard cannot remake the world.

Yet the way Pettit and Sugden incorporate this insight into the postulated reply and their response to it continues to reflect a degree of conventionalism that is unappealing. In both the reply and the response, the inevitability of rational behavior is secured by knowledge of the participants' rationality. The institutional realist would question this, arguing that since the world of players is as it is, and since knowledge presumably must be knowledge of truths, then what needs to give way is not strategic freedom, which players have as much of as ever, but the definition of rationality, which cannot be a context-free property of players.

Abstract knowledge of rationality does not eliminate the strategic freedom to maneuver, for what is rational is, in part, a function of that maneuvering. In other words, knowing that A is rational is not the same as knowing what A will and must do in the literal sense of behavior since it is not to know of a particular *mechanism* in A's head prior to the game.[22] Institutional realism does not deny that human behavior can be predicted; it does question whether a context-free definition of rationality can always succeed in this respect. In such cases, knowledge of A's rationality does not restrict the anticipated course of play as much as Pettit and Sugden perhaps imagine.

From the standpoint of institutional realism, Pettit and Sugden as well as their imagined critics have all bought into a mistaken conventionalism. This standpoint, one might object, is unfair since a full-fledged conventionalism can use the full-fledged apparatus of counterfactual logic to transcend the limitations imposed by the common knowledge condition. As I read the conventionalist analysis of rationality by Gibbard and Harper (1978), for example, B is still free, given known truths about A's and B's behavior in the actual world, to contemplate what would happen conditional on alternative actions in other possible worlds. Predictions of what would happen might, in fact, include changes in A's behavior.

But does not A's and B's knowledge of each other's beliefs and rationality preclude them from anticipating any changes in behavior? Not if knowledge is equivalent to what Gibbard and Harper (1978:154–55) mean by certainty. Certainty or knowledge is epistemic, they argue, whereas the effects of B's actions on A (and vice versa) reflect the objective causal relations among these players. So long as the epistemic and the objective are carefully distinguished, knowledge of the game—in this case, of each player's rationality—cannot be equated with objective relations. In short, knowing that some action is rational for A and that A is rational does not preclude B from asking what would be the case if A were to behave differently.

At first sight, Gibbard and Harper's distinction between the epistemic and the objective is quite congenial to institutional realism. In fact, its real impact is to deepen the conventionalist interpretation of games. For the ability of agents to choose freely among strategies is now understood as the capacity to leave this world, so to speak, for an alternative possible world in which some other course of action takes place.[23] Objective causal relations remain independent of knowledge. But according to this interpretation of games, each player's choice, as an objective fact, is detached from the decision context. The context is incorporated into the decision as background information—indeed, in the case of role-induced interdependencies, inert background information.[24]

Thus we return to the issues surrounding evidential decision theory that I addressed a chapter back. Here I want to indicate the extent to which these problems afflicting a conventionalist rational choice theory of institutions are not confined to any particular example, like the iterated prisoners' dilemma, but pervade much of contemporary game theoretic analysis. In this sense, institutional realism does not invent complaints against the standard approach so much as reinterpret problems already discovered. These problems have a deeper, social scientific significance.

Let me, then, pose the problems associated with the iterated prisoners' dilemma in a broader context. Institutions, in the conventionalist view, are equilibria or solutions of games. Solutions, in turn, are determined by the rationality of the players. Since these games are by definition played by rational players, it is unclear why anything but equilibria should arise. Yet key solution concepts like the Nash equilibrium seem to be plausible predictions of the actual outcome of the game only when players are pushed away, so to speak, from those alternative outcomes not satisfying the solution criteria: "Where there are no equilibrating forces, equilibrium in this sense is not a relevant concept" (Bernheim 1984:1008). In other words, what makes a particular equilibrium reasonable is, in part, the way rational agents contemplate the consequences and therefore the possibility of out-of-equilibrium beliefs. Rational players, on the other hand, should not expect to find themselves out of equilibrium.

In their widely discussed work, Reinhardt Selten (1975) and David Kreps and Robert Wilson (1982) take the idea of mistakes seriously and thereby acknowledge a discrepancy between what is officially rational behavior and the way agents may actually behave. In Selten's analysis, for instance, each player calculates her optimal response not only to the possible rational choices of the other players but also to their choices subject to the possibility that they make mistakes, that their hands tremble, to use Selten's evocative image. Selten argues that postulating this revised calculus assures the reasonableness of the equilibria postulated by game theory.

One problem with the Selten approach is its failure to clarify how the generation of out-of-equilibrium beliefs might be rationalized. Kreps and Wilson, accordingly, tackle this issue more directly, but the challenge they face is formidable. As they well understand, they are attempting to make sense of beliefs that are conditioned on out-of-equilibrium events that within the model have a zero prior probability. This makes for a certain indeterminacy, mathematical and otherwise. In fact, it is widely acknowledged that their approach does not exclude unreasonable beliefs out of equilibrium.[25]

In fairness, there is a sense in which any out-of-equilibrium belief is unreasonable within conventionalist game theory. Elon Kohlberg and Jean-Francois Mertens (1986:1005) reassert this "classical point of view" by insisting that the possibility of mistakes built into a game theoretic analysis "must not be interpreted as the probabilities that the players will actually err in choosing their strategies." Everything the players know and believe must be derived from the game as modeled.

In fact, to maintain this internal point of view, Kohlberg and Mertens assume that in each game a referee presents players with a recommended vector of mixed strategies and tells them that this vector is a stable equilibrium "expected to be adhered to by all parties." Assuming that people bother to show up for this charade, how do Kohlberg and Mertens propose to handle real-life deviations? In conventionalist style: "In principle, in situations where this restriction is not met, the game tree is just used as a shorthand notation for the rules of a much bigger 'extended game.'"

According to this analysis, deviations from the equilibrium path are not viewed as temporary lapses, with subsequent play following as closely as possible ordinary lines of rational decision making. Rather, the justification of the solution concept presupposes that players will be calculating the game along lines that assume that rational strategies are being played throughout (see van Damme 1989:478–83).[26] As van Damme notes, deviations basically serve "as a computational technique for checking [the] self-enforcingness" of the equilibria presented to the players.

There are two immediate conclusions to draw from these and other twists in contemporary game theoretic debates. One, a "merely" philosophical concern about the ontological status of games is not in any sense ancillary to the theory of games. Although game theorists may not consciously address the philosophical nature of this concern—and we see how even that is changing—it continues to haunt specific attempts to grapple with definitions of rationality and equilibrium. The possibility of out-of-equilibrium events in a world of perfect rationality, for example, has implications for the existence of the game in the conventionalist interpretation. The question it raises is not only whether players should reasonably anticipate or rationally react to this possibility. Rather, the underlying problem is the ontological status of that part of the structure of the game that cannot be reached, that is ruled *impossible*. Why and in what sense can an impossible belief play a role in defining the game? Alternatively, if players' trembling and irrationality are anticipated, how does the psychology of these same players still define the range of possible behavior and outcomes in a world defined by rational players?

Two, although rationality defines solutions, increasingly solutions and rationality are defined simultaneously. A rational player becomes the sort of person who when guided by the solution concept can figure out or anticipate the behavior of others. Sometimes the mirroring between solution concept and rationality is preserved by tightening up the beliefs associated with rational participation; sometimes considerations of plausibility external to the model maintain harmony within. As Bernheim (1984:1010) observes, "even if some technique always isolated unique equilibria, it would represent a psychological hypothesis rather than a characterization of rationality, and would be empirically relevant only if it formalized characteristics that are universally perceived as salient" (cf. the notion of caution in Pearce 1984).

If games are products of agents' minds and are played within them, then indeterminacy becomes a basic challenge to conventionalist assumptions, not just a feature of particular solution concepts. Thus Pearce (1984:1030) notes, "Once one admits the possibility that a player may have several strategies that he could reasonably use, expectations may be mismatched. Player i's strategy will then be a best response to his (possibly incorrect) *conjecture* about others' strategies, not the actual strategies employed."

From the standpoint of institutional realism, the essential difficulty is that the real social situations in which people find themselves are supposed to be defined and determined by the individuals involved, yet this stipulation makes it very hard to make sense of social situations that are not so defined and determined, or at least have drifted away from their predetermined course. Players may even be asked to confront "impossible" events; in that case, their reactions are somewhat indeterminate, the very possibility is simply defined out of existence, or the independently defined rationality scheme that is supposed to dictate behavior is supplemented by an ad hoc imputed psychology.

Ken Binmore's (1987) approach, adapted to the iterated prisoners' dilemma, seems closer to the mark. When, owing to A's cooperative behavior, B reaches an intuitively plausible situation that should not have occurred if all players are rational, B may have to reassess the definition of rationality rather than the assumption of its universality. "One might say she is subject to trembles in what she supposes to be the correct way to play" (1987:203).[27] The institutional realist might say that she faces the predicament of behaving rationally in a situation in which even her rationality has a strongly contextual component. In this respect, her own rationality is as much a discovery as a state of mind. Self-definition, in short, goes the way of designer institutions.

7.

Details about institutional rules, information, ideologies, and rationality should not be allowed to obscure the larger message of institutional realism that these details reflect. Institutions are aggregates of human beings satisfying certain relational and dispositional descriptions. The institutional structure is, in effect, the set of behavioral channels or alternative actions open at various stages of the game. This structure is determined by the array of behavior and behavioral dispositions each player faces, while information, rules, and ideology may allow the player to face it more successfully.

Institutional realism, like the players it models, is relatively indifferent to the history of these dispositions (except of course when there is learning within the game). Given a strict understanding of what counts as explanation, these dispositions may even be socially inexplicable, indeed psychologically inexplicable given a traditional notion of psychology. In particular, the idea of rationality is used by institutional realists to characterize dispositions within game theoretic settings, not to explain the behavior they produce. So long as a rational player enters an institution, the institution, if truly stable, should be able to assure his conformity given the alternatives he is presented.

By the same token, institutions do not require more than adaptive behavior from participants. Rational players do the best they can within the institution using the information they have and their understanding of the rules; nonrational players generally fail to do the best they can. The game itself need not become an object of thought, let alone choice or preference. Each player as player works within the game rather than on it. By adding an iterated hierarchy of beliefs to account for actual behavior, one does not probe more deeply into the rational foundations of the game; rather, one lets the imputed psychology reflect the behavioral interconnections so characteristic of institutional situations.

The institution, in short, defines the player's set of feasible social alternatives. Each rational player is assumed to behave so as to maximize his conditional expected utility with regard to these alternatives. Within the institution, players are thus modeled as if they strive to fulfill their intentions. To preclude any misinterpretation, then, I use the traditional psychological terminology ultimately for convenience and for greater intelligibility to social scientists (myself included) and others: the key issue is what behavioral output we can expect given a particular series of inputs. By the same token, the convenience of this terminology is no small matter. Indeed, I concede that there is nothing on the horizon ready to replace the familiar folk psychology.

Not every social arrangement is an institution. A convention, for example, exists because the participants know it exists and want it to continue. It is an object of their actions. Institutions rely on a much more limited brand of loyalty. Since each agent faces the institution as a fact, albeit a social fact, players are required only to make the local decisions the institution presents to them.[28] Each player acting in this way, or disposed to act in this way, helps produce the institutional conditions confronting other players in the form of an institutionally determined range of alternatives. Thus the institution reproduces itself.

The institutional game confronts each player as a given. It is even a given for the players collectively insofar as they must operate collectively through existing institutional forms. Do not players facing conventions similarly operate within rather than on their coordination game? Yes and no. Yes, because they are assumed to choose from among the alternatives the coordination game presents to them; no, because players in a convention are doing more than optimizing relative to the alternatives they happen to be offered. They are seeking to reproduce a regularity involving the behavior of all. This regularity is the object of their intentions; hence the knowledge conditions for conventions are crucial.

In a convention, members decide whether to (re-)create the convention. The decision is not merely how to do one's best given the existing regularity or the reactions one anticipates by virtue of being within an institutional structure. Lewis emphasizes this game theoretically by insisting on the arbitrariness of the regularity in question—that is, the availability of a satisfactory alternative. If a convention were not arbitrary, players "would conform to it simply because it is the best thing to do" (1969:70).

Still, I do not want the convention-institution distinction to depend on the availability of alternative regularities. Arbitrariness is more a symptom than a defining characteristic of this distinction. In the case of conventions, the definition of the equilibria, of the recurrent situations, and of the alternative actions is all conventional since the participants do the defining. In the case of institutions, these features are discovered and, in a weak sense, produced by participants. They do not exist or become distinguished simply by virtue of the intentions of participants.

A convention, in sum, is not merely a special case of an institution. It heralds a fundamentally different understanding of social and political order. For even though conventionalists recognize tacit and potential knowledge, the paradigm convention remains the explicit and pure example we associate with the signals for Paul Revere's ride. All the rest is a concession to reality disguised by the flexibility of the psychological terminology.

If knowledge can be potential or tacit, the institutional realist asks, is not the next logical step to say that knowledge need not exist at all? As a complex pattern of social interaction, an institution can certainly make use of the beliefs and knowledge that agents bring or may develop. Yet the institution can also rely on habit, reflex, ignorance, and laziness. The knowledge and belief that conventionalists see as the core of social order are, to the institutional realist, two of the ingredients sustaining an institution. Though they may help produce it, they do not define it.

As I have already conceded, the existence of institutions more than likely depends on mechanisms that working social scientists have to characterize in richly psychological terms. This is an empirical issue, which the preceding analysis of mediating instruments such as information and rules only partly addresses. As an additional concession, I can easily imagine conventions arising prior to any institution, particularly in the context of small-group interactions. Even in this case, though, institutions can later do the "work" of maintaining the associated regularity (an outcome conventionalists may continue to credit entirely to knowledge and desire). Institutions develop in the wake of conventions as knowledge, or at least knowledge requirements, recede. Only institutions, in the end, fully permit the complex interdependencies of action that can emerge behind the backs of participants.

In a somewhat similar fashion, the anthropologist Arnold Gehlen (1964) suggests that institutions relieve individuals of the burden of stabilizing a meaningful and productive social organization. This *Entlastung,* or relief is at once required and possible, he argues, because of the plasticity of human nature. Humans are not furnished with strong instinctual drives that might otherwise guide us through thick and thin. (In later work, Gehlen modifies this claim.) For my own brand of institutional realism, the biological characteristic in question is simply the cognitive capacities and limits of humans. People are capable of producing complex social interactions that they cannot survey, control, or design at will—certainly not on a daily basis. Institutions make such supervision unnecessary.

6.

Electoral Institutions and Voting

Although institutional order would seem to face chronic subversion from free riders and other opportunists, institutional realism alerts us to a mechanism of social control able to pick up the slack: a rational choice analog of the sociological concept of an institutional role. In occupying a particular place within the institution, be it voter, mail carrier, or air force pilot, the participant may be cued into stochastic dependencies specific to the institution.

Insofar as institutions are maintained in relatively impersonal and complex ways, these institutionally secured dependencies must arise among actors who do not know each other and hail from very different backgrounds. They have to rely on cues that go beyond the recognition of personal relations or shared personalized identities. In fact, if the institution is to reproduce itself under these conditions, the sheer fact of common or related institutional identities must "socialize" members into institutionally appropriate behavior. These more abstract commonalities may need to become as salient to these members as the common physical characteristics that bound their ancestors.

An institution of this sort is not a social club. Unlike marriage, for example, it does not exist through face-to-face contact alone. Indeed, in one modern institutional arena, mass democratic elections, anonymity has become self-conscious and even sacrosanct. Not surprisingly, accounting for mass participation in this institution has posed a formidable challenge to standard rational choice theory, which sees anonymity as an opportunity for shirking and free-riding—in brief, for abstention. Formal theory has had a notoriously difficult time getting voters to the polls.

The case of mass elections is not only empirically significant but has theoretical importance as well. In chapter 4 I argued that a combination of two factors protects institutions from the potential disintegration associated with an encompassing prisoners' dilemma: members' higher expected utility due to rational role expectations within the institution and their lower expected utility due to transaction costs faced outside the institution. The institutional constraints on them are thus only partial and, accordingly, the distinctiveness of institutional realism, vis-à-vis Shepsle (1989), is blurred.

All that changes in the case of mass elections. First, in a country like the United States, the voter's decision—participate or abstain—is completely internal to the institution. Both courses of action are legally sanctioned. This means that rational role expectations should have their most clear-cut effect. Second, transaction costs work against participation. In particular, the standard rational choice analysis assumes that voters will not organize joint participation. Third, the existence of the institution is still at stake. I assume, in other words, that an electoral institution in which no one shows up is an institution in name only. Fourth, the standard analysis does in fact deliver a zero or negligible level of turnout from voters having a net positive cost of voting.

As Anthony Downs (1957) first described the problem, there is a minuscule probability that one voter will affect the outcome of a mass election. If so, the expected benefits of participation, when the act itself is not especially rewarding, will be swamped by the ordinary costs of voting associated with expenditures of time and money. Voting, Downs concludes, is irrational or at least largely noninstrumental (Riker and Ordeshook 1968). Yet if it is irrational, then millions of people proudly demonstrate their irrationality every election year. If it is essentially noninstrumental, then turnout should be insensitive to the closeness of the election, the political difference between the candidates, or relatively small variations in cost due to such factors as weather.

The problem of mass irrationality is not merely a passing diversion for rational choice theorists. Presumably, this result would concern anyone who thinks that the normative theory of democratic consent ought to have some relation to reality or that participants ought to have a justified sense of efficacy. Some, like Howard Margolis (1984), also argue that the failure to explain turnout is symptomatic of the inability of the standard theory to comprehend situations in which the agent's identification with a larger group matters.

Of the numerous and ingenious proposals for rescuing rational choice theory, only one is particularly important to the theory of institutional realism developed in chapter 4. In a majority-rule, two-candidate election, a single voter can hope to affect the outcome only by breaking or creating a tie. Downs took the probability of this happening as fixed and given. In his model, the voter decides whether to participate by comparing the result of voting with the result of not voting, given all possible vote totals. When the outcome cannot be affected by a single vote, participation makes no difference, but it is still costly. The decision to participate thus boils down to the voter's estimate that one of the single-vote situations will occur. With a large electorate, these situations are extremely rare (see Chamberlain and Rothschild 1981).

Yet even as Downs (1957:267) recognized in passing, this representation of the voter's choice actually assumes a degree of irrationality. The probability of affecting the election's outcome is not fixed and given but endogenous to the electoral process. For a voter can validly estimate that probability only after factoring in the parallel estimates made by the other voters, who presumably make their own decisions accordingly. The key point for institutional analysis is that an election is a game (Ledyard 1981; 1984; Palfrey and Rosenthal 1983) and therefore should be grist for the institutionalist's mill.[1]

Although the move from decision theory to game theory had initially positive results, the so-called paradox of not voting has not been resolved. Given realistic assumptions about each voter's level of information about other voters, expected turnout from those who are instrumentally rational approaches zero as the number of potential voters increases (Palfrey and Rosenthal 1985). The application of game theory using the standard rational choice analysis has failed to solve the original problem.

This standard analysis assumes that voters are concerned solely with the causal impact of their actions on the outcome of the election. They are causal decision theorists who discount the utility of alternative outcomes by the probability that the acts in question will bring them about. Suppose, however, that potential voters are evidential decision theorists. If these voters see their own behavior as providing evidence about the likely behavior of others occupying the same role, they will calculate the conditional expected utility of their acts in light of their rational role expectations rather than in terms of what the causal consequences of their acts might be. Under these circumstances, electoral participation can become one of those key situations in which the predictions of conventionalism and institutional realism diverge.

Insofar as the act of voting provides differential evidence concerning the behavior of other potential voters, a rational voter will welcome indications that his side will win. Given rational role expectations, the likelihood of a voter's preferred candidate winning is larger than the individual vote would suggest.

For present purposes, the American electoral institution will be understood as classifying an otherwise heterogeneous collection of voters into supporters of the Republican candidate and supporters of the Democratic candidate. In principle, this classification is entirely synthetic: a candidate's supporters may have nothing in common besides their support. Yet however artificial from a social point of view, this institutional classification may still lead an individual voter to believe that his decision to vote raises the conditional probability of the chosen candidate winning beyond what the single vote would indicate.

Given the institution's classification—the institutionally defined choices—there are only three alternatives any voter can have: vote for the Democrat, vote for the Republican, and abstain. The fate of sharing a role thus is determined by sheer sameness of political preferences that can be revealed within the institution. The voter's role, nonetheless, may offer sufficient information to prompt participation. This is not to say that subgroupings of the population along the lines of race, ethnicity, occupation, class, religion, and gender do not matter. Yet each of these will be funneled through and scattered by the simple preference partition. This institutionally induced classification by preference is my main focus in this chapter. Accordingly, I shall assume that each voter has a strict preference for one of the two candidates.

Institutional realism suggests that voters are influenced by their institutionally defined roles. What follows is one possible way of integrating this institutional effect into a model in which the voters accept stochastic dependencies but nonetheless remain sensitive to the strategic possibilities inherent in the institutional game. Specifically, I (1) modify the game theoretic model mentioned above by incorporating a version of the decision calculus associated with evidential theory, (2) show that the modified model explains positive turnout by voters who have a net positive cost of voting, and (3) indicate some implications for candidate strategies, for the influence of institutional membership on political behavior, and for the problem of supplying public goods.

Although the model recognizes that each voter has only incomplete information about the preferences and costs of the other voters, it still provides each with a comprehensive reading of the institution as a whole. Voters understand their institutional interdependence and incorporate it in fairly sophisticated calculations.[2] Tracking these calculations sometimes gets a bit technical, but there is no other theoretically convincing way to show that the institutionalization of the electoral game influences turnout despite strategic thinking on the part of voters. (Those readers who are willing to take my word for it may choose to skip the next three sections and appendix 2.)

There is one important limitation on the otherwise substantial degree of rationality imputed to the voters. In a full rational expectations model, voter estimates of costs, preferences, and beliefs would also be endogenous to the model. I believe that the simpler model developed in this chapter is sufficient to make the points that need making. In the concluding section, however, I do introduce one new institutional factor weighing on the voter's calculation of expected utility, since this will allow us to consider an important application of the idea of institutional ideology developed in chapter 5.

1.

I am interested in evidential decision theory solely as an empirical theory of electoral participation. Still, its claim to resolve the paradox of not voting depends, in part, on the accuracy of its claim to model normatively rational choice. With this in mind, I first want to motivate this application of evidential theory by tailoring to the voting case some of the abstract considerations I have already advanced in favor of that theory.

Consider a voter who has already decided to vote and, if she decides to walk to the polls, would like to run into a particular neighbor who walks there. Unfortunately, she has no direct information about which of several routes the neighbor will take. If she were to learn that the two of them are remarkably similar in their views about the attractions of walking, the kind of scenery they like, and so on, then presumably this would increase the subjective probability that the two will take the same route. Would a rational voter refrain from taking this increased probability into account? Should, for instance, her reservation price for not walking to the polls—the minimum payment she requires to drive instead—remain the same after learning about the neighbor? Evidential decision theory endorses an increased reservation price even though the voter's choice of routes has no causal impact on the neighbor's decision.

By election day, a registered voter may have information about characteristics she shares with other citizens. In some cases, they occupy the same institutional role. This coincidence, in turn, may suggest that the decision of these fellow citizens to take one route (viz. voting) rather than another (viz. abstaining) stochastically depends on her own. The conditional expected utility of participation will be revised upward in light of this information. Accordingly, institutional realism sanctions participation even though the voter's decision has no causal impact on the decisions of others.

Causal decision theory—the standard analysis—insists that the price a rational individual is willing to pay to take the gamble called voting—namely, the cost of voting—is unaffected by the increase in conditional expected utility associated with these rational role expectations. As in the case of the neighbor, the voter's decision to take one route rather than another will have no casual impact on the decisions of others, and therefore she should ignore any stochastic dependence. Rational strategic behavior, in this view, dictates abstention.

Institutional realism counters that this kind of strategic thinking is self-defeating because those who maximize conditional expected utility will do better, on average, than those who are guided solely by causal considerations. Whatever their ultimate decision, it will continue to increase the subjective probability that their counterparts will act the same way.

Returning to Levi's (1982) example, we can see why voters might legitimately consider only the lottery aspects of their choice rather than its causal impact. Suppose, once again, that an agent is given a choice between two lotteries. Alternative 1 delivers one dollar plus either one million dollars or zero. The latter amount has already been determined but is unknown to the agent. His subjective probability distribution on the outcomes is a 10 percent chance of the million and a 90 percent chance of nothing. Alternative 2 delivers either one million dollars or zero, similarly determined by a draw, this time to a distribution that gave a 90 percent chance of the million and a 10 percent chance of nothing.

I trust that no rational agent would be fooled by his causal inefficacy into selecting alternative 1. Although he is too late to influence the two draws, he will forgo the certainty of the dollar and opt for the higher conditional expected utility of alternative 2. This is exactly the basis on which I am supposing that voters with institutionally induced role expectations opt for the better lottery called electoral participation.[3]

There is, we have seen, a way for those who emphasize the causal impact of choice to rationalize alternative 2: describe the agent as facing a choice between causally activating one of two alternatives, in which case the decision's causal influence on the outcome is restored. Yet when the same agent decides whether to vote, this decision also causally activates one of two lotteries having different expected utilities. So whoever prescribes alternative 2 in the artificial example ought to prescribe electoral participation. For if the relevant probability is not confined to the likelihood of personally causing the million to be drawn, it should not be confined to the likelihood of causing the preferred candidate to win. I grant that the latter probability is negligible in mass elections; but if that is the concern, do not recommend alternative 2 since the probability of causing a million in that case is zero. Nonetheless, I suggest, rational voters can vote as well as select alternative 2.[4]

In modeling terms, stochastic dependence must be treated as a parameter, just as preferences in the standard theory are modeled as

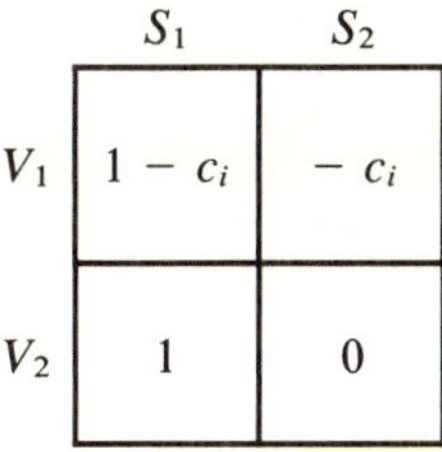

Figure 4. Participation Decision

parameters. In a dynamic setting, which the present model does not develop, agents are free of course to learn about the value of this parameter. But at the moment of decision, the parameter represents a fact about decision makers that, for reasons noted above, they cannot merely think away. Even causal decision theory has no basis for believing that stochastic dependence disappears, though it does ask agents to ignore it in their calculations.

2.

I shall assume that each of the N potential voters occupies one of two institutionally defined roles, R_1 and R_2.[5] That is, there is a two-candidate majority rule contest in which the occupants of R_1 and R_2 prefer candidates C_1 and C_2 respectively. In the event of a tie, candidate C_2 wins. Later I shall discuss an alternative tiebreaker, a coin toss giving each candidate an equal chance of winning.

Potential voters decide whether to participate by comparing the conditional expected utility of voting and abstaining. The utility for i of candidate C_j winning, $U_i(x,C_j)$, is a function of the position of the candidate and the voter's personal characteristics x, usually understood as the voter's ideal point. Assuming that costs enter the voter's utility function linearly, I normalize each voter's utility function, assigning 1 as the net utility for each voter i of having his candidate win, 0 as the net utility of that candidate losing, and c_i as the cost of voting.[6]

A potential voter $i \in R_1$ thus faces the decision problem shown in figure 4. In this setup, V_1 stands for participation, V_2 for abstention; S_1 is the state such that C_1 wins (that is, the final number of votes for C_1 is greater than the number for C_2), S_2 the state such that C_2 wins (that is, the final number of votes for C_1 is less than or equal to the number for C_2).

As long as the net costs of voting are positive ($c_i > 0$), V_2 strictly dominates V_1. The catch is that the two alternative states S_1 and S_2 are not independent of the agent's actions. The standard solution, we have seen, is to disaggregate these states into those in which the agent's vote would make or break a tie, causing a change in payoff, and those in which the agent cannot affect the outcome.

An analysis in terms of rational role expectations, by contrast, is not sensitive to the different ways that states of the world can be partitioned (this is one of its practical advantages). Each potential voter i is only interested in comparing the expected outcome given i's participation with the expected outcome given i's abstention. Maximizing conditional expected utility is the criterion.

Selecting the dominant act as such is still a mistake, though, insofar as rational role expectations suggest that S_1 and S_2 are not stochastically independent of the agent's actions. The agent's vote alters the probabilities slightly and, more important, it is statistically relevant to the behavior of other occupants of the role. Agents belonging to the same institutional role all rank the candidates the same way and may be similar in the beliefs and other preferences from which this specific inclination derives. In the interest of greater generality, I shall also assume that there may be stochastic dependencies between voters in R_1 and R_2. They participate in the same institution and, as registered voters, have similar roles. Interrole dependence does not fundamentally affect the results. In any case, an agent's decision to vote will in general provide her with information about the decisions made by others. Later I shall discuss some of the empirical support for this assumption.

Guided by rational role expectations, voter $i \in R_1$ votes if and only if

$$prob(S_1|V_1) (1 - c_i) + [1 - prob(S_1|V_1)] (-c_i)$$
$$= prob(S_1|V_1) - c_i > prob(S_1|V_2)$$

where prob $(S_k|V_1)$ $(k = 1,2)$ is the probability of S_k given V_1.[7] Thus voter i votes whenever

$$prob(S_1|V_1) - prob(S_1|V_2) = P_{C1} > c_i \tag{1}$$

that is, whenever the increase in the conditional probability of i's candidate winning occasioned by i's voting is more than the cost of the act itself, given normalized utilities. In short, P_{C1} is the increase in expected utility associated with i's participation. The possibility of stochastic dependence means that $prob(S_1|V_1)$ and $prob(S_1|V_2)$ are not necessarily equal even allowing for i's one-vote increment to C_1.

To determine how voter i estimates $prob(S_1|V_1) - prob(S_1|V_2)$ I shall assume that, in addition to the structure of the model just outlined, certain information is exogenously given to this voter. First and foremost are i's valid rational role expectations: he may correctly believe there is an unavoidable stochastic dependence between his decision to vote and the decision of any randomly selected occupant of R_1. If so, i's private information about his own decision provides additional insight into the participation decisions of other occupants of the role. Specifically, if Q_1 is the common probability estimate of a randomly chosen individual voting for C_1 given universally available information about the distribution of voting costs and the number of occupants in the role, then $r_{p1}Q_1$ ($r_{p1} \geq 1$, $0 \leq r_{p1}Q_1 \leq 1$) is i's revised estimate given i's participation, and $r_{a1}Q_1$ ($0 \leq r_{a1} \leq 1$, $0 \leq r_{a1}Q_1 \leq 1$) is i's revised estimate given i's abstention.[8] When $r_{p1} = r_{a1} = 1$, i's own participation provides i with no additional information about the likelihood that other occupants of R_1 will participate. In general, $r_{p1}Q_1 < 1$ and $r_{a1}Q_1 > 0$ since i's actions will provide him only imperfect information about the rate of participation from other occupants of the role.

If Q_2 is the common probability estimate of a randomly chosen individual voting for C_2 given universally available information about the distribution of voting costs and the number of occupants of R_2, then the intrarole estimate for occupants of R_2 is determined by r_{p2} and r_{a2} applied to Q_2, with analogous restrictions. Occupants of both roles also have shared symmetric beliefs about interrole dependence, determined by r_{p3} and r_{a3}, which are applied to the universal estimate for the opposing role. These parameters, then, are common knowledge.[9] On the other hand, the idea that voters have strict point estimates on the r_{pk} and r_{ak} is quite implausible. Later, this assumption will be modified.

Recall that the dependence parameters reflect the statistical impact on voting behavior of contemporaneous institutional facts about the voters' shared circumstances. It is worth emphasizing that the standard rational choice analysis, even in its game theoretic applications, has no basis for treating these parameters as manipulable at the point of decision. Since the voter is embedded in the electoral institution, they are not choice variables but when inserted into the calculation reflect some of the perceived structural conditions under which she decides to participate. As a result of her institutional position, this decision gives her private information about the probability that other institutional members will participate. Although causal theory advises agents to ignore this institutional information, it cannot pretend to eliminate it.

By assumption, the voting costs for occupants of R_1 are independent and identically distributed (i.i.d.) according to the continuous probability density function $h_1(c)$ for $-\infty < c < \infty$; the costs for occupants of R_2 are also i.i.d. and given by the density function $h_2(c)$.[10] Although each voter has only common probabilistic information about the costs of others, she of course has private information about her own. Voters are similarly uncertain about the number of occupants in each role. Their shared information is summarized by $g(x)$, a probability density function over the unknown voter characteristics that in effect defines the relevant estimate.[11]

Finally, given the stress that institutional realism places on intra-role identity, it is natural in this case to adopt Ledyard's (1984) and Palfrey and Rosenthal's (1985) simplifying assumption that at equilibrium all occupants of a role decide to participate based on a common way of relating the cost of voting to the utilities represented by the two candidates. Specifically, I assume that $[U_i(x,C_1) - c_i]/[U_i(x,C_2) - c_i] = [U_j(x,C_1) - c_j]/[U_j(x,C_2) - c_j]$, $i,j \in R_1$ or $i,j \in R_2$. This assumption of symmetry allows us to use the same c to represent any role occupant's criterion for voting.

To determine (1), I calculate the probability of i's candidate winning with i's participation, $prob(S_1|V_1)$, and from it subtract the probability of i's candidate winning without i's participation, $prob(S_1|V_2)$. These estimates are influenced by the stochastic dependencies among individuals occupying a role. Both probabilities are calculated as multinomial distributions.

The first probability is given by

$$\sum_{k=0}^{\|(N-1)/2\|} \sum_{n=0}^{N-2k-1} \frac{(N-1)!}{(k+n)!k!(N-2k-1-n)!} \cdot$$

$$(r_{p1}Q_1)^{k+n}(r_{p3}Q_2)^k(1 - r_{p1}Q_1 - r_{p3}Q_2)^{N-2k-1-n}$$

where $\|(N-1)/2\|$ is the greatest integer $k \leq (N-1)/2$; n is the vote difference between the candidates; and $r_{p1}Q_1$ (resp. $r_{p3}Q_2$) is the probability that a randomly selected voter from R_1 (resp. R_2) votes given i's participation. Thus, the probability of C_1 winning by n votes with i's participation is calculated as the probability of winning by $n - 1$ without.

From this sum I subtract the probability of C_1 winning without i's participation. This reflects the stochastic dependence between i's abstention and the turnout for both candidates. The sum of this second series is

$$\sum_{k=0}^{\|(N-1)/2\|} \sum_{n=1}^{N-2k-1} \frac{(N-1)!}{(k+n)!k!(N-2k-1-n)!} \cdot$$

$$(r_{a1}Q_1)^{k+n}(r_{a3}Q_2)^k(1 - r_{a1}Q_1 - r_{a3}Q_2)^{N-2k-1-n}$$

Letting $f_1(Q_1, Q_2, r_{p1}, r_{a1}, r_{p3}, r_{a3})$ represent the difference between the two series, we have, in effect, the expected difference i's voting makes:

$$P_{C1} = f_1(Q_1, Q_2, r_{p1}, r_{a1}, r_{p3}, r_{a3}) \tag{2}$$

There is an analogous calculation for occupants of R_2, except for C_2's winning in the event of a tie. In this case, voter $j \in R_2$ votes if and only if

$$prob(S_2|V_1) - prob(S_2|V_2) = P_{C2} > c_j. \qquad (3)$$

The sum for the first series is

$$\sum_{k=1}^{\|(N-1)/2\|} \frac{(N-1)!}{k!(k-1)!(N-2k)} (r_{p3}Q_1)^k (r_{p2}Q_2)^{k-1}(1 - r_{p3}Q_1 - r_{p2}Q_2)^{N-2k}$$

$$+ \sum_{k=0}^{\|(N-1)/2\|} \sum_{n=0}^{N-2k-1} \frac{(N-1)!}{k!(k+n)!(N-2k-1-n)!} \cdot$$

$$(r_{p3}Q_1)^k (r_{p2}Q_2)^{k+n}(1 - r_{p3}Q_1 - r_{p2}Q_2)^{N-2k-1-n}$$

From this I subtract a second series representing the probability of C_2's winning without j's participation. This sum is given by

$$\sum_{k=0}^{\|(N-1)/2\|} \sum_{n=0}^{N-2k-1} \frac{(N-1)!}{k!(k+n)!(N-2k-1-n)!} \cdot$$

$$(r_{a3}Q_1)^k (r_{a2}Q_2)^{k+n}(1 - r_{a3}Q_1 - r_{a2}Q_2)^{N-2k-1-n}$$

Letting $f_2(Q_2, Q_1, r_{p2}, r_{a2}, r_{p3}, r_{a3})$ represent the difference between these two series, we have

$$P_{C2} = f_2(Q_2, Q_1, r_{p2}, r_{a2}, r_{p3}, r_{a3}) \qquad (4)$$

If there is complete stochastic independence ($r_{p1} = r_{p2} = r_{a1} = r_{a2} = r_{p3} = r_{a3}$), the model reduces to the Ledyard (1984) and Palfrey and Rosenthal (1985) models for the relevant tiebreak rule.

Finally, voters must estimate Q_i. This is calculated from

$$Q_i = \int_{x_i} \int_0^{P_{C_i}} h_i(c)g(x)dcdx \equiv t(P_{c_i}, g, h_i), \; i = 1,2 \qquad (5)$$

where $x_i = \{x: U(x,C_i) > U(x,C_k)\}$. Sometimes I will refer to the inside integral involving $h_i(c)$ as $H_i(c)$.

3.

A voter's decision to participate is a function of the expected turnout, which in turn is a function of each agent's decision. Mathematically speaking, P_{Ci} is a function of Q_1 and Q_2 while Q_i is a function of P_{Ci}, as described in (5). There exists what is termed a Bayesian equilibrium when there are Q_1^*, Q_2^*, P_{C1}^*, and P_{C2}^* that solve (5) for $i = 1,2$, and solve (2) and (4). At equilibrium, each voter's beliefs and actions are fully consistent and each likewise believes in the consistency of all other voters.

PROPOSITION 1: There is a Bayesian equilibrium. (Proof: See appendix 2.)

The next proposition implies that voters with net positive costs are voting at the equilibrium:

> PROPOSITION 2: If $H_i(c) > 0$ for all $c_i > 0$ $(i = 1,2)$, then equilibrium turnout is positive. (Proof: See appendix 2.)

For the operative tiebreak rule, the following are conditions for a positive turnout for both candidates:

> COROLLARY A: If $r_{p3}Q_i < 1$, $H_j(c), > 0$ for all $c_j > 0$, and $r_{p3} > 0$, then $Q_j > 0$ $(i = 1,2; j = 2,1)$. (Proof: See appendix 2.)

The antecedent of corollary A assumes that abstainers will always be with us, or at least expected to be with us. When a coin toss is the tiebreaker, the effect on turnout is the same:

> COROLLARY B: If the tie-breaker is a coin-toss, $r_{p3}Q_i < 1$, and $H_j(c) > 0$ for all $c_j > 0$, then $Q_j > 0$ $(i = 1,2; j = 2,1)$. (Proof: Parallels the proof of corollary A.)

These propositions recapitulate the positive results on turnout derived by John Ledyard (1984). Thomas Palfrey and Howard Rosenthal (1985) add the crucial negative result that turnout from voters with net positive voting costs goes to zero as the size of the electorate goes to infinity. The introduction of rational role expectations thwarts this result:

> PROPOSITION 3: If $r_{pi}Q_i > r_{p3}Q_j$ and $r_{ai}Q_i \leq r_{a3}Q_j$ or $r_{pi}Q_i = r_{p3}Q_j$ and $r_{ai}Q_i < r_{a3}Q_j$, for $(i = 1,2; j = 2,1)$, then equilibrium turnout does not limit to 0 as $(N - 1) \to \infty$. (Proof: See appendix 2.)

The sufficient condition for the truth of proposition 3 is quite plausible, particularly since both $r_{pi} > r_{p3}$ and $r_{ai} < r_{a3}$ are plausible. For the proposition to obtain, the potential voter either (1) expects to win given participation and expects a tie or worse without participation, or (2) expects a tie with participation and a loss without it. In large electorates, (1) is more relevant. But in either case, the essential point remains. Although the occupants of each role are not only aware of their own intra- and interrole dependencies but are also aware of the other role's parallel dependencies, the original decision theoretic intuition survives. Institutionally induced rational role expectations can lead to positive turnout in mass elections.

While the introduction of role expectations can solve this particular collective action problem, it is no panacea. If stochastic dependence is sufficiently high, for instance, the winning side may wind up with a larger turnout than is numerically necessary. The present model offers no antidote to this (although the existence of other forms of stochastic dependence involving race and religion, for example, may allow individuals to be somewhat more subtle in their calculations). The temptation to free-ride on the winning surplus is nullified by the recognition that this decision is likely to be made by other occupants of the role. In short, a surplus at equilibrium does not imply that agents are failing to optimize. The winning side has simply decided to live with its success.

4.

The prediction of positive turnout for mass elections accomplishes our main mission. In one respect, however, it is a Pyrrhic victory. The proof of proposition 3 implies that whenever there is positive turnout, everyone for whom $c < 1$ will be voting—that is, unless some specific equalities involving Q_1 and Q_2 obtain. The implication is that voters are grossly insensitive to the costs of voting. The equalities that might rescue the model, moreover, are empirically doubtful in the case of the United States given the recent pattern of Republican victories in presidential elections and the incumbency advantages for Congress. Nor is it easy to attribute the discrepancy to noise in each election: various hypothesized variations in turnout do not substantially affect outcomes (Wolfinger and Rosenstone 1980; Squire, Wolfinger, and Glass 1987; Teixeira 1989).

It would be a mistake to dismiss the familiar knife-edge condition of equality as an artifact of proofs involving limits. Elementary statistics tells us that the problem the model identifies is closely approximated by any reasonably large electorate. The more likely culprit, therefore, is the working assumption that each voter knows the r_{pk} and r_{ak} ($k = 1,2,3$) with certainty. If, more realistically, we assume uncertainty about these parameters, the alternative expected utilities— 1, $\frac{1}{2}$, and 0—should be weighted by the cumulative probability that the restrictions imposed by proposition 3 will be satisfied. This produces a more realistic sensitivity to cost on the part of voters.

One possibility is to develop a more general version of P_{Ci}—call it $E(P_{Ci})$—based on separate distribution functions for each parameter. In lieu of this complicated task, let us simply assume that the cumulative probability that the parameters satisfy the restrictions of proposition 3 has already been calculated and is a common expectation. There are then three possible outcomes: the relevant candidate wins with probability 1, probability $\frac{1}{2}$, and probability 0. This can summarized by

$$\begin{aligned}
E(P_{C1}) = \ &prob(r_{p1}Q_1 > r_{p3}Q_2 \ \& \ r_{a1}Q_1 < r_{a3}Q_2 | Q_1^* \text{ and } Q_2^*) + \\
&\tfrac{1}{2}prob(r_{p1}Q_1 > r_{p3}Q_2 \ \& \ r_{a1}Q_1 = r_{a3}Q_2 \text{ or} \\
&r_{p1}Q_1 = r_{p3}Q_2 \ \& \ r_{a1}Q_1 < r_{a3}Q_2 | Q_1^* \text{ and } Q_2^*)
\end{aligned} \tag{6}$$

$$E(P_{C2}) = prob(r_{p2}Q_2 > r_{p3}Q_1 \ \& \ r_{a2}Q_2 < r_{a3}Q_1 | Q_1^* \text{ and } Q_2^*) +$$
$$\tfrac{1}{2}prob(r_{p2}Q_2 > r_{p3}Q_1 \ \& \ r_{a2}Q_2 = r_{a3}Q_1 \text{ or} \tag{7}$$
$$r_{a2}Q_2 = r_{a3}Q_1 \ \& \ r_{a2}Q_2 < r_{a3}Q_1 | Q_1^* \text{ and } Q_2^*),$$

where, for simplicity, $Q^* = (Q_1^*, Q_2^*)$ is the unique equilibrium value derived in conjunction with (5′) below. Under these circumstances, it is plausible that $0 < E(P_{Ci}) < 1$, which implies more realistic sensitivity to cost.

Of course, (5) will have to reflect each voter's belief that other voters face similar uncertainty in calculating P_{C_i}:

$$Q_i = \int_{x_i} \int_0^{E(P_{c_i})} h_i(c)g(x)dcdx \equiv t[E(P_{c_i}), \ g, \ h_i], \ i = 1,2 \tag{5′}$$

Propositions 1–3 can be proved *mutatis mutandis*.

5.

Because of the rational role expectations built into proposition 3, there will be positive turnout at equilibrium regardless of the size of the electorate. This otherwise modest result owes its significance to the importance of mass voting for the study of politics, to the role of mass participation as a central example in debates over the general validity of rational choice theory, and, most important, to the usefulness of turnout as an illustration of the effect of institutional roles. The present model, in short, not only indicates that institutional embedding matters in a world congenial to methodological individualism, but also demonstrates why that is so.

The model presupposes a fair degree of rationality, even if only in a behavioral sense. It would be easy to lighten the voter's burden by reverting to the original decision theoretic model supplemented by the insights of evidential theory. Given sufficient stochastic dependence, voters in this model would also turn out. Is it plausible, however, for intrarole stochastic dependencies to rationalize positive turnout when, presumably, each voter is aware that occupants of the other role can also take advantage of dependencies? The two sets of dependencies might cancel each other. Only a game theoretic model can answer this question. In any case, an objection to excessive rationality changes the terms of debate. The original problem was turnout from rational agents; now those agents turn out but may be too rational.

I am more concerned about the opposite complaint, that the game theoretic model permits irrationality. Insofar as $g(x)$, $h(c)$, r_{pk}, and r_{ak} are given exogenously, the present model, like typical Bayesian models, may not incorporate fully rational expectations. Clearly, the behavior of the dependence parameters is the most intriguing consideration. Given the secrecy of the vote, what rational expectations about r_{pk} and r_{ak} would mean is not that these parameters become endogenous at the point of decision, but rather that over an election campaign or series of elections voters will accurately estimate them, rationally altering their current strategies in light of evolving information.[12]

An agent's beliefs about appropriate role expectations need not be conditioned solely on direct information about political behavior. But past turnout is certainly the most relevant basis for forming expectations about the dependence parameters. Without loss of generality, we can focus on the perceptions of $i \in R_1$.

I conjecture that if r_{pk} and r_{ak} initially motivate positive turnout, an updated estimate of them will not disturb this qualitative result. In any given election it is very likely that the number of occupants of R_1 who vote will not equal the number who abstain.[13] The resulting majority will, by definition, find the behavior of a majority of the occupants consistent with its own, a finding that tends to reinforce the original intrarole estimates. For that same majority, conversely, the behavior of R_2 lacks this direct association and therefore is likely to be more volatile, relative to a randomly chosen i, than the behavior of R_1. So the expected sufficiency of r_{p3} and r_{a3} will also tend to be reinforced. Isolated conjectures about the time path of these parameters, of course, are no substitute for actual analysis.

6.

Individuals who emigrate from the state of nature to the United States do not simply become voters. They are likely to be fathers or mothers, Protestants or Catholics, wage earners, and owners of property. These same human beings spend different time slices of their lives enmeshed in various institutional settings, each imposing its own ideological stamp. How do people negotiate among these forms of institutional participation? How do voters, in particular, reconcile their various institutional identities when contemplating political participation?

According to the usual story, each voter calculates the net difference between parties or candidates in terms of her expected after-tax income stream, calibrated by the relevant utility function. Thus, in deciding what the best political choice would be—and whether to vote at all—the voter's budget constraint is her individual endowment, while the prices of goods or policies offered by politicians are their tax prices. In other words, this standard economic model recognizes, or assumes that voters recognize, the difference between collective and market choice by using tax prices instead of true costs in its representation of the voter's calculus.

Yet this means of recognizing the institutional difference is only a halfway measure. It fails to appreciate that whatever about politics allows a voter to command resources nominally belonging to others undermines the idea that tax prices represent payments out of the particular voter's private resources.[14] After the votes have been aggregated into a political decision, of course, the resulting allocation of the political budget is now a parameter for these voter-consumers, who must make consumption choices based on their after-tax, market-defined income. Arthur Denzau and Robert Parks (1979) rightly complain that many voting models ignore this second stage by treating political decisions as if they occurred in isolation from market choices. It may also be a mistake, however, to interpret political decision making in terms appropriate to markets. The fact that consumers work with after-tax income in the market does not mean that they vote based on before-tax income as defined in the private sector.[15]

To apply this distinction, let us return to the problem of mass participation in elections. To repeat the traditional version of the story, a potential voter in a two-party election is apparently being offered a p chance (quite small) of producing a benefit B (the difference between the two candidates) complemented by a $1 - p$ chance of producing no benefit. The cost of this gamble, C, is the cost of voting. Apparently, a benefit sufficient to induce participation must be huge. Indeed we can calculate the minimum benefit by the formula $B \geq Cp^{-1}$.

The tricky issue is to determine how this lottery is integrated into the voter's wealth position. Individuals are being offered a lottery involving a gain if they are decisive and a loss if they are not. Yet these different outcomes may induce appropriately different understandings of the credibility of the offer's gain and loss components. In the case of gains, which are net additions to current wealth, the credibility of the offer hinges on the wealth of the offerer—in effect, the two political parties. Let us assume that offers of gain in the situation under consideration are credible. The credibility of the loss component, however, depends on the wealth of the taker—namely, the voter. For takers with finite wealth, there are limits on the real losses they can sustain regardless of the nominal losses defined by the prospect. These limits may represent the point of bankruptcy as normally understood.

Suppose there is a lower bound to possible wealth, while utility functions defined on this wealth are also bounded from below, which might mean, for example, that losses beyond the initial bankruptcy point do not decrease utility below some level.[16] The implication is clear. No matter how risk-averse agents are over broad ranges of positive wealth, they will nonetheless prefer to accept fair lotteries whose nominal losses bankrupt them. Behaviorally, this means a lower segment of their utility functions will be strictly convex from below or risk-acceptant (Ross 1974).

To take a simple example, imagine a 50-50 bet with a win yielding $B and a loss yielding $-$B. Although the expected value is $0, otherwise risk-averse decision makers who are almost bankrupt will pay some amount of money for the opportunity to take the bet. These decision makers act as if they are risk-acceptant even though "subjectively" the gamble does not involve a loss beyond the point of bankruptcy. This distinction between gains and losses has a bearing on the paradox of not voting. For the crucial consideration is that voters, as decision makers, may behave as though they are risk-acceptant over prospects when, subjectively, they are not.

A potential voter is offered a choice between two outcomes lying on the budget plane defined by the political institution, that is, alternative ways of allocating the entire tax yield from the society. In this sense, even purely self-interested voters vote as if the tax yield is theirs and is to be allocated toward one of the candidate's policies. Thus the official gamble of voting is defined by prospects on the budget plane associated with the political process translated into appropriate utility streams.[17]

Now let us introduce an ideologically relevant notion of party identification. Since Downs (1957), it has been customary within rational choice theory to think of party identification in purely instrumental terms as a substitute for costly information about the party's candidates. It can also be treated as a form or reflection of ideological identification. To the extent voters identify with a party, they believe that they have won when their party does, that its allocation of the political budget is their own preferred allocation given the feasible alternatives associated with competing parties, in short, that *their* budget constraint is still defined by the political context when their party wins.

If, however, a participant should lose the gamble, she does not have to spend an amount equal to the political budget on the winning candidate's policies. After the opposing candidate's victory, she is, ideologically speaking, restored to her private, market-defined income. The winning political position is still officially determined by the larger political budget yet this sum is now perceived to come out of the individual's private budget in the form of taxes. The result is an official, ideologically sanctioned bankruptcy, with the voter's actual expenditure toward the winning position reduced to a fraction of the original, political amount. Voters do integrate their options into their final wealth positions, as expected utility theory demands. But there is an ideological cast to their understanding of their wealth.[18] This ideological cast, in turn, reflects an institutionally dictated aggregation of the budget as an object of electoral control.

In sum, potential voters face an ex ante loss of the full party differential; voters ex post only have to pay their taxes, which puts a bound on their loss far within the actual dollar loss calibrated as political money. Successful voters control the allocation of the political budget. Unsuccessful voters count their blessings that they are not responsible for the complete tab. They are protected by the political version of the bankruptcy institution and become risk-acceptant. And arguably, they are quite willing to take a big gamble, which costs C, to protect against the possible loss of control over the political budget.[19]

This speculative analysis of voting leaves us with several ideological messages. First, electoral institutions may induce citizens to be risk-acceptant when faced with the gamble of participation (cf. Schwartz 1987:108–09). Second, party identification should increase turnout (see, for example, Abramson and Aldrich 1982, who also find a link with government responsiveness). Third, there is a certain "civic duty" component to voting, albeit not one that enters the voting calculus in a neat, linear fashion. The notion of a government budget being one's own budget, a party's victory being one's own victory, requires, conformably with self-interest, an ideological sense of identification with the public arena, a way of thinking that seems to be cognitively associated with a sense of civic duty though by no means equivalent to it (cf. also the notion of sociotropic voting introduced by Kinder and Kiewiet 1979). This civicmindedness, in turn, reflects the way political and economic rights are institutionalized.

The preceding analysis, of course, assumes that voters identify with political parties and political budgets in a rather extreme sense. A more realistic portrait of voters would recognize that they have a more subtle relation with the political arena. By the same token, the unrealistic starkness of the analysis highlights the institutional and ideological influences on turnout that may continue to affect voters who are not caricatures.

In sum, I have explored two possible institutional effects in the electoral arena. The first involves turnout. Potential voters understand the institutional game they are playing, the institutional constraints imposed on them, and their strategic options. Athough they exploit these constraints in a sense, they cannot dissolve them. In other words, the voters would be quite willing to free-ride, but the institution makes the ride too costly. The result is positive turnout.

The second institutional effect is ideological. Since property is institutionally mediated, different institutions become associated with different kinds of property. Democratic elections, in particular, give voters collective control over assets which thereby become collective as well. My analysis of this political bankruptcy institution shows that the resulting relations between markets and political institutions can affect the behavior of the property holders. Armed with an appropriate ideological reading of their environment, these voter-consumers make appropriate adjustments in their understanding of their two kinds of property, altering the degree of risk aversion they display when deciding whether to participate in elections.

7.

Self-Control

Any argument against the conventionalist approach runs the risk of turning individuals into institutional puppets. Since this is both normatively and empirically unpalatable, the risk has led some to see the defense of conventionalism not just as a scientific but also as a moral imperative. By design, institutional realism does not in fact replace the human subject with an institutional one. Still, if it avoids backing into an old-fashioned holism, it cannot avoid questions about the potential control individuals have over the conditions of their lives in the face of institutional constraints.

This is an issue on which conventionalists are pretty close to being intrinsically optimistic. If the individuals of a society wish to change their social condition and this condition is their product, says the conventionalist, then what can stand in their way when they have the requisite knowledge and will? True, forces may conspire to weaken and deceive even rational agents. Yet when "man is at last compelled to face with sober senses, his real conditions of life, and his relations with his kind" (Marx and Engels 1968:38), the forces of constraint cannot long survive.

Notwithstanding this valedictory promise of a world set free, or of one much more to our liking, an institutional realist is less inclined to be optimistic. As it turns out, this is not the same as counseling pessimism or despair.

1.

Although individuals try to do the best they can, they must work within limits. Some limits are psychological. People can be mentally deficient, or act on mistaken beliefs, out of ignorance or weakness of will, or behave irrationally. They may have preferences that in some sense are inappropriate to their situation. There are also limits external to the individual—limits set by physical circumstance and, most intriguing, institutional constraints on the set of feasible alternatives.

In social settings, these institutional constraints often work as a matter of course. Everyday exchanges typically reproduce market institutions, for example, without much soul-searching or self-consciousness on the part of traders. Taking advantage of this, neoclassical economics adopts the simplifying assumption that all exchanges are uncoerced, that initial endowments, including property rights, are undisputed, and that pure markets exist in abundance (Arrow and Hahn 1971). For our purposes, this often-remarked indifference to variations in the institutional features of the market is better viewed as a presumption of institutional stability.

Actual social arrangements, of course, do drift and evolve. Although this drift can often be accommodated within existing institutions, sometimes a new institutional pattern must coalesce around the new behavior. Yet one general point about the stability of social institutions remains, with or without drift. There is generally neither need nor warrant to presume that participants are making global judgments about their institutional surroundings.

Traditional sociologists are apt to supplement the economist's analysis of the market precisely with this kind of presumption (see, for example, Smelser 1963:40–44). To them, stability implies a normative underpinning to the market and perhaps even a positive judgment among traders about the institution's legitimacy. To the institutional realist, however, what is intriguing about neoclassical assumptions is not their psychological insight into the typical trader's apathy but the institutional facts they reflect. The alternatives faced by traders usually define changes within the institution, not fundamental changes of the institution. Typically, there is no behavioral opportunity for participants to vent their feelings about the institution as a whole.

As Kenneth Arrow (1963:18) observes, the "market mechanism . . . takes into account only the ordering of tastes," which concern "the direct consumption of the individual." For the most part, protest is through "exit" (Hirschman 1970), and exit in the market is hard to distinguish from mere shopping around. Indeed, the purer the market, with fewer quality or price differences among substitute goods, the less can be said for exiting. In any case, exit and voice tend to be directed at firms rather than the market as a whole. More abstract preferences can only be expressed symbolically, after a lot of hard "symbol building," since the institution itself does not afford any direct way of making institutional judgments.[1]

Political institutions, by contrast, typically do afford a way of making choices about institutions. Politics can serve as the "consciousness" of society, the arena in which social relations and institutional forms, including those of politics, become objects of decision.[2] Or to put the matter somewhat differently, politics provides the institutional ballast for social thought, conversation, and action concerning the alternatives the individual confronts. As such, it is the crucial instrument enabling agents to make explicit decisions about the preservation, modification, or destruction of their institutional environment. Although Marx welcomed the withering away of the state, he appropriately scoffed at those who ignored the political character of any serious attempt to achieve it.

2.

When political stability is the rule, the differences between conventionalism's analysis of institutional modification and institutional realism's may seem academic. Under stable conditions, conventionalism does saddle participants with a global acceptance of political institutions as a whole; but this acceptance is usually implicit, which generally means it adds no testable weight to the analysis. Of course, voting on institutional rules can still run into structural constraints that affect rational role expectations. Still, on either approach, agents use existing political institutions to effect changes in social institutions or in parts of the political system.

Revolution, on the other hand, seems to bring out an important difference between the two approaches. Conventionalists are not fazed by revolution, since they are always prepared to look outside the institution for explanations of change or stability. Since stable institutions are anchored by stable values or stable beliefs and preferences, institutions become unstable when their supporters have a change of mind or heart. When the set of political institutions is itself the object of change, however, the institutional realist can no longer rely on this institutional framework to understand the associated activity. How, then, does the institutional realist make sense of global institutional change?

Actually, even the existence of ordinary politics poses awkward questions about the nature and limits of institutional constraint. If institutional constraints are subject to political control, in what sense are they decisive or inevitable? The case of revolution is more awkward still. When a revolution shatters its own context, from where is it supposed to derive its social identity if not from the actors themselves?

The institutional realist's best response is to turn these questions around: how, apart from context, is an act supposed to obtain a social identity? Institutional constraints can be purposefully modified through politics because political institutions, in connection with the target institutions, give the relevant acts their social meaning. The revolutionary destruction of institutions, says the realist, is no different on this score. However explosive and unusual, a revolution does not get its social identity by magic. As with any social act, there is no political homunculus in the individual agent or body politic unilaterally determining the identity of the revolution; there is no mental beam illuminating otherwise meaningless behavior. Collective acts with collective consequences, revolutions are not exempt from the realist's questions about social identity that can be raised in the more usual case of intrainstitutional action.

The same point can be made in terms of alternatives. Within such nonpolitical settings as the market, individuals choose "locally" by selecting from among a set of alternatives. When agents choose "globally," taking institutional arrangements as the objects of choice, they do not thereby acquire a new power to define their own alternatives. If they had this power, most of the constraints and trade-offs we associate with choice would no longer play the role they do. Indeed the notion of choice would lose much of its sense and poignancy. So long as the behavioral changes instigated through politics are socially meaningful, the institutional realist will want to analyze even large-scale changes contextually in terms of other social or political institutions.[3]

My answer to the challenges posed by revolution, in sum, is that I do not see the challenge. Revolutionary acts are as clearly defined, or as ambiguous, as the context allows. Institutional realism, moreover, cautions us not to underestimate the enduring efficacy of the context even when there is revolution. The linguistic, social, and political continuities undergirding political change tend to rely on existing meanings, absent what one might call a total revolution. There is, in Craig Calhoun's (1988:131) phrase, a "paradoxical conservatism in revolution."

The possibility of total revolution, which theoretical considerations alone cannot rule out, is the real test for institutional realism.[4] For in the case of a societal grand mal, the sociopolitical context presumably is so fluid that it can no longer institutionalize the meaning of behavior. Yet this fluidity, says the institutional realist, is a two-way street. Not only is the environment's defining grip on a participant's actions weakened; participants find that their grip on the definition and determination of events is also weakened. The physical world they confront, of course, is no less determinate or determined. Yet when the social structure of the environment does not reveal a clear rational connection between behavior and determinate social outcomes, participants likewise can no longer make decisions about the causal processes and determinations that matter to them.

Some social theorists believe that the elimination of institutional constraint redounds to the benefit of participants, who are free to reinvent or redefine the alternatives they face (e.g., Unger 1987; Przeworski 1985). Institutional realism clearly takes a more somber view. Lacking an institutional anchor and never having had a fully psychological one, the social identity of behavior under total revolution simply becomes more transient and inchoate. In these "moments of madness" (Zolberg 1972), the menu of alternatives from which participants can choose is not just radically expanded but also rendered fuzzy and ill-defined. Focusing on May 1968 in France, Zolberg suggests there are times when it seems as though "anything is possible." In one sense, no doubt, such moments may infuse participants with the power to shape events; in an another sense, people become powerless when anything is possible.

Granted, the linguistic resources of imaginative individuals can outstrip their particular institutional opportunities. Yet linguistic behavior must get its content somewhere. Actions speak louder than words, in part, because words divorced from clearly defined behavior become more ambiguous. What Eric Hobsbawm (1971:2) says of the "primitive rebels" against early European modernization tends to be true of participants in total revolutions: they "have not yet found, or only begun to find, a specific language in which to express their aspirations about the world." I suggest that finding a language in these circumstances is not quite the same as creating a language. A language needs public referents.

Total revolution sets changes in motion behind the backs of the revolutionaries. Even the leaders of the revolution do as much adapting as leading. Since the institutional framework destroyed by the revolution was also a source of social meaning, the new meaning must await the emergence of a new framework. Marx describes this phenomenon in a famous passage about a less than total revolution, this time in 1848 in France:

> The tradition of all the dead generations weighs like a nightmare on the brain of the living. And just when they seem engaged in revolutionising themselves and things, in creating something that has never yet existed, precisely in such periods of revolutionary crisis they anxiously conjure up the spirits of the past. . . . In like manner a beginner who has learnt a new language always translates it back into his mother tongue. (Marx and Engels 1968:97)

This speaking in tongues disappears as new relations crystallize along with an appropriate language to describe them.

3.

There is both a conservative and a liberal thrust to these observations. On the one hand, institutional realism emphasizes the extent to which the social identity of alternative actions, revolutionary and conformist, depends on the stable or settled pattern of interaction into which those actions are inserted. In unstable situations, of course, observers of behavior can still discover interesting, albeit temporary, patterns subject to fascinating interpretations. What makes the ascription of meaning and pattern scientifically useful rather than gratuitous, however, is in part the stability of the objects identified, stability serving as the anti-essentialist counterpart to the notion of substance or natural kind (see chapter 1).

On the other hand, institutional realism recognizes the extent to which emancipation from the confines of an institution can initiate a new openness regarding possible meanings and patterns of behavior. Institutions coalescing in the aftermath of revolution may differ markedly from those antedating them. This liberal dimension holds out hope for those who wish to see ordinary people have a greater role in the design or selection of the institutions influencing them.

The Marxist tradition expands this liberal hope into the possibility of deinstitutionalizing society altogether. Yet if institutional realism is correct, institutions provide the necessary framework for actively assessing or controlling social and even political institutions. Their role cannot be attributed solely to the exceptional power that institutionally well-connected people can wield, or even to the subtle, tacit ways in which institutions constrain action. Institutions insinuate themselves into the very conceptualization of alternatives, into the language of choice. Although it certainly is possible to look beyond what currently exists, the very formulation of alternatives will bear an institutional stamp, at least insofar as the formulation is translated into a shared language connected to action (again, see chapter 1). Although liberal ambitions, it seems, will be fulfilled only by agents who can conceptually detach themselves from the political institutions they are trying to assess, institutional realism questions whether such completely extrainstitutional judgments are possible.

Is it possible for individuals to sit in judgment over the societies in which they are embedded?[5] If a society has institutions for making collective decisions, can its self-evaluation include those same institutions? Analytically speaking, what seems to distinguish philosophical liberals and Marxists is their insistence on the desirability and possibility of a truly complete assessment.

A total assessment is desirable, in this view, since no social or political institution should be immune to critical scrutiny or accepted simply because it is. In order to breach the immunity of the status quo, evaluators need a standpoint for judging society as a whole, its family structure, its distribution of wealth, its sexual relations, its mode of intellectual production, and so on. By the conventionalist logic of this view, such a full-scale judgment is not only desirable but also possible. If society is a construct, then presumably the Archimedean point for its radical evaluation exists in principle.

According to this brand of conventionalism, then, it is intellectually irresponsible for appraisers of society to presuppose the existence or legitimacy of any of society's social parts save as a pragmatic concession to the shortness of life. To institutional realists, this refusal to presuppose ignores the extent to which the individuals making a comprehensive judgment bring not only their preferences, willpower, beliefs, and biology but also, in aggregate, their institutions, which are the critical parts of a functioning society. Institutions are not just objects of choice. They form the backdrop for choice or, more accurately, they are the aggregate of their choosers. By all means, one should avoid the fallacy of composition: an institutional aggregate of agents is not itself an agent directing their evaluations. Yet this aggregate is something those agents cannot, on pain of self-destruction, simply nullify.

The rational choice approach, fortunately, has already developed an excellent instrument for assessing the limits and possibilities of collective self-determination. Collective choice theory, consisting of social choice theory (e.g., Arrow 1963) and public choice theory (e.g., Buchanan and Tullock 1962), seeks to explore the process by which individuals adopt an external vantage point for choosing or rating possible institutional arrangements. Both variants of the theory are used to explain and evaluate existing social order.

Collective choice theory is also an ideal vehicle for documenting why it is so difficult to make sense of an extrainstitutional standpoint. Specifically, in neither of the two main variants of the theory do individuals attain the necessary analytical distance from the society they are judging. Each variant builds into its analytical apparatus a distinctive institutional relation between individuals and the societies they are supposed to evaluate.

There is a more familiar way to say this: collective choice theory is ideological. I hesitate to use the term, since in a certain narrow sense this charge is manifestly untrue. Collective choice theory has not been confined to conservatives (e.g., Buchanan and Tullock 1962), but has been pursued by modern liberals (e.g., Arrow 1984:303–18) as well as Marxists (e.g., Roemer 1982). Yet since neither of its main variants truly allows individuals to escape the institutional bonds of society, each inevitably builds institutional presuppositions into a scheme it portrays as a-institutional.[6] The social choice approach analyzes politics and society in political terms; the public choice approach commits the opposite sin, analyzing politics and society in social, specifically market terms. Neither variant is institutionally neutral.

Fearful of institutional presuppositions, collective choice theory misses the opportunity to avoid analytic bias by equally embracing both kinds of institution within one framework. True, the two factions of collective choice theory are aware of their differences, and the resulting internal squabbles have already exposed serious weaknesses in each approach. Yet the key to understanding the full implications of this debate is to see each side's victories against the other as symptoms of a deeper weakness afflicting both attacker and defender. Every success in the ongoing dispute reaffirms the validity of a third position, institutional realism.

4.

To the social choice theorist, collective choice encompasses any and all social processes leading from individual preferences to social or political outcomes. Institutions, in particular, are understood as mechanisms for making social decisions; and every institution, in turn, is understood as the product of a social decision, a product that can be recalled. From this overarching perspective, any collective process can be judged "externally" by the extent to which it meets certain ethically attractive criteria, say, being nondictatorial. This evaluation, whether conducted by observers or participants, thus subsumes the entire social structure insofar as it classifies each of society's component processes as a decision-making mechanism. Politics and markets are both "regarded as special cases of the more general category of collective choice" (Arrow 1963:5).

The attempt to reach a verdict on every part of society would be idle if there were an institution, set of institutions, or social outcome that was not, in principle, subject to evaluation or decision. This is why social choice theorists are unable to understand how unanimous consent can be a legitimate decision rule. The symptomatic problem with unanimous consent has been noted by many observers in and out of the social choice tradition, and is easily stated. Suppose, on the basis of this rule, a decision to depart from the status quo S to a new state S' is vetoed by one voter; then the status quo prevails. This is incoherent, say critics of unanimous consent, since the individual who exercised the veto has decided for all. The supposed rule of unanimous consent issues in its opposite, dictatorship. Thus, Douglas Rae (1975:1282) concludes, "unanimous universal consent has the logical form of the square circle."

Here is the three-step argument that social choice theorists use to transform this paradox of unanimous consent into a parable about the comprehensiveness of social decisions. First, in the example just considered the outcome of inaction was determined by one individual's preferences. Second, however, "government *inaction* is as much a choice of policy as government action" (Dahl and Lindblom 1953:338). In other words, "Abstention from a decision cannot exist; some social state will prevail" (Arrow 1963:118). Third, therefore, unless unanimity prevails, the unanimous consent rule does not live up to its billing as a coherent decision rule.

The key to this argument is its second premise. Ultimately, it says, any prevailing social state reflects a social choice, because any social state, including the status quo, is explicitly or implicitly the product of the society's collective decision procedures. This premise, however, is by no means obvious. There is a clear, intuitive difference between failing to choose S' and choosing *not-S'*, which is to say, S. Ruth Millikan's (1984:61–62) analysis of the parallel case of belief illustrates this nicely. If I go to sleep, I do not believe Jack the Ripper is under my bed. This is not to say, however, that if I go to sleep, I believe Jack the Ripper is not under my bed. As Millikan observes, this conclusion does not follow since, for example, I may never have heard of Jack the Ripper. So not believing (choosing) S' is not equivalent to believing (choosing) *not-S'*. The argument of social choice theory, in short, says less about the incoherence of universal unanimous consent than about the incoherence of equating all social conditions and outcomes with social decisions.[7] The fact that the status quo prevails does not imply that it was chosen.

My point, of course, is to defend the coherence of unanimous consent, not its normative value. Values aside, then, why would social choice theorists, in violation of intuition, ever suppose that the status quo must be labeled as a choice whenever it is the outcome of a decision process? Their latent assumption must be that a proper collective choice ultimately has command over the status quo. Decision rules cannot just fail to operate, says the social choice theorist, since the failure is itself a decision.

Still, why equate a failure of these rules with a decision made within them? After all, an ordinary social institution such as a market takes some social outcomes for granted—individual endowments, for instance. The answer is that social choice theory is ultimately an institutionally loaded analysis, in particular a politically loaded analysis. For only in the political arena is it even conceivable that each possible social outcome is the result of an implicit or explicit decision and therefore is necessarily within the purview of a decision-making process.

As a consequence, social choice theory's account of nonpolitical institutions must repeat its original analysis at a higher level of abstraction: when failing rules of unanimous consent or the market are allowed to fail, this represents a political decision to retain them. In other words, if society cannot simply abstain from choice, it must in principle have incredible power over the very institutions undergirding it. Evidently, this implies not only a pervasive politics superordinated to social states of affairs but a pervasive politics of politics. For the persistence of political institutions themselves must, in the social choice account, result from *acts,* albeit acts of omission. There cannot be simple, unglorified omissions.

The failure to change a set of rules is to the critic of unanimous consent a political decision not to change them. Likewise, the continuing existence of a political mechanism, nondecisions and all, is a social choice in support of that mechanism and its consequences. At least, "such valuation . . . seems to be implicit in every stable political structure" (Arrow 1963:90). Social choice via the unanimous consent rule, specifically, is a collective choice of that rule and the consequences of using it. It goes without saying that this conception must rely on the implicit character of the metadecision.

To institutional realists, by contrast, the push to make every decision a metadecision misconstrues political institutions as objects of choice rather than as the frameworks necessary to make the very idea of collective choice meaningful. So ultimately, alleging the incoherence of the unanimous consent rule reflects a failure to appreciate fully the existence of institutional facts of life.

There is, I grant, a certain plausibility to social choice theory's thoroughgoing sense of politics. Does not pervasive racial discrimination, for instance, reflect a society's refusal to eliminate this injustice? Surely, it will be said, "We did not consider it" is no answer, since a deeper social decision must lie behind a society's failure to address the issue. Similarly, a society's maintenance of an unfair distribution of wealth seems to imply an unjust decision mechanism behind it: "a society must have some social product over any interval of time, and [therefore?] must have some set of rules for its allocation" (Rae 1975:1278).[8]

What lends legitimacy to these reconstructions of society's thinking, I suspect, is in part the historical fact that explicit but unofficial decision making often lies behind official nondecisions. Social choice theory, I also suspect, is guided by the very sensible intuition that the political decision rules sanctioning discrimination or inequality are not inexplicable brute facts but result from some social process. There is nothing ordained about the political status quo. Like any social outcome, it is in general socially determined. Yet it would be a serious mistake to interpret this reasonable assertion as equivalent to the claim that every social state of affairs is determined by a collective choice mechanism. I acknowledge the social determination of social states of affairs. It takes place whenever the processes of society map its preference profile and other social features onto the range of social outcomes. But collective choice, in the sense I am considering it, requires more than this.

What qualifies a procedure as collective choice is the existence of actual mechanisms for making choices *about* the relevant social and political outcomes. If institutional realism is correct, the two processes are not equivalent.[9] A political mechanism, in particular, may be socially determined without being an object of collective decision. After all, not every description of society someone can cobble together designates the specific output of a decision process.[10]

The conflation of social determination and social choice mechanisms represents more than conceptual expedience. It is a twofold weapon. By assimilating mechanisms to determination, it lulls us into denying the possibility of unchosen outcomes, since the denial becomes a matter of simple logic. Likewise, by assimilating social determination to mechanisms, the conflation buttresses the idea that ostensibly unchosen outcomes are really the result of social decisions. Social decisions in the conventionalist's sense look like social decisions in the ordinary sense.

To sum up, if we choose *not-S'* whenever we do not choose *S'*, the status quo is never a condition of life but always a continuing object of choice. It is a latent object of decision even when it comprises the institutional framework for decision. Social choice theorists' verdict on unanimous consent, in other words, goes beyond a formal ruling on how to categorize nondecisions. It presupposes a deeper understanding of the nature of this or any collective choice mechanism and its relation to the rest of society.

This understanding, of course, is by no means unique to social choice theory. All variants of conventionalism assume that thoughts and intentions concerning politics and society always antedate or at least outrun existing institutional arrangements. Among traditional political sociologists, these considerations are quite explicit and are summarized by the notion of political legitimacy. Parsons's political sociology, we have seen, solves the "Hobbesian problem of order" by finding a normative consensus behind every stable social arrangement. The participants produce social order with their eyes open. And if politics represents a coercive element in social order, it too is bound by norms and regulated by values. Under stable circumstances, the existence of politics and its role in society are due to the legitimacy widely attributed to it.

Of course the Parsonian style of sociology no longer holds the position it once did, though its intellectual legacy is stronger than one might imagine. It emerges in social choice theory and elsewhere in the rational choice literature. Indeed, Ronald Rogowski's (1975) notion that agents are always measuring existing regimes against hypothetical alternatives is a self-conscious rational choice analog of the concept of legitimacy. Similarly, Arrow (1974) argues that although authority is necessary in a complex society, authority cannot survive solely through the threat of sanctions.[11] "Ultimately, it seems to me, authority is viable to the extent that it is the focus of convergent expectations" (Arrow 1974:72).

From the standpoint of institutional realism, all sides have gone overboard. The option to evaluate an institution is not always exercised, nor is there always an option. A specific institutional framework such as the unanimous consent rule allows one voter to maintain the status quo, *but only given that decision rule and every other voter's preferences*. The dissenter does not individually decide this outcome or the use of the unanimous consent rule. What decides it, so to speak, is the collection of all voters including the dissenter, the institutionalized rule, and the history producing the status quo. To state the claim more succinctly, it strains the notion of decision to say that unanimous consent makes the dissenter a dictator.

Finally, I should note an interesting distinction introduced by Amartya Sen (1982:306–07). Social choice, he argues, can be interpreted in terms of institutional mechanisms, as I have done, or as an ethical judgment about social welfare distinct from the mechanisms producing it. The finding that social choice has an unavoidable institutional dimension, one might argue, is an artifact of adopting an institutional, rather than ethical, interpretation. Does my analysis beg the question?

It begs the question only if there are institutionally innocent principles of ethical judgment. Social choice theory, I have suggested, is far from institutional innocence, establishing in effect a political position vis-à-vis society. In making a principled judgment about society, it inevitably makes assumptions about the propriety of society's underlying institutional arrangements. Social choice theory, for example, cannot pretend to incorporate institution-neutral conceptions of individual property or rights. Granted, it may in the end judge markets and private property to be best. But this conclusion must emerge from a collective choice evaluation of the institution, whose associated rights, in the meantime, are trumped by an analysis that has the right not to rule in their favor. As a result, individual property is analytically collectivized in order to evaluate the system of property rights in competition with other values.

By implicitly denying any *presumptions* about property rights, social choice theory's brand of ethical analysis has already introduced its own presumptions. It forecloses the possibility that individuals might be entitled to, rather than just permitted, their property under the status quo. Their rights are not allowed to negate the application of social choice ethics itself. Although these rights are assumed by the market, for example, they are not considered justified unless first subjected to an overarching collective choice analysis that is intrinsically political.

Assessing Robert Nozick's (1974:166) claim that his choice of residence should not be a matter of social consideration, Sen (1982:306) reaffirms the priority of a social choice analysis: "But one can also argue that, if I believe that it is a better society which—given other things—lets Nozick decide where he wishes to live, then I must *assert* that it is socially *better* that Nozick should be permitted to live in Massachusetts as desired by him." Yet, asks the institutional realist, who exactly does the permitting and why should the issue be posed in those terms? Choosing the lesser of two evils, Nozick would acknowledge that it is a better society that permits freedom of residence. A still better society, he would argue, does not presume it is society's role to grant permission in the first place. Note, by the way, that whether Nozick is correct is beside the point. What is important is the conflict between Sen's approach and Nozick's. In less adversarial terms, Sen's social choice approach is not institutionally neutral.

5.

Social choice theory tries to perch "above" the societies it surveys. The public choice approach, the other variant of collective choice theory, finds its extrainstitutional vantage point "below," conceiving the choice of political institutions as analytically prior to the very existence of society. As before, I want to show that this alternative approach, otherwise known as state-of-nature theory, is institutionally biased, though now in favor of society over politics. Fortunately, in the case of public choice theory, the foundation for this indictment has already been laid.

As noted in chapter 3, Buchanan and Tullock (1962) and Buchanan (1975) derive collective choice mechanisms from state-of-nature equilibria, which determine individual rights or control over property and endowments. This state of nature defines the base point against which individuals assess the value of creating political institutions. Public choice theorists argue that since the state of nature is always available by default, any movement from what Buchanan calls anarchistic equilibrium must be by unanimous consent.

Most important, Buchanan and Tullock's state-of-nature approach is not designed just to provide a historical scenario for the initial emergence of politics. It purports to represent the underlying relation between any political institution and its participants, whether the relation is primordial or civilized. In other words, the state of nature is the extrasocietal Archimedean point against which participants and observers judge whether institutions should persist.

As we have seen, the unanimity rule is not in fact analytically privileged but rather is simply one specific collective choice mechanism among others. Moreover, when public choice theory welds this mechanism to a status quo embodying individual property rights, the resulting market institution is analytically superordinated to politics. Under public choice theory, in other words, unanimous consent is not merely a rule respecting the autonomy of individual preference that is capable of being implemented through markets or politics alike. Its ostensibly a-institutional character masks its specific connection with markets.[12]

This claim should be distinguished from the familiar objection that public choice theory is biased toward bourgeois individualism (e.g., Macpherson 1962). Public choice theory's problem is not its excessive institutional content; rather, it suffers from insufficient institutional content. By giving the market institution analytic priority, it fails to recognize political and social institutions as coequal partners.

As a point of further clarification, the unanimous consent rule invoked by public choice theory is not biased per se in favor of markets. The rule in fact is institutionally flexible, with its institutional content determined by the objects over which individual preferences range. In public choice theory, it is true, this abstract rule is fleshed out with market-like constraints. On the other hand, by introducing this same rule into a very different institutional setting, Rawls (1971) achieves the opposite effect, the subordination of markets to politics.

In the well-known original position, decision makers select the basic principles governing society while remaining ignorant of any socially relevant facts about themselves. In Rawls's mind, this procedure eliminates bias. Yet it also embodies a particular presumption about property, resources, and personal endowments (Nozick 1974:183–231; Sandel 1982:66–103). The original position is quintessentially political.

We have already seen this kind of politicization in the case of social choice theory: the collectivity can have the right to choose principles for allocating these assets only if the assets are ex ante collective, or in the formulation that public choice theorists would prefer, ex ante collectivized.[13] In short, the rule of unanimous consent must be distinguished from the sheer coincidence of opinion when everyone happens to agree (Reiman 1972:10–12 and Wolff 1976:88 provide additional support for this distinction). In Rawls's hands, the rule is politically based. In the hands of public choice theorists, it is market-based. The institutional setting is decisive.

If social choice theorists are unable to get a noninstitutional, bird's-eye view of society, public choice theorists equally fail in their attempt to get a total assessment from "below," that is, from the presocial world of the state of nature. The reasons for this failure should be clear. State-of-nature theorists may be able to tell us why we have a society or polity. But they cannot characterize current decisions about political institutions without making assumptions about the property rights inscribed in the institutional status quo ante, about the political mechanisms these imply, and therefore about the institutional relation between politics and society. Even if unanimous consent in the state of nature had causal priority over political institutions, this rule is not automatically appropriate for the analysis of current relations.

My earlier distinction between the value of unanimous consent and its coherence continues to hold, of course. It still may be that "only through the securing of unanimity can any change be judged desirable on the acceptance of the individualistic ethic" (Buchanan and Tullock 1962:261). This ethic, however, does not ground—indeed it presupposes—a view of the proper balance between politics and society. For some time now, if the truth be told, there have been no preinstitutional actors available to establish a new political world from scratch, unanimously or otherwise.

I can now sum up the effort of collective choice theorists to establish an extrainstitutional Archimedean point for making decisions about society as a whole. As public choice theorists see it, individuals control their social circumstances through the threat of exit, not only from current political arrangements, but even from society. As social choice theorists see it, the only true answer to the problem of control is to design institutions properly in order to minimize their distortion of people's preferences. In either case, institutions are at the mercy of the participants' or designer's choices. Or as Arrow (1974:73) puts it, "The emphasis on convergent expectations as the source of authority implies its fragility."

No one, of course, wants to live with an institution that is out of control. True control, however, must be exercised, finally, within an institutional framework. The preceding analysis of collective choice theory certainly suggests that save for periods of total revolution, where control must still be distinguished from destruction, institutions are wholesale targets only relative to an implied institutional baseline of institutionally entailed property, objects, and alternatives.

The leading variants of collective choice theory assume that their baselines are institutionally neutral. In the case of social choice, however, the real presumption is that markets and the form of property they recognize are implicitly products of political decision making. Property is ex ante collective. In the case of public choice, the real presumption is that property is ex ante private, and collective uses of it are ultimately sanctioned by the unanimous consent given to political institutions.

The individuals making these decisions and giving their consent are of course distinct entities, not just creatures of a social system. Institutions, I insist, are likewise distinct entities. Collective choice theory should count them when it counts what is really there. Social order may be fragile at times, and it certainly has its problems. But institutions are not second-class citizens of society, and their problems are not ontological in character.

6.

People systematically control their circumstances through institutions. It has not been my purpose to adjudicate between the two different visions of how this control is best exercised, one analytically weighted toward markets and one analytically weighted toward politics. Rather, I have highlighted the effect of conventionalist assumptions on both variants of collective choice theory. Whatever their other disagreements, both assume that the idea of control, in its broadest sense, is noninstitutional. Each also calls attention to the institutional naiveté of the other.

Thus, according to public choice–inspired conservatives, what drives the sympathy of modern liberalism for government action is the presumption that property is intrinsically public: liberals always know good ways to spend your money, and they treat what remains in private hands as the result of a tax loophole. Hence liberals are bound to believe that when Mr. Fat Cat, with a marginal income tax rate of x percent, makes a donation to charity, x percent of his largesse is really being paid by the public.

According to social choice–inspired liberals, on the other hand, what drives libertarian conservatives is the presumption that all property is intrinsically private. These conservatives view virtually any social claim or mandatory form of public responsibility as a form of theft. Hence conservatives commonly believe that we should not expect corporations to do more than satisfy their owners.

Liberal talk of loopholes and conservative talk of theft jointly assume there is one "natural" form of property or control which is defiled by the other side. Recognizing the coexistence of both political and market institutions, institutional realism happily bifurcates the notion of control into its market and political versions. The resulting analytic equality between the two kinds of institution arguably offers a framework for assessing normative claims that is less likely to be pushed toward extremism. For the same reason, it is less likely to interpret normative moderation as a violation of fundamental principles reeking of compromise and ad hockery. Institutional realism, in short, is entirely comfortable when individuals control their circumstances through both institutions, though it thereby surrenders any pretense of adopting a radically extrainstitutional position.

Suppes (1988:90) puts the case against ethical extremism nicely: "Too much discussion of matters of justice and equity has centered on unrealistic ideas such as those of Rawls concerning the initial distribution under the veil of ignorance, or, to take a quite different example, Nozick's idealized and equally unrealistic concept of entitlement. . . . [W]e are always rebuilding the equity ship at sea. We are not going to run ourselves aground and start afresh." To be more than plausible, this alternatively grounded normative theory would have to grapple with a number of thorny issues, most immediately the problem of defining a proper balance between the control individuals exercise over their lives and circumstances through markets and the control they exercise through politics. Rather than pursuing this issue, however, let us stick with empirical theory.[14]

The Marxist theory of revolution nicely illustrates the empirical relation between institutions and self-control.[15] Why do workers put up with capitalism? Tired of excuses, some Marxists have conceded that workers may perceive capitalism to be a better economic deal than socialism, particularly when workers factor in disturbances to production during the revolutionary and postrevolutionary periods. "Is it not an absurdity that they would consent to capitalist relations, that they would not use their political rights for 'social emancipation' if there did not exist a real possibility for realizing their material interests [under capitalism] in some foreseeable future?" (Przeworski 1985:147). Retaining capitalist constraints, then, is a matter of decision: "while social relations constitute a structure of choices within which actors choose, their choice may be to alter social relations" (1985:96).

The parallel with McKelvey and Ordeshook (1984:201), discussed in chapter 3, is striking: "And when such [preferred] outcomes cannot be attained under them and when some set of persons possesses the appropriate means, those institutions will either be modified or bypassed." Political science, evidently, makes strange bedfellows. In truth, both positions are nurtured by a belief in the power of human choice to transcend institutional constraint.

Yet before I contrast this belief with institutional realism, I ought to remove the air of utopian innocence I have given it, which is misleading. There are important obstacles to worker control that conventionalism is well equipped to acknowledge. Watkins's (1968:271) definition of methodological individualism nicely captures the intuitively reasonable core of this down-to-earth conventionalism: "no social tendency exists which could not be altered *if* the individuals concerned both wanted to alter it and possessed appropriate information." The power to alter constraints is not absolute but conditioned on preferences sufficiently spread among the population and on the information possessed by the appropriate parties (what McKelvey and Ordeshook call "means").

Rational choice theorists can point to important reasons for thinking information will in fact be a serious problem. For one thing, information is costly. In addition, workers must use the information they extract to build an accurate model of the system. Even after they have the information and model, workers may still be unable to provide themselves with the collective good of revolution. And different initial endowments are apt to encourage disagreements.

So Watkins's "if" is a big one: capitalist constraints will be altered if workers want to do so, can produce the collective good of organization, and possess appropriate information, as opposed, say, to laboring under "false consciousness" (see Przeworski 1985:136). Conventionalists will concede, conversely, that so-called capitalist constraints will become binding when these conditions are not met. The flip side of this concession, however, is the notion that "institutional constraint" is shorthand for the failure of Watkins-like conditions to be met. When his conditions are satisfied, institutional constraints dissolve. At that point, according to Marxists in particular, humanity leaves the realm of unintended consequences for an arena in which it truly makes its own history.

The conception of institutions I have proposed does not, of course, take a specific stand on the myopia or disorganization of workers, however important to the power of capitalist institutions they are alleged to be. Yet it does cast doubt on the general significance of Watkins-like conditions. To the conventionalist, these conditions mark the *extent* to which workers have been constrained by institutions. To the institutional realist, these conditions mark the *way* workers have been constrained by institutions. In general, institutional constraints change rather than ebb and flow.

I have already noted the sense in which institutional realists would expect the content of workers' choices to be parasitic on their institutions rather than the other way around. The same holds for the global models workers may build or the "appropriate information" they may extract.[16] Even the problem of collective goods clearly depends on the arrangement of property, which the institutional realist suspects will be institutionally defined. We cannot strictly separate (1) organizational obstacles and the perception of these as obstacles and (2) the institutions of property these organizational problems presuppose.

In short, we must surrender the view that individuals can mentally detach themselves from their obstructive institutional environment while retaining all the characteristics that define them as individuals. In reality, the institutions that represent collective obstacles to reaching collective goals are the same institutions that help constitute the individuals who encounter those obstacles. Even political revolution, Michael Oakeshott notes, must appear within a given society having a given way of doing things. He appeals to the familiar ship metaphor: "In political activity . . . men sail a boundless and bottomless sea; there is neither harbour for shelter nor floor for anchorage" (Oakeshott 1962:127), neither a suprainstitutional dock for making complete repairs à la social choice theory, nor a preinstitutional anchor for getting control of the boat à la public choice theory.[17]

The institutional obstacles and the individuals facing them are two sides of the same coin. *Pace* conventionalist hopes, there is no radical, ex ante choice concerning the institutions under which individuals live. There is no choice before all choices, even when this ex ante choice is qualified as collective. The collectivity is not a primordial mass but is institutionally structured. In other words, with collective freedom of choice comes the responsibility of choosing with the preferences, means, and alternatives the decision makers inherit.[18] Marx's claim, quoted above, is still correct: "The tradition of all the dead generations weighs like a nightmare on the brain of the living." However, it weighs not only on the brain of the living but also on the world the living experience.

The conventionalist is apt to see the limits to social and individual transformation as the limits dictated by individual or collective resources. Limits imply either that there is an individual failure of imagination, ability, or will, or that barriers posed and defined by the decisions of others restrict the opportunities open to those interested in change. The institutional realist does not see individuals as unilaterally or collectively defining their alternatives and choices. Although they can use their social resources imaginatively and creatively, they cannot will them into existence. In the end, the social content of their beliefs and preferences is defined in relation to the institutional setting. Thus, this "barrier" to the fulfillment of their goals is also the structure within which their goals ultimately receive their sociopolitical meaning. Institutions are not merely barriers to actors, or instruments, but conditions under which full social choice is possible.

7.

The institutions that politically minded citizens attempt to control are distinct entities. Indeed, they are physical objects. When discussing and using rational choice theory, I have assumed that individuals have a fairly accurate reading of these institutions. My reasoning is the reverse of the conventionalist's. Rather than seeing accuracy as a natural consequence of understanding institutions as human products, I see it as a natural way to make sense of the stability

I ascribe to them without seeming to beg the rational choice theorist's questions. By imputing a reasonably realistic understanding to participants, I interpret them as fulfilling, at least in an "as if" sense, the individual preconditions for the institution's persistence. Still, institutional realism lives up to its name by acknowledging the possibility of a serious discrepancy between participant psychology and particular institutions. Stated less controversially, participants may have only a piece of the puzzle.

Oddly enough, this broad philosophical principle also suggests one more way in which the prospects for controlling collectivities might be limited. Ontological realism recognizes that participants and outside observers can carve up a given human aggregate in different ways. My discussion of ideology shows that rational agents can maintain these differences without necessarily destabilizing the institution or changing their minds. A given institution can coexist with distinct and competing constructions of it.

If this is possible, then it is also possible for the very institution that participants are trying to control to be quite different from one, noted by outsiders, that continues to constrain. There are, of course, numerous methodological constraints—simplicity comes to mind—restricting the number of variant interpretations that can be imputed to participants and observers. Yet broadly stated, the only question ontological realism allows us to ask is whether the objects a given institutional conception marks out exhibit the relations between participants and institutions which the associated theory posits.[19]

Workers may see capitalist institutions as instruments for achieving greater material success, whereas some Marxist theoreticians may dismiss this as an illusion reflecting systematic institutional constraints—education, family, religion, culture—beyond the control of these agents. As I see it, there is no a priori basis for denying the prospect of multiple institutional conceptions, each with its own plausible evidence. This, after all, was the moral of my discussion of ideology.

There is usually more than one way to look at the world, but this does not give workers or other participants extreme license. Within limits, they can differ over how the objects they face are to be interpreted, but they cannot will the objects away. If the objects have an effect, they have an effect. This means that the conventionalist counter that "truly free" individuals will define their own institutions and thereby determine which interpretation is correct just begs the question. A judgment that individuals are truly free in the appropriate sense is relative to the institutional configuration they are judged to be confronting.

Free people, it is widely felt, can use politics to control the institutional conditions of their lives. The conventionalist view of institutions has encouraged this conviction on the assumption that what people have created and understood—what they have defined—they can master. "Mankind thus inevitably sets itself only such tasks as it is able to solve" (Marx 1970:21). Yet the possibility that chosen institutions coexist with unseen or ignored constraining ones suggests that the converse may also be true: mankind only solves such tasks as it sets itself.

Earlier, I argued against the assumption that understanding implies political control. As we now see, the optimistic view of self-control also makes the illicit assumption that there must be only one institutional arrangement for participants to discover and master. The prospect of multiple institutional conceptions makes this assumption problematic, because in abolishing one set of institutional necessities society may be reflecting another set. This does not mean that any particular institution is, in principle, beyond change. It does raise the question whether all institutional configurations could simultaneously be objects of decision. Institutional necessities may accompany any expansion of political possibilities. When this happens, the optimist and the pessimist will each find reason to be satisfied.

I conclude with an awkward question: insofar as pessimists recognize multiple institutional conceptions of the same physical reality, do they not themselves become conventionalists of a sort? After all, conventionalism need not have been inspired by ontological realism in order to be rescued by it. My answer is in three parts. First, conventionalism has been more than uninspired by realism. The correct institutional conception is supposed to be the one affirmed by the participants because conventionalism sees social order as a projection from the minds of those who create and reaffirm it. By the same logic, when these minds are uniform, the social order will be uniform as well. In the latter case, conventionalism is forced to deny the very grounds on which it might be given new life.

Second, ontological realism is not the only obstacle to conventionalism. For even if social concepts are, up to a point, philosophically arbitrary, they are in fact historically well rooted. Schemes of thought too far removed from the existing categories will not appear as alternative social scientific conceptions but as odd intellectual exercises, if they can be understood at all. Institutional realism, I believe, is best able to make sense of the socially relevant categories we inherit: social meaning, rational action, choice, and the like. These ultimately are specified in relation to the world to which they are applied. To keep this language, we need to jettison its conventionalist underpinnings.

Third, institutional realism's surprising degree of conventionalism is dampened by its respect for reality. Although we climb up the ladder of familiar language and may hesitate to kick it away, institutional realism suggests that there can come a point where the familiar is no longer sufficient. Alien and unexpected institutional conceptions can force themselves on us. At that point, we should accede to the demands of science by acknowledging these newly understood constraints, even if believing in them violates our own sense of self-control. In any case, how we discover institutions and what we discover are again shown to be distinct questions. And this distinction prevents a fuller reconciliation between institutional realism and its popular competitors. Its ontological individualism does not lose sight of social wholes, while its interest in the possibilities of human freedom does not become other-worldly, grounded in introspection, or even asocial.

8.

Let me summarize the essential distinctions between institutional realism and conventionalist rational choice theory, its principal rival and inspiration. Ultimately, the conventionalist approach is unable to recognize institutions as distinct objects having the distinct power to constrain individual behavior. In order to explain institutions away, this approach is forced to invest the human creators of institutions with extraordinary psychological powers. Given the inherent implausibility of this psychology, this approach is also forced to adopt an "as if" instrumentalism about its assumptions. The resulting psychological theory of institutions lacks both institutions and a psychology.

Institutional realism happily embraces the "as if" psychology in order to put the focus where it belongs, on institutions. It can do so because it recognizes institutions as having full ontological status. As a result, it only needs to impute just enough psychology to explain actual behavior. This contrasts with the conventionalist approach, which requires additional and empirically questionable psychological ballast just to keep the creators of institutions in the game. The first major distinction, then, is between institutional realism's more pragmatic approach to psychology and conventionalist rational choice theory's counterfactual, philosophically driven approach.

Moreover, individuals without institutions cannot be fully embedded in them. Conceptually speaking, the rational decision makers of the conventionalist approach are always outsiders who continually evaluate and reassess the institutions they have created and must reaffirm. As the paradox of not voting and other examples show, however, even the enormous psychological capacities of these outsiders cannot overcome the a-institutional isolation that has been analytically imposed on them. Institutional realism can more genuinely embed participants in their institutions. It is thereby in a better position to recognize that agents acting truly within institutional collectivities are better able to overcome their collective action problems. Institutional realism is in a better position to recognize that institutions matter.

Appendix 1

The proof of proposition 1 (chapter 5) relies on straightforward algebraic manipulation.

$$\text{dc}(E, H\&K) = prob(H\&K|E) - prob(H)\,prob(K|H)$$

$$= \frac{prob(K|H)\,prob(H)}{prob(E)} - prob(H)\,prob(K|H)$$

$$= \frac{prob(K|H)\,prob(E|H)prob(H)}{prob(E)} - prob(H)\,prob(K|H)$$

$$= prob(K|H)\,[prob(H|E) - prob(H)]$$

$$= prob(K|H)dc(E,H) \quad \text{Q.E.D.}$$

Appendix 2

The proof of propositions 1 and 2 (chapter 6) parallels Ledyard (1984).

Proof of proposition 1 [existence of equilibrium with positive costs of voting]:

First define the functions:

$$P_{C1} = F_1(P_{C1}, P_{C2}) = f_1[t(P_{C1}, g, h_1), r_{pm}, r_{am}; t(P_{C2}, g, h_2), r_{an}, r_{pn}]$$

$$P_{C2} = F_2(P_{C1}, P_{C2}) = f_2[t(P_{C2}, g, h_2), r_{pn}, r_{an}; t(P_{C1}, g, h_1), r_{pm}, r_{am}]$$

where $m = 1,3$; $n = 2,3$. Note that F_1 and F_2 are continuous in (P_{C1}, P_{C2}): f_1 and f_2 are continuous because they are polynomials (see Rudin 1976:87–88) and, since the $h_i(c)$ are continuous, t is continuous in P_{C1}. Since (F_1, F_2) maps $[0,1] \times [0,1]$ into itself, and $[0,1] \times [0,1]$ is compact and convex, then by Brouwer's fixed-point theorem there exists at least one point $P^* = (P_{C1}^*, P_{C2}^*)$ such that $P_{C1}^* = F_1(P_{C1}^*, P_{C2}^*)$ and $P_{C2}^* = F_2(P_{C1}^*, P_{C2}^*)$. Finally, define $Q^* = (Q_1^*, Q_2^*)$ such that $Q_1^* = t(P_{C1}^*, g, h_1)$ and $Q_2^* = t(P_{C2}^*, g, h_2)$; then (P^*, Q^*) is a Bayesian equilibrium. Q.E.D.

Observe that the same result holds for the alternative tiebreak rule involving a coin toss.

Proof of proposition 2 [positive turnout when $H_i(c) > 0$ for all $c_i > 0$]:

To show positive turnout at equilibrium, assume there is no turnout, i.e., $Q_1 = Q_2 = 0$. Then $P_{C1} = 1$. But when $P_{Ci} > 0$, then from the assumption on $H_i(c)$ and (5), $Q_i \neq 0$. This is a contradiction. Q.E.D.

Proof of corollary A [positive turnout for C_1 and C_2 when $r_{p3}Q_i < 1$, $H_j(c) > 0$ for all $c_j > 0$, and $r_{p3} > 0$]:

If $r_{p3}Q_2 < 1$, then $P_{C1} > 0$; along the same lines as proposition 2 this implies $Q_1 > 0$. If $r_{p3}Q_1 < 1$ and $r_{p3} > 0$, it similarly follows that $P_{C2} > 0$, which in turn implies $Q_2 > 0$. Q.E.D.

Palfrey and Rosenthal (1985) prove there is positive turnout for C_1 and C_2 under both tiebreak rules, but they make somewhat stronger, albeit plausible, assumptions about the distribution functions for the costs of voting; of course they do not have r_{pk} and r_{ak}. Their assumptions would work for the propositions above as well.

Proof of proposition 3 [positive turnout when N tends to infinity]:

Proposition 2 tells us there is positive turnout at equilibrium and that this turnout will limit to zero only if P_{Ci} limits to zero for $i = 1,2$. The behavior of P_{Ci}, therefore, is the focus of our concern. Denote the sum of the first series for candidate i as Σ_i^p and the sum of that candidate's second series as Σ_i^a. Now consider the two tiebreak rules, beginning this time with the coin toss.

(a) *Coin toss tiebreak.* In this case, Σ_1^p becomes:

$$\sum_{k=0}^{\|(N-1)/2\|} \sum_{n=1}^{N-2k-1} \frac{(N-1)!}{(k+n)!k!(N-2k-n)!} \cdot$$
$$(r_{p1}Q_1)^{k+n}(r_{p3}Q_2)^k(1 - r_{p1}Q_1 - r_{p3}Q_2)^{N-2k-1-n}$$

$$+ \frac{1}{2} \sum_{k=0}^{\|(N-1)/2\|} \sum_{n=0}^{1} \frac{(N-1)!}{k!(k+n)!(N-2k-1-n)!} \cdot$$
$$(r_{p1}Q_1)^k(r_{p3}Q_2)^{k+n}(1 - r_{p1}Q_1 - r_{p3}Q_2)^{N-2k-1-n}$$

Similarly, Σ_1^a becomes:

$$\sum_{k=0}^{\|(N-1)/2\|} \sum_{n=1}^{N-2k-1} \frac{(N-1)!}{(k+n)!k!(N-2k-n)!} \cdot$$
$$(r_{a1}Q_1)^{k+n}(r_{a3}Q_2)^k(1 - r_{a1}Q_1 - r_{a3}Q_2)^{N-2k-1-n}$$

$$+ \frac{1}{2} \sum_{k=0}^{\|(N-1)/2\|} \frac{(N-1)!}{k!k!(N-2k-1)!} \cdot$$
$$(r_{a1}Q_1)^k(r_{a3}Q_2)^k(1 - r_{a1}Q_1 - r_{a3}Q_2)^{N-2k-1}$$

A parallel calculation for Σ_2^p gives:

$$\sum_{k=0}^{\|(N-1)/2\|} \sum_{n=1}^{N-2k-1} \frac{(N-1)!}{k!(k+n)!(N-2k-1-n)!} \cdot$$
$$(r_{p3}Q_1)^k(r_{p2}Q_2)^{k+n}(1 - r_{p3}Q_1 - r_{p2}Q_2)^{N-2k-1-n}$$

$$+ \frac{1}{2} \sum_{k=0}^{\|(N-1)/2\|} \sum_{n=0}^{1} \frac{(N-1)!}{(k+n)!k!(N-2k-1-n)!} \cdot$$
$$(r_{p3}Q_1)^{k+n}(r_{p2}Q_2)^k(1 - r_{p3}Q_1 - r_{p2}Q_2)^{N-2k-1-n}$$

Likewise for Σ_2^a:

$$\sum_{k=0}^{\|(N-1)/2\|} \sum_{n=1}^{N-2k-1} \frac{(N-1)!}{k!(k+n)!(N-2k-1-n)!} \cdot$$

$$(r_{a3}Q_1)^k (r_{a2}Q_2)^k (1 - r_{a3}Q_1 - r_{a2}Q_2)^{N-2k-1-n}$$

$$+ \frac{1}{2} \sum_{k=0}^{\|(N-1)/2\|} \frac{(N-1)!}{k!k!(N-2k-1)!} \cdot$$

$$(r_{a3}Q_1)^k (r_{a2}Q_2)^k (1 - r_{a3}Q_1 - r_{a2}Q_2)^{N-2k-1}$$

Theorem 3 of Palfrey and Rosenthal (1985) shows, *mutatis mutandis*, that those terms above that are multiplied by $\frac{1}{2}$ limit to zero as $N-1$ approaches infinity, so they can be disregarded. On the basis of the strong law of large numbers (see Hinich 1977:212–13; Ledyard 1984:20–21), we can conclude, therefore, that when $N-1$ approaches infinity, then for $i \epsilon R_1$,

$$(1) \quad \lim_{(N-1)\to\infty} \Sigma_1^p = \begin{cases} 1 \text{ when } r_{p1}Q_1 > r_{p3}Q_2 \\ 0 \text{ when } r_{p1}Q_1 < r_{p3}Q_2 \\ \frac{1}{2} \text{ when } r_{p1}Q_1 = r_{p3}Q_2 \end{cases}$$

Likewise,

$$(2) \quad \lim_{(N-1)\to\infty} \Sigma_1^a = \begin{cases} 1 \text{ when } r_{a1}Q_1 > r_{a3}Q_2 \\ 0 \text{ when } r_{a1}Q_1 < r_{a3}Q_2 \\ \frac{1}{2} \text{ when } r_{a1}Q_1 = r_{a3}Q_2 \end{cases}$$

It follows that:

$$(3) \quad \lim_{(N-1)\to\infty} (\Sigma_1^p - \Sigma_1^a) > 0 \text{ when } r_{p1}Q_1 > r_{p3}Q_2 \ \& \ r_{a1}Q_1 \leq r_{a3}Q_2$$

$$\text{or } r_{p1}Q_1 = r_{p3}Q_2 \ \& \ r_{a1}Q_1 < r_{a3}Q_2$$

Similarly,

$$(4) \quad \lim_{(N-1)\to\infty} (\Sigma_2^p - \Sigma_2^a) > 0 \text{ when } r_{p2}Q_2 > r_{p3}Q_1 \ \& \ r_{a2}Q_2 \leq r_{p3}Q_1$$

$$\text{or } r_{p2}Q_2 = r_{p3}Q_1 \ \& \ r_{a2}Q_2 < r_{p3}Q_1$$

(b) C_2 *wins when there is a tie.* Compared to (a), this case:

1. inflates both Σ_1^p and Σ_2^a by $\frac{1}{2}$ the probability of a tie vote when there are $N-1$ voters in the respective calculations;
2. deflates both Σ_2^p and Σ_1^a by $\frac{1}{2}$ the probability of a tie vote when there are $N-1$ voters in the respective calculations;
3. deflates Σ_1^p by $\frac{1}{2}$ the probability of i's creating a tie;
4. inflates Σ_2^p by $\frac{1}{2}$ the probability of j's creating a tie.

Palfrey and Rosenthal's (1985) theorem 3 again implies that each of the probabilities in 1–4 limits to zero as $(N-1) \to \infty$. Thus the limits described in equations 1–4 for case (a) apply in case (b) as well. Q.E.D.

Notes

Chapter 1: Philosophical Preliminaries

1. This characterization of modern skepticism glosses over some finer distinctions between conventionalism as an epistemological doctrine and antirealism as an ontological doctrine (see Horwich 1986). For present purposes it is worth trampling on the conceptual niceties, particularly since conventionalism and antirealism are strongly linked in social science where, conventionalists insist, the objects are also object-creating subjects (e.g., Parsons 1968).

2. The message of the constellation example is actually nominalistic, not anti-ontological (Goodman is also a nominalist, but that is another matter). To a nominalist, connections among things do not exist alongside the things themselves. In this sense a pattern-giving description of stars is imposed and arbitrary.

3. Davidson (1980) strongly develops this theme. Incidentally, although the ostensibly identical behavior is likewise thought to be denuded of its original social meaning when it occurs in a different context, this second act is not literally the same physical event but, at best, an analog. Physical nonidentity is a necessary condition for social nonidentity. From a realist's perspective, judgments of sameness and difference presuppose an underlying distinction between same and different physical events.

4. Weber (1968) handles this problem in a remarkably direct manner. Yes, he admits, agents need not attach subjective meaning to all the important causal processes affecting social behavior. He simply rules that these processes are outside the purview of sociology.

5. Richard Rorty (1979), one of the leading lights of "irrealism," argues precisely against any attempt by science or philosophy to mirror a preexisting reality. Yet this mirroring is particularly important in the case of social phenomena, which are supposed to reflect the concepts of social actors.

Subtract the idea of a preexisting reality and, ironically, conventionalist social theory comes close to insisting on a mirroring relation.

6. In a sense, I would grant, there is only a fine line between the scientifically mediated version of realism and the specific version of irrealism Fine (1986) calls the "Natural Ontological Attitude." The latter welcomes debate on specific existence claims but does not see any implications in this debate for existence claims as such. Yet for present purposes, realism makes a difference. The modern version continues to insist that objects, including social objects, are not constructed or constituted in any sense that justifies regarding the correctness of a culture's beliefs, or hypotheses about them, as self-confirming. A scientifically mediated realism simply rejects the thesis that reality itself is relative to theories or interpretations (see Field 1974; 1975, who perhaps takes more seriously than Quine himself the preceding distinction between the epistemology and the ontology of science). Insofar as realism finds the notion of ontological relativity to be incoherent, the line between irrealism and realism, however fine, still distinguishes institutional realism from modern conventionalism.

7. Cultural factors, of course, can be intervening variables in explanations of why particular social objects exist. To explain why something exists is not necessarily to impugn its ontological status.

8. Conventionalists are not the only ones who shy away from this idea of a common world, at least in all its glory. Some realists do as well. A world that holds still when people categorize and interpret it incompatibly can also be a world that does not admit of one right interpretation, one correct or distinguished cognitive relation between it and observers. Such a world does not come prepackaged in a unique set of categories called properties (cf., e.g., Armstrong 1978).

9. Cf. the suggestive remark of Quine (1981:13) and the wider discussion by Noonan (1980) concerning the justification for this sort of identification. For completeness, it may be useful to define institutions a little more broadly to include not just human beings but also some of the implements of their institutional activity like levers in voting booths, documents, and uniforms. This specification is drawn from Grafstein (1988).

10. The work of Talcott Parsons, as we shall see, demonstrates chronologically the conversion of social structure and system from analytic abstractions to distinct, active entities.

11. To dot one of the philosophical i's here, social science, in this interpretation, is concerned with particular collections of physical objects, whereas physics posits what social science should accept as the basic building materials of these collections. This approach may smack of ontological physicalism—the doctrine that there are only physical objects—by definition. In a certain sense, this is precisely what I intend: "If the physicist suspected there was any event that did not consist in a redistribution of the elementary states allowed for by his physical theory, he would seek a way of supplementing his theory. Full coverage in this sense is the very business of physics, and only of physics" (Quine 1981:98). The science of building materials, by whatever official name, is what deserves to be called physics.

12. Exactly how or whether one needs an explicit theory of reference tying individual categorizations to the world is an issue I must sidestep here.

See, for example, Leeds (1973; 1978), Devitt (1983), Glymour (1982), and Field (1986a).

13. Thus, compare Huntington's (1968:12) conventionalist definition of institutions as "stable, valued, recurring patterns of behavior."

14. For this identification of events with four-dimensional objects, see Quine (1981:11–12). He has modified his position, worrying that it permits the same event to be, say, both rapid and slow, as when a given four-dimensional object like a steel ball rotates rapidly while warming slowly (1985). I think Quine hit the brake on his original analysis too quickly, because describing the same event as rapid and slow is only superficially problematic. Or it is no more problematic than saying that a comet is small when considered as a celestial object, whereas it is big when considered as a missile striking the earth. Just as the same object can rotate rapidly and warm slowly, so can the same event be a rapid rotation and a slow warming.

15. I understand a situation in this case as a spatiotemporal segment of an aggregate of people.

16. Lewis (1969) adds numerous refinements, while Lewis (1975) emphasizes there can be conventions of belief as well as action. Sugden (1986) expands Lewis's analysis of conventions beyond those coordination problems in which the participants are relatively indifferent among the coordinated outcomes, including situations where there is not a unanimous interest in conformity. My analysis in this chapter is not sensitive to these distinctions.

17. Gettier's (1963) important objection to this view has stimulated an enormous discussion. The role of common knowledge assumptions about every participant's rationality also figures in game theoretic models of institutional phenomena. I shall take this up in chapters 3 and 4.

18. Obviously, in making this point I am not particularly concerned whether the equilibrium is a coordination equilibrium or some other kind, say a Nash equilibrium in a prisoners' dilemma, which is discussed in chapter 3. In fact, even the idea of equilibrium is not crucial, although it is convenient. What is at stake is the more general idea that when a regularity of behavior is defined by participants one has somehow avoided the problem of external description.

19. Lewis's definition of a convention requires an alternative regularity to which conformity is also preferable (for example, if stop on green and go on red is the regularity, it is still preferable that everyone conform). When I refer to alternative regularities in the text, I have in mind regularities that play no role in the characterization of the convention.

20. This may also account for the previously noted affinity between some versions of conventionalism and a Wittgensteinian emphasis on social practices, rules, and patterns of interaction as the loci of ostensibly psychological terms like meaning and concept. Depsychologizing the psychological in this way takes the pressure off the individuals who otherwise would have to maintain all this in their heads.

21. The whole issue of stretching beliefs and distinguishing between the explicit and implicit varieties not only is methodological but, in my opinion, suggests something important about the social nature of belief (interesting in this respect are Stich 1983; Field 1986b; Burge 1979). For this reason, I am

somewhat sympathetic to the socialization of psychology discussed in the preceding note.

22. Lewis's analysis of conventions, in fact, is designed primarily to develop a theory of language. Lewis (1969) and Schiffer (1972), among others, have shown that a coherent, though not necessarily persuasive, conventionalist account of the birth of language is in fact possible. Since the creation of a common language arguably relies on linguistic signaling, their work helps allay a persistent concern about infinite regress in language theory that goes back at least to Rousseau (1964:120–26) and still surfaces from time to time (e.g., Holmes 1989:34). I mention this because the infinite regress problem can and has been treated as a point against methodological individualism and, more substantively, as evidence for the inherently social nature or essence of human beings. My beef with conventionalism is different.

23. As Elster (1983a:32–33) observes, social stability can arise when society depends on individuals but is not affected by the actions of any one individual.

24. I want to emphasize that the question is whether there need be a distinct psychological *mechanism* corresponding to crucial psychological attributions. Though in each and every case individual behavior is produced through some process, this process is not necessarily realized through a distinct and persistent mechanism.

Chapter 2: The Sociological Solution

1. There is something of a new interest in Parsons's work: "one of the most visible trends in social theory today is the prime part played by views drawn more or less directly from Parsons" (Giddens 1984:xxxvi; see also Alexander 1983).

2. Elster (1989), in effect, partly supports Parsons, as does Hardin (1982).

3. In Parsons's (1968) neo-Kantian language, these distinct "frames of reference" correspond, respectively, to the "objective" and "subjective" points of view.

4. For an even more radical notion of constitution from existing possibilities, see Luhmann (1976). A comparison of his work with that of Parsons makes clear the degree to which the constructivist idea criticized in the discussion of Goodman in chapter 1 does tap the crucial philosophical presuppositions of Parsonian theory, presuppositions that Luhmann to some extent wants to transcend.

5. Galtung (1959) notes that values can be reciprocally adjusted rather than shared. Why, then, does Parsons emphasize common values? Social order, in his view, is ultimately defined, not merely explained, by values; and conventionalism notwithstanding, Parsons is not eager to embrace the idea of multiple worlds, an idea entailed by the idea of multiple values. The logic of this position begins to unravel when a multiplicity of values is shown to be compatible with order, which is analogous to what we saw when examining conventions in chapter 1.

6. Black (1961:286) suggests that the notion of implicit choice implies "a disturbing element of the fictitious." In his early writing particularly, Parsons tries to sidestep the problem by appealing to a Freudian notion of the

subconscious. The strategy of one-downmanship succeeds, if only in an analytic sense, so long as this appeal can reconcile the idea of objective psychic processes and subjectively meaningful categories. Habermas (1971:214–73) argues that Freud himself failed on this score.

7. See also Parsons and Smelser (1965:69) and Parsons, Bales, and Shils (1953:228).

8. Scott (1963) argues there is in fact a break between the earlier "subjective" Parsons and the later "systems" Parsons.

9. Note the phrase "abstractly *defined.*" As we have seen, Parsons (1954:341–42) uses the idea of analytic abstraction to advance the claims of methodological individualism. In section 3 I consider the definition of structure as an abstract entity.

10. Grafstein (1981a) makes an analogous point about Weber's conception of legitimacy.

11. Grafstein (1982a) attempts to tease out structuralism's structural ontology, which is resisted by Mayhew (1982). In response, see Grafstein (1982b).

12. For further discussion of the issue, see Aune (1984) and Schiffer (1987:234–39). Putnam (1975:305–22) argues for the importance of properties in causal explanation and in empirical statements equating, for example, temperature and mean kinetic energy. I think that Field (1985) considerably weakens the force of this argument.

13. By way of analogy, Giddens mentions the tacit knowledge employed by language users, although claims in linguistics about the existence and scope of this knowledge have proved very controversial. See, for example, Searle (1971), Stich (1983), and Churchland (1986).

14. This section draws from Grafstein (1988).

15. I will only add one observation to this debate. As we saw in the case of Parsons, the appeal to functions can itself have a function, namely, to sustain a macro-level analysis without detailing the macro-level mechanisms involved. Functional analysis thus allows the conventionalist to sidestep the awkward questions raised by the existence of these mechanisms.

16. Cohen (1978:220) defines a power simply as an ability. Rights are considered effective in social contexts only insofar as they are coupled with appropriate powers.

17. Explanations, of course, are verbal phenomena and perhaps pragmatic at that. But explanations, in this case, are presumably designed to say how one thing influences or is connected to another. The reader should compare this breezy appeal to causation with the ontological stipulations of chapter 1 and the discussion of evidential decision theory in chapter 4, where only causal *norms* for explanations are recognized.

18. For a similar distinction, see Przeworski (1985:245–46). Discussing the crucial difference between social form and material content, Cohen (1978:91–92) offers the analogy of a statue with respect to which one can abstract a form and a content. Yet both form and content, as he notes, are abstractions. The statue is spatially distributed matter, which means there is no raw "stuff" constrained by the statue's form. This suggests two things. One, his nice description of communism—"the form is now just the boundary created by matter itself"—is generally true of the form-content distinc-

tion. Two, he has not shown how form constrains. Whatever constraining forces there are will have to be realized by the "matter" itself, which is the idea behind my physicalist characterization of institutional ontology in chapter 1.

19. For a more refined discussion of this contrast, see, for example, Przeworski and Wallerstein (1988); see also Przeworski (1990).

20. I believe the same judgment must be made about some recent attempts to introduce neo-institutionalism into public law. Smith (1988), for example, relies on many of the developments discussed here and, in particular, on Huntington's (1968:12) conventionalist definition of institutions cited in chapter 1.

21. If anything, my qualms concern the underlying notion of intentions.

22. Taylor (1988) criticizes Skocpol for thinking that the idea of unintended consequences is inimical to rational choice explanation, let alone that it absolves her from furnishing an explanation at the individual level.

23. See Grafstein (1981b) for one nonconventionalist version of legitimacy.

24. See, for example, the skeptical epistemological comments of Harré (1981).

Chapter 3: The Rational Choice Solution

1. There is now, in fact, a substantial rational choice sociology. It was ignored earlier since what I have to say about it can be subsumed under my criticisms in the present chapter.

2. To anticipate one important corrective to this endorsement of instrumentalism: presumably, even instrumental assumptions cannot demand that agents have information about the institutional environment they could not have acquired. As we shall see, this becomes an important issue in evaluating rational expectations models.

3. I am assuming that probabilities play a role, though in some games they do not. Determining the proper role of probabilistic beliefs has been a matter of debate; see, for example, Aumann (1987). For one attempt to achieve a fully decision theoretic foundation for game theory, see Tan and Werlang (1988).

4. I think it is fairly well agreed that Howard's (1971) metagame attempt to dodge this equilibrium through additional levels of reflection is unsatisfactory. The crucial point, in the end, is that the prisoners' dilemma, as a noncooperative game, does not allow binding agreements. Since the binding character of coalitions, which are associated with cooperative games, is not something given by nature, it is widely felt among game theorists that noncooperative game theory is more basic.

5. The psychologizing of game theory becomes even more apparent with the introduction of mixed strategies, that is, plans assigning probabilities to the individual ("pure") strategies or plans of the agent. Although mixed strategies are crucial to solving certain kinds of games, at one time they had a disputed status (Luce and Raiffa 1957:74–76; Owen 1974). Part of the reason is that while an agent can, in a formal sense, choose a mixed strategy, mixed strategies are indistinguishable from pure ones when the game is actually played. Rather than constituting a true strategy within the

game, a mixed strategy, it is now generally believed, is just a way of preventing other players from discovering the agent's proposed course of action. Standard formalizations of game theory will not reveal this distinction, however, since they treat pure strategies merely as a special case of the mixed. The psychological thus absorbs the behavioral. Since Aumann's (1987) Bayesian approach to game theory will come up later, I should mention that an alternative interpretation of mixed strategy is that it directly represents the *other* player's uncertainty about the mixed strategist's behavior (see notably Pearce 1984:1034).

6. The preceding characterizes a static, one-shot game with no history and no future. Later, I shall accommodate sequences of games into this conventionalist portrait.

7. Ostrom (1986:5–6) similarly complains about the failure of game theory to differentiate between physical laws and made-up rules. The distinction requires treating rules ambiguously as mental representations and as shared norms. This will become clear in section 3.

8. For a more recent example, Harsanyi and Selten (1988:10) say games of incomplete information arise because *inter alia* "players may have limited information about . . . the *physical consequences* to be produced by alternative strategy combinations."

9. As we shall see later, Harsanyi (1967–68) introduces an intermediate case in which an agent playing a game of incomplete information calculates the likely behavior of others based on his beliefs about shared attributes. But this agent can exploit these correlations by acting independently of them. Harsanyi also ingeniously circumvents the anticonventionalist implications of having a game that is only indeterminately defined by the players' knowledge: each is endowed with a subjective probability distribution over a common set of possible games. The uncertainty, in other words, is embedded in a larger game.

10. The following material on the von Neumann-Morgenstern interpretation is drawn from Grafstein (1983a).

11. For a good survey of the different senses of common knowledge, see Brandenburger and Dekel (1989).

12. Actually, there can be some variation in the common knowledge assumptions that deliver Nash and correlated equilibria (e.g., Tan and Werlang 1988). This variation, on the other hand, demands a more explicitly modeled infinite recursion on beliefs (e.g., I know that he knows that I know . . .) which, if anything, intensifies the conventionalist quality of games, as noted in the analysis of Lewis, and weakens its possible behavioral interpretation.

13. To say that players have common knowledge of each other's information partitions is not to say that each player knows what the other players know. Knowing a player's a priori limits is not the same as knowing the information revealed to her in a particular play of the game.

14. To put the institutional realist's two cents in, Nau and McCardle (1990) do not make entirely clear how, in using an observer to "characterize the mutually expected rationality in the game" (p. 429), they define the options that rational players will not in fact offer their fellow players. This problem of out-of-equilibrium behavioral paths will again arise in chapter 4.

15. Usually, preferences are also taken as givens, although rational choice theory is open to the idea of endogenous preference formation. In the latter approach, e.g., agents arrive on the scene with general and primitive preferences, whereas the specifically expressed preferences ascribed to them reflect their information and opportunities (Stigler and Becker 1977).

16. For a game theoretic analysis of Hobbes's state of nature, see Taylor (1987). Taylor, among others, has questioned whether individuals contemplating long-term iterations of the prisoners' dilemma would be so myopic about the long-term consequences of their antisocial behavior. I shall take up this "internal" resolution of the prisoners' dilemma shortly.

17. There is actually a third problem: it is particularly difficult for residents of the state of nature to reach an effective agreement to transcend the prisoners' dilemma when society is more realistically sized than the one just considered. This problem is substantial, notwithstanding the possibility of selective incentives offered by organizations and the efforts of political entrepreneurs (see Hardin 1982; Hechter 1987; Coleman 1988:266–76).

18. Obviously, a fully expanded game would have to include impure outcomes in which some agree to the institutional regularity and some do not. The entire distinction between unanimity and every other percentage shall be addressed shortly.

19. Schmidt-Trenz (1989) has shown in detail how calculations leading to state-of-nature equilibria are affected by institutional possibilities, just as equilibrium institutions are affected by the possibility of anarchy.

20. As an exegetic point, Buchanan and Tullock (1962) focus on uncertainty about the future as the basis for defining the rights embodied in the state of nature's unanimous consent, whereas Buchanan (1975) emphasizes the equilibrium dimension.

21. Since I take this fundamental claim for unanimous consent seriously, I am ignoring otherwise reasonable suggestions about the use of intermediate organizations and communities to bootstrap individuals out of the state of nature (e.g., Hechter 1987; Taylor 1988). I shall return to this in chapter 4.

22. Tversky, Slovic, and Kahneman (1990) argue that preferences are in fact sensitive to the context or way in which they are elicited.

23. I believe that Buchanan and Tullock's justification for ignoring the development of institutional pockets within the state of nature is that although people in the state of nature can leave in subgroups, this is not important for a fundamental account of politics. For when subgroups leave, the result is not so much a new case within the Buchanan and Tullock model as an ambiguous one. Within the group, there is a contractual relation. Externally, the individuals who remain and the subgroup considered as a single actor constitute the original state of nature.

24. Institutions do not evolve as solutions to prisoners' dilemma games but are supposed to emerge full-blown from the heads of the participants. Shepsle (1989:138–43) remarks that the resulting ex ante deliberations about the creation of an institution are subject to great uncertainty, and hardly any resulting institution can be expected to be truly "renegotiation-proof." This only extends the range of psychological demands on social contractors who must anticipate that the original setup may encompass a procedure for insti-

tutional change (such as amendments) that makes the process of renegotiation part of the institution.

25. There is an additional problem if psychological content is dependent on context, as was discussed briefly in chapter 1.

26. Accordingly, two institutions can in principle be behaviorally equivalent but nonetheless count as different institutions (Schotter 1981:62–63).

27. Following Davis and North (1970), Bromley (1989:22–23) notes the possible confusion between institutions as rules and institutions as the organizations defined by those rules. Like most in the rational choice tradition, he opts for the former. Vanberg (1986:78) is better on this: "it is not 'the rule,' as such, that can explain behavioral regularities, but the social facts or constraints that induce individuals to act in accordance to the rule."

28. Note that the dual status of rules and regularities also parallels the dual status of norms in Schotter's (1981) setup. Sometimes norms, at least conceptually, seem to have an active, public character: "For instance, the norm 'honor among thieves' is a code or norm existing in societies that informs criminals what type of behavior can be expected from their colleagues" (1981:52; see also 109–43). Yet technically, a norm is just a vector of the subjective probabilities each player places on the behavior of the other players at any given time (1981:86). So norms per se do not inform; they are probabilities summarizing the agent's beliefs.

29. For attempts to introduce learning into rational expectations analysis, see Bray and Savan (1986) and Marcet and Sargent (1989). Their results are not uniformly positive even for highly simplified models, whereas the models of learning are not always fully rational.

30. Put another way, institutions serve to reduce transaction costs, leading to additional gains from trade; for one formulation of this important approach to institutions, see North (1981).

31. The "trembling hand" condition discussed in the next note is interesting in this respect. Participants do not interpret it as a sign of irrationality but continue to respond as though all behavior is dictated by rational choice. This helps preserve the idea of institutions as the product of choices.

32. As we have seen, Schotter (1981) does insist on one arguably important qualitative distinction for institutions: they are reproduced with probability 1 (certainty). When he gets to modeling the emergence of institutions as a diffusion process, this distinction is both reinforced and weakened (see 1981:100–109). It is reinforced by Schotter's condition 2, which in effect assures a degree of irrationality analogous to Selten's (1975) "trembling hand" but only for behavior sufficiently removed from institutional equilibria. It is weakened since Schotter's condition 1 requires that outcomes having nearly the certainty of the institutional equilibria be treated as equivalent to the institutional equilibria. This, of course, is a natural continuity assumption, but continuity between what readers may see as qualitatively different situations (see the previous note).

Chapter 4: The Return of Institutions

1. Kirzner (1962) argues that insofar as Becker assumes that consumers facing a budget constraint are price takers, he is assuming rational be-

havior on the part of producers. This is irrelevant to my concern, the effect of the budget constraint rather than its source.

2. A contrasting idea is deinstitutionalization through self-understanding modeled on Freudian therapy (Habermas 1971). Deinstitutionalization is addressed in chapter 7.

3. Grafstein (1983a) presents a formal axiomatization of games consistent with institutional realism, except that the axioms characterizing the game's structure refer to abstract entities. As I have indicated, I now believe an appeal to behavioral dispositions can do the same job (see also Grafstein 1988). There is a disagreement among game theorists whether it is best to proceed using the extensive or normal form of the game, but no one to my knowledge questions the extensive form as the underlying structure.

4. The standard approach, as I noted in chapter 3, also includes as part of the extensive game the information players have about their own previous choices as well as those of other players. The role of information shall be examined shortly.

5. I am assuming some fixed descriptive vocabulary, concerning which see the discussion in chapter 7. For a more formal rendering of the idea of determination, see Hellman and Thompson (1975).

6. For an appropriate behavioral interpretation of information, see Grafstein (1981b).

7. The notion of games of incomplete information does recognize a certain lack of intentional control over the definition of institutions. It is particularly useful for modeling the effects of other choices that have an impact on the player but that she does not model as the distinct or intended effect of choices made by an actual player. Yet this is accomplished by giving each player a probability distribution over a domain of alternative games. Insofar as this domain is common to the players, conventionalism achieves closure on its original scheme. Indeed, as Bernheim (1984:1024) observes, there is characteristic homogenization of beliefs insofar as all players ascribe the same beliefs and actions to each "type" of player. The underlying common knowledge assumptions are addressed in chapter 3, and additional problems with the generic notion of incompleteness are discussed in chapter 5.

8. I have structured the example to avoid an empirically significant complication: the possibility that defectors from an institution may get sustenance (higher expected utility due to rational role expectations) from other institutions. Think of the Mafia or, on a more positive note, the family.

9. For an example from the Western hemisphere of restrictions on alternatives apparently promoting stability, see Mintz and Wolf (1957).

10. The proposed institutional constraint does not preclude altruistic concern for others or local organizational constraints induced by effective monitoring. In fact, the different influences need not be simply additive. The incentive to sacrifice for kin at home, for instance, can be magnified by the threat of institutional failure conditional on evidence of individual shirking.

11. Chapter 2 casts doubt on whether it can be achieved by some important non–rational choice alternatives. I shall remain agnostic on a different question, whether social scientific explanations can be reduced to physical (that is, neurophysiological or biological) explanations. Ontological

physicalism does not preclude a negative answer so long as the notion of explanation is taken seriously (see Hellman and Thompson 1977).

12. Clearly, a nominalist would need to do more work, such as translating talk of propositions. In this context, however, I am concentrating on differences between Jeffrey's decision theory and the more conventionalist approach.

13. This is not to deny the utility of what might be called a causal norm orienting scientific research (Skyrms 1980:109–27). Yet if Quine (1969:114–38) is right, successful scientific research replaces causation with explicit descriptions of physical structure.

14. According to the four-dimensional ontology proposed in chapter 1, all of spacetime is ontologically equivalent. The future, in particular, does not present us with an open horizon of unactualized possibilities. This makes some people nervous over issues of free will, fatalism, and the like. Williams (1966:274) and Smart (1963:141–42) address these concerns.

15. Schiffer (1987) elaborates the distinction between ontological physicalism about individual psychology, which he supports, and the possibility of reducing psychology to internal physical or functionalist mechanisms, which he strongly denies.

16. Technically, one's reasons, R, for desiring treatment screen off the statistical relation between illness, I, and going to the doctor, D, if $prob(I|D \& R) = prob(I|\neg D \& R)$.

17. Aside from the technical complications, there are of course more ordinary reasons for uncertainty about one's preferences. For example, do teenagers know whether they really have the urge to smoke or whether they seek social acceptance? Perhaps in some circles they smoke to enjoy the image of being nonconformist. I assume we all have been unclear about our own motives at some time or another.

18. Jeffrey (1983) introduces a similar notion he calls ratifiability. The act an agent has chosen but not quite undertaken may, under some circumstances, give the agent valuable additional evidence about the best choice to make. A ratifiable choice is one that does not change given this additional information. Rational agents, Jeffrey contends, should make ratifiable choices. There is a causal version (e.g., Skyrms 1982), which will not occupy us.

19. Nor do I deny that agents may acquire the relevant information after encountering the decision problem but before having to act. Their prior probabilities will have to be revised in light of this new information (Eells 1985b:195–97 is instructive). Yet the resulting revision establishes a new decision problem; it does not reflect the dynamics of the old one.

20. Jeffrey (1988) seems to return to this idea, characterizing the estimation process as a "two-level probability model"—one level determining the probabilities for another level which bears directly on action. Jeffrey, though, winds up endorsing the prescriptions of causal decision theory in those divergent cases discussed later. His specific recommendations in these cases have less to do with his general approach, however, than with the particular setup of his model.

21. This is the beginning of an answer to Horwich's (1985) earlier noted objection. If the agent is somewhat ignorant, he argues, objective propensi-

ties may be screened off whereas subjective statistical relations survive. What this shows is that in some cases the task of assigning conditional probabilities is quite difficult, whether the decision maker subsequently tracks causal or evidential theories (again see Price 1986).

22. The updating process mentioned in the text is Bayesian conditionalization. Viscusi (1989) is interested in rationalizing certain experimental results widely viewed as contradicting expected utility theory.

23. Bayesian conditionalization assumes that incoming evidence is associated with a particular degree of belief (probability) for specific sentences. Some think that this theory must be supplemented with an account of how degrees of belief are assigned to raw input (Field 1978b). Similarly, one might object to the notion expressed in the text that agents first have to determine their initial probability assignments before making a rational decision. One might ask, Using what process and which prior beliefs? Based on considerations similar to those adduced in arguing for the social content of rationality, I join Jeffrey in questioning the utility of understanding this underlying mechanism as a deeper form of conditionalization preceding the regular decision-making process. Indeed, Jeffrey (1983:183) calls these ostensibly raw inputs into the process of initial belief formation "epistemological geegaws that do no work." A more moderate interpretation is that ordinary inductive operations belong to a behaviorally interpreted psychology, whereas the creation of *prior* beliefs remains a physiological notion.

24. Unless otherwise noted, evidential decision theory shall henceforth be equated with the version I have defended.

25. The key, again, is to show evidential decision theory's legitimacy, not its absolute superiority. I tend to agree with Horwich (1985) and Price (1986), who both prefer the evidential approach, that our guiding intuitions about rationality are so weak in the cases I shall now discuss that pragmatic considerations count heavily when making comparisons. In an informal poll of his colleagues, Nozick (1969) found that intuitions were evenly divided. Lewis (1981), a supporter of causal decision theory, concludes that the debate between the competing intuitions is "hopelessly deadlocked." So in complex cases of divergence, one might recognize different solutions when intuitions falter and common solutions when they do not (see Price 1986 and Talbott 1987).

26. As I pointed out earlier, Jeffrey (1988) does not recommend cooperation, but he assumes stochastic independence in the calculation of the joint probabilities of similar actions.

27. I grant that there is a certain fuzziness inherent in this belief for the general case. Intuitively, it means prisoners expect to engage in the same behavior without exception. Yet in the face of standard probability theory, as many have acknowledged, intuitions falter. Consider, for example, a trillion real numbers lying between 1 and 2. There is a zero probability of randomly picking one of these from a choice confined to that interval. Intuitively speaking, however, these impossibilities, in the sense of probability = 0, seem to be possible.

28. For analogous reasoning, see Levi (1975) and Seidenfeld (1985).

29. This distinction is brought out in Sobel (1985). As he observes, the conditional relation entails, but is not entailed by, what I have called the

coincidental relation. To see this, observe that if the conditional relation is true, $prob(A_1 \& B_1) = prob(A_1) \cdot prob(B_1|A_1) = prob(A_1)$; likewise, $prob(A_2 \& B_2) = prob(A_2) \cdot prob(B_2|A_2) = prob(A_2)$. Since $prob(A_1) + prob(A_2) = 1$ and $prob[(A_1 \& B_1) \& (A_2 \& B_2)] = 0$, $prob[(A_1 \& B_1) \text{ or } (A_2 \& B_2)] = 1$. Q.E.D. concerning the claim of entailment. The coincidental relation does not entail the conditional relation, since, for example, the high probability of the former may hinge on $prob(A_1 \& B_1)$; see Jeffrey (1981:485). Contrast the coincidental argument for symmetrical outcomes discussed in chapter 3. There is another difference between that argument and the present one. The case for evidential decision theory is based on behavior, not on some generalized commonality in thinking styles such as common rationality.

30. The comparison to reasoning by means of subjunctives refers to Gibbard and Harper (1978), whose analysis shall be discussed briefly in chapter 5.

31. Compare the analysis of character planning by Elster (1983b), who recognizes the limits on this process.

32. Eells (1985a) does not actually discuss the prisoners' dilemma; the example he uses shall be addressed shortly.

33. Another apparent reason for Eells's common cause interpretation concerns a technical feature of Jeffrey's (1983) version of introspection. Introspection requires agents to contemplate the probability of an outcome conditional on an action they have, at that moment, chosen *not* to perform. Yet for introspection to matter, there must still be some possibility of the action occurring. Otherwise, the conditional probability would be undefined. Jeffrey justifies this possibility by arguing that agents do not always succeed in carrying out their plans. If their slips, as well as their intended actions, must be predicted, Eells may reason, only some common cause could drive the other agent to track both the rational process and its various breakdowns (cf. Jeffrey 1983:25). See chapter 5 for additional discussion of this issue.

34. Harsanyi (1967–68:322–29) assumes that agents playing games of incomplete information will incorporate statistical dependence among player attributes into their calculations of expected utility. In a sense, I have proposed extending these calculations to cover rational behavioral dispositions as attributes. In a full rational expectations model, of course, these probability distributions would be inferred from information players receive in the model.

35. In particular, by most standard approaches one player can eliminate the possibility that another player will use dominated strategies, given the fact that the other player is rational. This kind of reasoning is implicated in the backward induction arguments discussed in chapter 5.

36. In chapter 6 I shall examine one particular game in which the required integration of beliefs takes place. The voting participation game discussed there is entirely intrainstitutional, so the analogy is imperfect. But in principle, the calculations are similar.

37. This can be viewed as expanding on an observation by Shubik (1982:250): "Sometimes one can step outside the usual conceptual framework of game theory and regard the probabilities [of mixed strategy equilibria] as subconscious behavioral parameters rather than conscious choices."

38. Counterfactual reasoning suggests to most of its practitioners that had the decision makers chosen one box under those circumstances it would still have been empty. Yet when one abjures this style of reasoning and the inherited problem of explicating the notion of same counterfactual circumstances, this response is unavailable. I shall stick with the facts of the matter.

39. This kind of issue is raised by the new classical analysis of labor markets. An ex ante choice about job search, career training, or employment can be rational even though it works out badly ex post. Many proponents of new classical economics therefore are disinclined to treat the inferior outcome, not getting a job, as an example of involuntary unemployment.

40. Orbell, Schwartz-Shea, and Simmons (1984), having enriched the prisoners' dilemma setup with an exit option, find not only a surprising amount of cooperation, like much of the literature, but also a failure by cooperators to exit even when doing so is to the subjects' distinct advantage. Their evidence indicates, however, that this greater reluctance to exit cannot be fully explained by higher optimism.

41. Quattrone and Tversky (1988), who believe their result contradicts rational choice theory, show in particular that voters think diagnostically. This is useful experimental evidence for the model of turnout developed in chapter 6.

42. For one careful attempt to sort out these distinctions, see Dawes, van de Kragt, and Orbell (1990).

43. It is understood, I assume, that this analytically useful contrast between the state of nature's prisoners' dilemma and institutional settings does nothing to dispel my earlier concerns about conventionalist formulations of institutional emergence and persistence.

Chapter 5: Rationality in Institutions

1. In some respects, denying an explanatory role for internalized grammar is similar to denying a language of thought to explain public language. Some indeed decry the idea of "Mentalese" as one step in an infinite regress (see Harman 1973; Dennett 1978; and Field 1978a:45).

2. The standard version of game theory does not claim complete comprehension either. It only says that players behave as if they have it (or have a well-defined probability distribution over a well-defined set of alternative games). In a sense, institutional realism simply draws out the full implications of this concession when any residual homogeneity of beliefs represents pragmatic simplification rather than a substantive theory of society.

3. The normal form of a game, which is designed to summarize all the relevant strategic possibilities detailed by the extensive form, is typically compatible with many extensive forms. This is another sense in which the same (normal form) institution is compatible with underlying (extensive form) changes. For the relation between these two game forms and the institutional interpretation of game theory, see Grafstein (1983a).

4. For further development of Quine's argument, see Jackson

(1987:115–26); for its application to jurisprudential debates about the role of rules, see Grafstein (1983b).

5. In describing rules as neither psychological nor constitutive of institutional structure, I have been rather cavalier about explaining exactly how they can work. Nominalism, moreover, puts severe constraints on the ontology available to any such explanation, which would have to appeal to inscriptions of sentences. Can one explain the informational use of rules in game situations without bringing in notions of proof and derivation involving arbitrary formulas or sentences? Players, after all, might know (or act as if they know) a little game theory. In characterizing the players of institutional games, I suspect that the conceptual-role semantics analyzed by Field (1977) is adequate. I would use this semantics to capture not how the brain concretely reasons with rules but the capacity of information encoded in rule statements to enhance the decision maker's behavioral competence. As for making sense of proofs and logical validity, nominalists may require elaborate and tricky devices I cannot discuss here (see Field 1989).

6. The idea of a conceptual scheme will raise a red flag for those philosophers such as Davidson (1980:183–198) who dislike the implied distinction between scheme (subjective) and content (objective). By conceptual scheme, I mean the language imputed to agents as part of an effort to explain their behavior (Quine 1981:38–42). Implicit "conceptual" classifications of stimuli are necessary even for simple conditioning; otherwise nothing in particular would be reinforced (Quine 1960:82–85).

7. Others, no doubt, will define ideology differently than I: Putnam's (1971) examination of the literature disclosed fourteen distinct characteristics that have been attached to the concept. Although the concept has often been associated with the idea of cognitive constraint (Converse 1964), its definers as a group evidently do not satisfy this criterion. One element some might add, certainly, is that ideologues have second-order preferences, that is, preferences about their preferences.

8. Bayesianism is a technical doctrine about the way rational agents should, or do, revise their beliefs in the light of new information (see DeGroot 1970). For a more complete discussion of the Bayesian problem of robustness discussed in the text, see Kadane (1984).

9. Shoemaker (1975) raises another interesting objection. Suppose emeralds observed *after* time *t* turn out to be green. It seems likely, he argues, that *grue* users still will not see it that way. They can interpret spectroscopic evidence, for example, as showing that emeralds have remained grue just as they expected. Yet it is also true that after time *t* an emerald is grue only if it is not green; and emeralds examined after *t*, we are assuming, will turn out to be green. The notion of a *grue* user is simply incoherent, says Shoemaker, given who we are as products of a particular natural history.

The answer I would offer is this. If the meaning of *grue* to a *grue* user is defined in terms of the reaction of the brain mechanism to emeralds observed before time *t*—to the light they emit and so forth—the *grue* user may behave much as Shoemaker expects, which suggests that *grue* is actually a synonym for *green*. On the other hand, the *grue* user may, quite logically, express disappointment over emeralds observed after *t,* in which case we have already rationalized the *grue* user's beliefs before and after *t,* but we are detaching this rationalization from the brain mechanism. The *grue* user's rationality becomes a behavioral phenomenon.

What agents mean, in short, is not what helps explain their behavior; their behavior helps us explain what they mean. The "as if" understanding of rational choice theory thus cuts rather deep, without in any way denying the reality of the neurophysiological mechanisms producing behavior. To conventionalists, by contrast, semantics is a one-way street, with meaning imposed on a meaningless world.

10. Strictly speaking, the grue hypothesis does not require the color constancy of emeralds (Goodman 1972:359). Furthermore, Goodman (1972:409–10) denies the substitutability of logical equivalents in this particular context, whereas Rosenkrantz relies on it.

11. Rosenkrantz's (1982:86–92) response is that our background knowledge is not just the symmetric fact that emeralds observed until now have been both green and grue, but includes the entire complex of relevant scientific theory concerning color, chemistry, and physics. "Goodmanizing" this background knowledge, he claims, as was done using *grue* and *bleen,* is too daunting a task. Yet this does not detract from the claim that had human kind begun with alternative, grue-like predicates, an equally imposing, confidence-inspiring scientific edifice might have been constructed. Goodman does not recommend abandoning current science in the face of these examples, but only suggests we recognize the absence of rational necessity in believing in its superiority.

12. Schick (1987) also uses Goodman to rationalize the related phenomenon of framing effects by observing that experimenters and their subjects may, in effect, be talking *green* and *grue* at one another. His formulation, however, is not completely persuasive. A rational agent, we have seen, can comprehend alternative frameworks within his own. In making choices, moreover, the subject's preference function will be defined over all characteristics of the outcomes presented to him, since the function, as Schick points out, determines not what the subject notices but its importance to him. If so, a given outcome will have the same properties, regardless of the way they are presented. Therefore, contrary to Schick, the agent should be indifferent among alternative descriptions of the outcome. Fully rationalizing framing effects seems to require the possibility of a positional characteristic like *grue* (cf. note 13).

13. On the role of imposed patterns in rational cognition, see Margolis (1987). Writing about framing effects, Machina (1987:146) suggests one way to integrate frames into rational choice theory is to think of the agent's choice as reflecting, in part, a preference among frameworks. From behavioral data about choice, observers can reconstruct the agent's preference for these frames. This analysis, however, does not show why a rational agent has these preferences in the first place. They appear as a *deus ex* Machina. Put another way, his procedure rationalizes the choice of one ideology over another without incorporating our claim that ideology plays an integral role in any rational decision.

14. That is, no distinct proposition combines all possible ideological characterizations. Recall the grue-green analogy: the agent does not have a

belief about an emerald's grue-greenness since there is no conceptualization spanning the two frameworks.

15. See Diaconis and Zabell (1982) for the mathematical conditions under which Jeffrey conditionalization is commutative. They also defend his approach by showing its greater generality and by linking it to less subjectivist conceptions of belief revision.

16. Typically, I suspect, ideological conversion involves changes in values as well as conceptualization, but if my notion of ideology is correct, it does not involve value change alone. Consider the case of Sidney Hook who protested against critics that his was not a conversion regarding fundamental values.

17. There may be opportunities for the evolution of ideological clusters of agents paralleling the evolution of strategic clusters analyzed, e.g., by Axelrod (1984).

18. When the exact number of finite iterations is unknown, the analysis is more complicated but probably the conclusion is the same (Thompson and Faith 1981). In a classic result, Kuhn (1953) uses a backward induction argument to show that any finite, two-person noncooperative game of perfect information (in extensive form) has a unique equilibrium. Kuhn's result is one reason the discussion in this section has implications far beyond the prisoners' dilemma.

19. The so-called "Folk Theorem" for prisoners' dilemma supergames implies similar variability (see, e.g., Friedman 1986: 103–104).

20. A game of imperfect information, of course, is no exception; in it players know and thereby define the game but anticipate not knowing all the details of how it plays out. On the conventionalist fiction, an umpire takes up the slack. Games of incomplete information represent a more serious information deficit. On Harsanyi's (1967–68) ingenious interpretation, this is handled by assuming there is a chance move selecting one of the possible games. This overarching game, as well as its component games, each constitutes a complete game. An umpire is still needed in order to "know" which game chance selected.

21. See Binmore and Dasgupta (1986:3–6) for a fuller discussion of the central importance of this assumption for game theory.

22. Of course, A's head is as it is; but A's head, whatever way it happens to be, is in the game. A particular feature of his brain cannot necessarily be identified as the rational component independent of that context.

23. For the specific bearing of this counterfactual logic on game theory, see Harper (1985).

24. Similarly, in the version Skyrms (1980) offers, which avoids counterfactuals where possible, freedom consists of the ability of agents to consider acts across the spectrum of alternative, unalterable conditions in such a way that their choices do not become part of those conditions.

25. To take up two related equilibrium refinements that confront the problem of unreasonable beliefs, Banks and Sobel (1987) assume that players encountering out-of-equilibria behavior decide who is responsible based on a determination of who, from an expected utility standpoint, is most likely to gain from deviation. This assumption might be justified by arguing

that within the model there is no other basis for distinguishing agents so each player might as well bet on that criterion. Yet the focus on purely within-the-model calculations is precisely what makes out-of-equilibrium behavior a problem. Cho and Kreps (1987), along the same lines, treat deviation not as a mistake but as a conscious attempt to signal other players about one's intentions. Here too we see reliance on extramodel conjectures about what a rational player would do. For a useful discussion of how explicit and speculative these conjectures can get, see Kreps (1989, e.g., 35–36).

26. Since the normal form of the game is central to the Kohlberg and Mertens (1986) approach, players do not have the opportunity to adjust behavior after their understanding or expectations are contradicted. In response to the signaling games discussed in the preceding note, Kohlberg and Mertens would model the signals that out-of-equilibrium behavior is supposed to send as specific behaviors within the game. Of course, the problem is that the sending of this kind of signal can itself be a signal, and so on.

27. See Binmore (1985) for further arguments against an independent notion of perfect rationality. Note Sugden's (1986:77) similar recognition that a player may not be sure about what type of player he is. Finally, Basu (1990) argues formally that rationality cannot be defined so as to apply to all strategic environments. Presumably, the definition has to be tailored to the game. Basu correctly notes, however, that one of his assumptions is likely to be contentiousness, namely, that players who reveal themselves to be irrational are less predictable than their rational counterparts. Is a player who has irrationally made a uniform choice over ten thousand iterations of the choice situation less predictable for being irrational?

28. The factual givenness of institutions is emphasized by Luhmann (1975).

Chapter 6: Electoral Institutions and Voting

1. Ferejohn and Fiorina (1974) also recognized this game theoretic element but thought that the resulting complications should be modeled as a decision problem under uncertainty.

2. For this reason, Ordeshook (1986) is skeptical of this kind of Bayesian model applied to mass elections.

3. The lottery in the voting case is likewise entirely a function of the voter's uncertainty since, I assume, it is timelessly true, though unknown before the election, that a certain determinate percentage of voters participates.

4. One moral is that the recommendation to maximize expected utility, which might seem to be violated by the choice of alternative 1, is ambiguous since it does not state what role causal factors should play. Should one choose so as to *cause* the highest expected utility or should one choose the option *statistically associated* with the highest expected utility? The argument in the text against the causal approach does not insist on one particular reading but only on consistency when analyzing the million-dollar lottery and voting. If maximizing expected utility demands alternative 2, then it recommends voting. This policy is then equivalent to maximizing conditional expected utility. A related moral, therefore, is that despite appearances, the

role and meaning of causation in causal decision theory is both delicate and ambiguous, as we saw in chapter 4.

5. The following model is based on Grafstein (1991) but with a different interpretation.

6. This normalization assumes that all voters perceive a difference between the candidates. Ideally, candidate strategies would be endogenous to the model. I think that the assumption is empirically reasonable.

7. These conditional probabilities do not model the causal efficacy of the alternative acts. When, for example, causal factors are formalized in terms of counterfactual conditionals, this distinction emerges as the difference between the probability of conditionals and conditional probabilities (Lewis 1976).

8. It would be natural to assume that $r_{p1} + r_{a1} = 2$, making the percentage increase in Q_1 due to participation equal to the percentage decrease due to abstention. However, this would preclude perfect stochastic dependence whenever $Q_1 \neq \frac{1}{2}$.

9. By common knowledge I mean universally held true beliefs. The common knowledge assumption appears in previous game theoretic models of turnout (Ledyard 1981; 1984; Palfrey and Rosenthal 1985). The r_{pk} and r_{ak}, of course, do not appear in these models.

10. When $c_i \geq 1$, i does not vote, whereas when $c_i < 0$, i always votes. The latter means that voting provides a net consumption benefit à la Downs (1957) and Riker and Ordeshook (1968).

11. The assumptions about costs and relative size are based on Ledyard (1984) and Palfrey and Rosenthal (1985), whose models are closely tracked in the text.

12. The perception of dependence can of course be influenced through educational programs, party organization, and the like. Candidates have certainly tried to increase their supporters' sense of intrarole dependence and even to lessen their sense of interrole dependence.

13. We come full circle: whatever the relative probabilities that occupants of a role will vote or abstain, it is highly unlikely, given a reasonably large group, that exactly $\frac{1}{2}$ will actually turn out.

14. For the notion of political property, see Aumann and Kurz (1977), Becker (1983; 1985), Hirshleifer (1976:244), and Peltzman (1976:212), who writes: "There is essentially a political auction in which the highest bidder receives the right to tax the wealth of everyone else." Although these models retain the notion of individual property, the ultimate budget constraint for political actors is defined by total tax revenues. By the same token, Peltzman's comment suggests an unfortunate conflation of the empirical and normative dimensions of property, the former revolving around institutionally mediated control. A parallel gap between Becker (1983) and the present proposal shows up in his assumption that political agents maximize their "full income" (what agents would have if they devoted every moment exclusively to generating money). If one treats income derived from politics and the market symmetrically, then full income is a function of the agent's possible choices involving both arenas. Yet as Becker (1983:374–78) portrays it, political income is simply a net addition to, or subtraction from, full income defined independently of political activity. This either violates his own as-

sumption of redistribution distortions induced by political subsidies or requires particularly strong assumptions about the "shadow price" of political activity (cf. Becker 1976:92–93).

15. The voter-consumers in question may still be entirely self-interested, so for better or worse this formulation departs from one by Margolis (1984), who has voters altruistically consider the complete "social difference" between the candidates.

16. Some versions of utility theory, such as the von Neumann–Morgenstern axioms, entail the boundedness of utility from above, and parallel arguments show boundedness from below.

17. In saying this, I do not ignore the very small likelihood that any one voter will actually bring about his preferred allocation of the budget. This does not necessarily indict the ideological picture I have presented, since the uncertain relation between actions concerning one's wealth and its consequences for one's wealth do not automatically undermine the claim to ownership. A hunter may feel entitled to shoot a raccoon on his own property even though his aim is so lousy that such an outcome is highly unlikely.

18. Fishburn (1988:33–34) argues against standard expected utility theory that it fails to acknowledge the significance of changes from the status quo since, for example, it hardly seems irrational to distinguish between falling down to a financial ledge and climbing up to it. If he is correct, the bankruptcy effect merely intensifies a more general phenomenon.

19. Friedman and Savage (1948) pioneered the analysis of utility functions that are not uniformly concave or convex, though the case and, therefore, the utility function they examined were different. Some, by the way, might be tempted to draw the perverse conclusion that turnout will be negatively associated with voter honesty, reflected in a refusal to accept gambles that are justified only by the possibility of welshing. This, however, is where ideology comes in: the difference in budget constraints before and after the election is perceived as a legitimate reflection of the voter-consumer's institutionally defined property, not as a test of personal honesty.

Chapter 7: Self-Control

1. Compare the discussion of various definitions of feasible alternatives in Schwartz (1986:226–27), where the interplay of internal and external factors is recognized, albeit in a very different way.

2. See Deutsch (1963) for this theme. By focusing on this function, I do not mean to imply a formal definition of politics. Obviously, politics performs other tasks as well.

3. If decisions about an institution are made with other institutions in the background, helping define alternatives, then rational choice theorists will have to be more sensitive to interinstitutional calculations; see Tsebelis (1990).

4. I am not suggesting that the idea of total revolution is really meaningful, but since I am introducing it as an objection to institutional realism I will give it the benefit of the doubt.

5. My discussion of this question is based on Grafstein (1990).

6. This is not the only charge of bias leveled at this approach. Some are unhappy with its model of preference aggregation, which, depending on

the observer, is either crude and distorting or elegant. For the former, see Elster (1986) and Frohock (1987); for the latter, see Sen (1986:232–37) and Grafstein (1989).

7. In a narrower interpretation, Rae (1975) and similar critics merely show it is not always possible to achieve unanimity under the unanimous consent rule. The argument I am considering aims at a less trivial conclusion, one that must equate nondecisions and decisions.

8. Another example that Rae (1975:1278–79) offers is the principle that actions not specifically illegal are legal. This however presupposes a deeper principle prohibiting ex post facto criminalization, which may be laudable but is hardly a conceptual necessity, as controversies over the Nuremberg trials, and natural law generally, suggest.

9. Chapman (1983:5) draws a similar distinction between social and legislative choice. Its importance is also reflected in the debate on nondecisions and political power (e.g., Bachrach and Baratz 1970; Wolfinger 1971).

10. The reader may wonder whether this distinction can be reconciled with my earlier analysis of rational choice, which treated the decision maker largely as a black box. There are, however, a few differences between the two cases. The rational choice I have discussed takes place in an institutional context delineating the relevant alternatives. Behavior is judged to be systematically rational, or not, relative to those alternatives. In the case of social determination, which social choice theorists blend in with collective choice, the set of alternatives is typically indeterminate (a point made by Polsby 1980:96–97 in his criticism of nondecisions). As a consequence, the notion of choice loses much of its theoretical bite. Moreover, although the institutional formulation spurns the idea that a specific kind of internal mechanism can necessarily be identified as rational for all individuals, or even for one individual over time, this does not preclude a more general distinction between a causal process that constitutes the (free) choice of an object and a process, such as being pushed down the stairs, that does not. Independently of any formal distinction, I assume that social choice theorists would concede the difference between, say, market processes, in which collective outcomes as such are not the objects of individual choice, and political processes, in which individual preferences do range over collective outcomes. Recall the complaint against unanimous consent that some *individual* can choose a particular outcome for all.

11. Along the same lines, Alexandre Kojève, a Hegelian, argues in a debate with Leo Strauss (Strauss 1963:152–56) that pure tyranny is impossible since personal control can only be exercised over a handful of people. There must be a system of authority cemented by a common idea. The notion of a common idea is functionally equivalent to Parsons's value system or the rational choice theorist's convention.

12. Buchanan (1987:1435) and Coleman (1988:243–76) do agree that unanimous consent allows the state of nature to mimic the structure of genuine markets.

13. Hare (1974:89–90) offers an interesting observation bearing on this interpretation. He points out that the veil of ignorance surrounding the original position could have imposed impartiality by allowing participants to know the full details of their society, including the distribution of its re-

sources and characteristics, but denying each of them knowledge of which particular individual he or she is. Rawls, however, opts for a more collective interpretation of endowments, which reflects "a political conception of justice," as he later put it (1985:224) when responding to Sandel (1982).

14. For a somewhat fuller discussion of the normative dimension, see Grafstein (1990). Cf. Walzer's (1983) notion of spheres of justice, although he is much more concerned with the distinct functions performed by an individual sphere than with its distinct institutional structure.

15. The material in the remainder of this section is drawn from Grafstein (1988).

16. A perhaps unnecessary reminder: although content is specified in relation to the agent's environment, relative to that specification we can continue to describe the agent as intending, desiring, and so forth. Intentions, desires, beliefs, and choices do not become unimportant simply because they acquire content by virtue of the agent's relations with the outside.

17. Interestingly, Otto Neurath's popular image of rebuilding a ship at sea is often used by Quine (e.g., 1960) to convey the social character of language. As a complementary point, I do not totally discount the "character planning" by which agents seek to mold their own preferences, or the making of "precommitments" to bind future actions (Elster 1983b; 1984). But agents do not thereby step outside themselves or their society; nor can they do so collectively without some definite collective means.

18. Cf. Arendt (1968:151): "Freedom as related to politics is not a phenomenon of the will." Arendt is responsible for one of the more interesting attempts in political philosophy to reconcile the public nature of political action and its power to transcend the existing menu of alternatives. For a critical discussion of this attempt, see Grafstein (1986).

19. Thus the possibility of competing conceptions does not necessarily undermine the possibility of truth. In the simplest terms, statements using different categorizations of the same world can all be absolutely true. Nor do scientific explanations of participant conceptualizations or ideologies necessarily undercut their status as theories (see Nozick 1981:332–48).

References

Abramson, Paul R., and John H. Aldrich (1982). "The Decline of Electoral Participation in America." *American Political Science Review* 76 (September): 502–21.

Alexander, Jeffrey C. (1983). *Theoretical Logic in Sociology.* Berkeley and Los Angeles: University of California Press.

Althusser, Louis (1970). *For Marx.* New York: Random House.

Althusser, Louis, and Étienne Balibar (1970). *Reading Capital.* New York: Random House.

Arendt, Hannah (1963). *Eichmann in Jerusalem.* New York: Viking.

——— (1968). *Between Past and Future.* New York: Viking.

Armstrong, D. M. (1978). *Universals and Scientific Reason.* Vol. 1. Cambridge: Cambridge University Press.

Arrow, Kenneth J. (1963). *Social Choice and Individual Values.* New Haven: Yale University Press.

——— (1974). *The Limits of Organization.* New York: Norton.

——— (1984). *Social Choice and Justice.* Oxford: Blackwell.

Arrow, Kenneth J., and Frank Hahn (1971). *General Competitive Analysis.* San Francisco: Holden-Day.

Aumann, Robert J. (1987). "Correlated Equilibrium as an Expression of Bayesian Rationality." *Econometrica* 55 (January): 1–18.

Aumann, Robert J., and Mordecei Kurz (1977). "Power and Taxes." *Econometrica* 45 (July): 1137–61.

Aune, Bruce (1984). "Armstrong on Universals and Particulars." In *D. M. Armstrong,* ed. Radu J. Bogden. Dordrecht, Holland: D. Reidel.

Axelrod, Robert (1984). *The Evolution of Cooperation.* New York: Basic Books.

Bachrach, Peter, and Morton S. Baratz (1970). *Power and Poverty.* New York: Oxford University Press.

Banks, Jeffrey S., and Joel Sobel (1987). "Equilibrium Selection in Signaling Games." *Econometrica* 55 (May): 647–61.

Basu, K. (1990). "On the Non-Existence of a Rationality Definition for Extensive Games." *International Journal of Game Theory* 19, no. 1:33–44.

Becker, Gary S. (1976). *The Economic Approach to Human Behavior.* Chicago: University of Chicago Press.

——— (1983). "A Theory of Competition among Pressure Groups for Political Influence." *Quarterly Journal of Economics* 98 (August): 371–400.

——— (1985). "Public Policies, Pressure Groups, and Dead Weight Costs." *Journal of Public Economics* 28 (December): 329–47.

Berger, Peter L., and Thomas Luckmann (1964). *The Social Construction of Reality.* Garden City, N.Y.: Anchor Books.

Bernheim, B. Douglas (1984). "Rationalizable Strategic Behavior." *Econometrica* 52 (July): 1007–28.

Bernstein, Basil (1964). "Elaborated and Restricted Codes: Their Social Origins and Some Consequences." In *The Ethnography of Communication,* ed. J. Gumphrey and D. Hymes. American Anthropologist Special Publication, no. 66.

Bicchieri, Cristina (1989). "Self-Refuting Theories of Strategic Interaction: A Paradox of Common Knowledge." *Erkenntnis* 30 (March): 69–85.

Binmore, Ken (1985). "Equilibria in Extensive Games." *Economic Journal* 95 (supplement): 51–95.

——— (1987). "Modeling Rational Players: Part I." *Economics and Philosophy* 3 (October): 179–214.

Binmore, Ken, and Partha Dasgupta (1986). "Game Theory: A Survey." In *Economic Organizations as Games,* ed. Ken Binmore and Partha Dasgupta. Oxford: Basil Blackwell.

Black, Max (1961). "Some Questions about Parsons' Theories." In *The Social Theories of Talcott Parsons,* ed. Max Black. Ithaca: Cornell University Press.

Blau, Peter M. (1970). "A Formal Theory of Differentiation in Organizations." *American Sociological Review* 35 (April): 201–18.

——— (1977). *Inequality and Heterogeneity.* New York: Free Press.

Blume, Lawrence E., and David Easley (1982) "Learning to Be Rational." *Journal of Economic Theory* 26 (April): 340–51.

Bourdieu, Pierre (1976). "Marriage Strategies as Strategies of Social Reproduction." In *Family and Society,* ed. Robert Forster and Orest Ranum. Baltimore: Johns Hopkins University Press.

Brandenburger, Adam, and Eddie Dekel (1989). "The Role of Common Knowledge Assumptions in Game Theory." In *The Economics of Missing Markets, Information, and Games,* ed. Frank Hahn. Oxford: Clarendon Press.

Bray, M. M., and N. E. Savan (1986). "Rational Expectations Equilibria, Learning and Model Specification." *Econometrica* 54 (September): 1129–60.

Brennan, Geoffrey, and James M. Buchanan (1985). *The Reason of Rules: Constitutional Political Economy.* Cambridge: Cambridge University Press.

Brenner, Robert (1986). "The Social Basis of Economic Development." In

Analytical Marxism, ed. John Roemer. Cambridge: Cambridge University Press.

Bromley, Daniel W. (1989). *Economic Interests and Institutions.* New York: Basil Blackwell.

Buchanan, James M. (1975) *The Limits of Liberty.* Chicago: University of Chicago Press.

——— (1987). "The Constitution of Economic Policy." *Science* 236: 1433–36.

Buchanan, James M., and Gordon Tullock (1962). *The Calculus of Consent.* Ann Arbor: University of Michigan Press.

Burge, Tyler (1979). "Individualism and the Mental." *Midwest Studies in Philosophy* 4: 73–121.

Cagan, Phillip (1983). "Comment." In *Individual Forecasting and Aggregate Outcomes,* ed. Roman Frydman and Edmund S. Phelps. Cambridge: Cambridge University Press.

Calhoun, Craig Jackson (1988). "The Radicalness of Tradition and the Question of Class Struggle." In *Rationality and Revolution,* ed. Michael Taylor. Cambridge: Cambridge University Press.

Calvert, Randall L. (1985). "Robustness of the Multidimensional Voting Model: Candidate Motivations, Uncertainty and Convergence." *American Journal of Political Science* 29 (February): 69–95.

——— (1991). "Elements of a Theory of Society among Rational Actors." Paper presented to the Public Choice Society, New Orleans, Louisiana.

Cartwright, Nancy (1983). *How the Laws of Physics Lie.* New York: Oxford University Press.

Chamberlain, Gary, and Michael Rothschild (1981). "A Note on the Probability of Casting a Decisive Vote." *Journal of Economic Theory* 25 (August): 152–62.

Chapman, Bruce (1983). "Rights and Constraints: Nozick versus Sen." *Theory and Decision* 15 (March): 1–10.

Cho, In-Koo, and David M. Kreps (1987). "Signaling Games and Stable Equilibria." *Quarterly Journal of Economics* 102 (May): 179–221.

Churchland, Patricia Smith (1986). *Neurophilosophy.* Cambridge, Mass.: MIT Press.

Cohen, G. A. (1978). *Karl Marx's Theory of History: A Defence.* Princeton: Princeton University Press.

Coleman, Jules L. (1988). *Markets, Morals and the Law.* Cambridge: Cambridge University Press.

Connolly, William E. (1981). *Appearance and Reality in Politics.* Cambridge: Cambridge University Press.

Conover, Pamela Johnston (1984). "The Influence of Group Identifications on Political Perception and Evaluation." *Journal of Politics* 46 (August): 760–85.

Conover, Pamela Johnston, and Stanley Feldman (1984). "How People Organize the Political World: A Schematic Model." *American Journal of Political Science* 28 (February): 95–126.

Converse, Philip E. (1964). "The Nature of Belief Systems in Mass Publics." In *Ideology and Discontent,* ed. David E. Apter. New York: Free Press.

Dahl, Robert A., and Charles E. Lindblom (1953). *Politics, Economics and Welfare.* New York: Harper & Row.

Davidson, Donald (1980). *Essays on Actions and Events*. Cambridge: Cambridge University Press.

Davis, Lance E., and Douglass C. North (1970). "Institutional Change and American Economic Growth: A First Step Toward a Theory of Institutional Innovation." *Journal of Economic History* 30 (March): 131–49.

Dawes, Robyn M. (1990). "The Potential Nonfalsity of the False Consensus Effect." In *Insight in Decision Making,* ed. Robin M. Hogarth. Chicago: University of Chicago Press.

Dawes, Robyn M., Jeanne McTavish, and Harriet Shaklee (1977). "Behavior, Communication and Assumptions about Other Peoples' Behavior in a Commons Dilemma Situation." *Journal of Personality and Social Psychology* 35 (January): 1–11.

Dawes, Robyn M., and Richard H. Thaler (1988). "Anomalies: Cooperation." *Journal of Economic Perspectives* 2 (Summer): 187–97.

Dawes, Robyn M., Alphons J. C. van de Kragt, and John M. Orbell (1990). "Cooperation for the Benefit of Us—Not Me, or My Conscience." In *Beyond Self-Interest,* ed. Jane J. Mansbridge. Chicago: University of Chicago Press.

DeGroot, Morris H. (1970). *Optimal Statistical Decisions*. New York: McGraw-Hill.

Dennett, Daniel C. (1978). *Brainstorms*. Cambridge, Mass.: MIT Press.

Denzau, Arthur T., and Robert P. Parks (1979). "Deriving Public Sector Preferences." *Journal of Public Economics* 11, no. 3:335–52.

Deutsch, Karl W. (1963). *The Nerves of Government*. New York: Free Press.

Devitt, Michael (1983). "Realism and the Renegade Putnam: A Critical Study of *Meaning and the Moral Sciences*." *Noûs* 17 (May): 291–301.

———— (1984). *Realism and Truth*. Princeton: Princeton University Press.

Diaconis, Persi, and Sandy L. Zabell (1982). "Updating Subjective Probability." *Journal of the American Statistical Association* 77 (December): 822–30.

Downs, Anthony (1957). *An Economic Theory of Democracy*. New York: Harper & Row.

Dunn, John (1978). "Practicing History and Social Science on 'Realist' Assumptions." In *Action and Interpretation,* ed. Christopher Hookway and Philip Pettit. Cambridge: Cambridge University Press.

Durkheim, Émile (1958). *Professional Ethics and Civic Morals*. Glencoe, IL: Free Press.

———— (1964a). *The Rules of the Sociological Method*. New York: Free Press.

———— (1964b). *The Division of Labor in Society*. New York: Free Press.

Dworkin, Ronald (1977). *Taking Rights Seriously*. Cambridge, Mass.: Harvard University Press.

Easton, David (1979). *A Framework for Political Analysis*. Chicago: University of Chicago Press.

———— (1990). *The Analysis of Political Structure*. New York: Routledge.

Eells, Ellery (1982). *Rational Decision and Causality*. Cambridge: Cambridge University Press.

———— (1985a). "Causal Decision Theory." *PSA 1984* 2:177–200.

———— (1985b). "Causality, Decision, and Newcomb's Problem." In *Paradoxes of Rationality and Cooperation,* ed. Richmond Campbell and Lanning Sowden. Vancouver: University of British Columbia Press.

Elster, Jon (1980). "Cohen on Marx's Theory of History." *Political Studies* 28 (March): 121–28.

———— (1983a). *Explaining Technical Change.* Cambridge: Cambridge University Press.

———— (1983b). *Sour Grapes.* Cambridge: Cambridge University Press.

———— (1984). *Ulysses and the Sirens.* Cambridge: Cambridge University Press.

———— (1985). *Making Sense of Marx.* Cambridge: Cambridge University Press.

———— (1986). "The Market and the Forum: Three Varieties of Political Theory." In *Foundations of Social Choice Theory,* ed. Jon Elster and Aanund Hylland. Cambridge: Cambridge University Press.

———— (1989). *The Cement of Society.* Cambridge: Cambridge University Press.

Enelow, James M., and Melvin J. Hinich (1984). *The Spatial Theory of Voting.* Cambridge: Cambridge University Press.

Ferejohn, John A., and Morris P. Fiorina (1974). "The Paradox of Not Voting: A Decision Theoretic Analysis." *American Political Science Review* 68 (June): 525–36.

Ferguson, Adam (1980). *An Essay on the History of Civil Society.* New Brunswick, N.J.: Transaction Books.

Festinger, Leon (1957). *A Theory of Cognitive Dissonance.* Stanford, Calif.: Stanford University Press.

Field, Hartry (1974). "Quine and the Correspondence Theory." *Philosophical Review* 83 (April): 200–228.

———— (1975). "Conventionalism and Instrumentalism in Semantics." *Noûs* 9 (November): 375–405.

———— (1977). "Logic, Meaning, and Conceptual Role." *Journal of Philosophy* 74 (July): 379–409.

———— (1978a). "Mental Representation." *Erkenntnis* 13 (July): 9–61.

———— (1978b). "A Note on Jeffrey Conditionalization." *Philosophy of Science* 45 (September): 361–67.

———— (1980). *Science Without Numbers.* Princeton: Princeton University Press.

———— (1985). "Can We Dispense With Spacetime?" *PSA 1984* 2: 33–90.

———— (1986a). "The Deflationary Concept of Truth." In *Fact, Science and Morality,* ed. Graham Macdonald and Crispin Wright. Oxford: Basil Blackwell.

———— (1986b). "Critical Notice: Robert Stalnaker, *Inquiry.*" *Philosophy of Science* 53 (September): 425–48.

———— (1989). *Realism, Mathematics and Modality.* Oxford: Basil Blackwell.

Fine, Arthur (1986). *The Shaky Game.* Chicago: University of Chicago Press.

Fishburn, Peter C. (1988). *Nonlinear Preference and Utility Theory.* Baltimore: Johns Hopkins University Press.

Fiske, Susan T., and Shelley E. Taylor (1984). *Social Cognition.* Reading, Mass.: Addison-Wesley.

Foucault, Michel (1970). *The Order of Things.* New York: Random House.

Friedman, James W. (1986). *Game Theory with Applications to Economics.* New York: Oxford University Press.

Friedman, Michael (1983). *Foundations of Space-Time Theories.* Princeton: Princeton University Press.

Friedman, Milton (1953). *Essays in Positive Economics.* Chicago: University of Chicago Press.

Friedman, Milton, and L. J. Savage (1948). "The Utility Analysis of Choices Involving Risk." *Journal of Political Economy* 56 (August): 279–304.

Frohock, Fred M. (1987). *Rational Association.* Syracuse, N.Y.: Syracuse University Press.

Frydman, Roman (1982). "Towards an Understanding of Market Processes: Individual Expectations, Learning, and Convergence to Rational Expectations Equilibrium." *American Economic Review* 72 (April): 652–68.

Frydman, Roman, and Edmund S. Phelps, eds. (1983). *Individual Forecasting and Aggregate Outcomes.* Cambridge: Cambridge University Press.

Galtung, John (1959). "Expectations and Interaction Processes." *Inquiry* 2 (Winter): 213–34.

Gehlen, Arnold (1964). *Urmensch und Spätkultur.* Frankfurt am Main: Athenäum.

Gettier, Edmund L. (1963). "Is Justified True Belief Knowledge?" *Analysis* 23: 121–23.

Gibbard, Allan, and William L. Harper (1978). "Counterfactuals and Two Kinds of Expected Utility." In *Foundations and Applications of Decision Theory,* ed. Clifford A. Hooker, James J. Leach, and Edward F. McClennen. Dordrecht, Holland: D. Reidel.

Giddens, Anthony (1981). "Agency, Institution, and Time-Space Analysis." In *Advances in Social Theory and Methodology,* ed. K. Knorr-Cetina and A. V. Cicourel. Boston: Routledge & Kegan Paul.

——— (1984). *The Constitution of Society.* Berkeley and Los Angeles: University of California Press.

Glymour, Clark (1982). "Conceptual Scheming or Confessions of a Metaphysical Realist." *Synthese* 51 (May): 169–80.

Goldberg, Victor P. (1985). "Production Functions, Transactions Costs and the New Institutionalism." In *Issues in Contemporary Microeconomics and Welfare,* ed. George R. Feiwel. Albany: State University of New York Press.

Goodman, Nelson (1972). *Problems and Projects.* Indianapolis: Bobbs-Merrill.

——— (1984). *Of Mind and Other Matters.* Cambridge, Mass.: Harvard University Press.

——— (1983). *Fact, Fiction, and Forecast.* Cambridge, Mass.: Harvard University Press.

Grafstein, Robert (1981a). "The Failure of Weber's Conception of Legitimacy: Its Causes and Consequences." *Journal of Politics* 43 (May): 456–72.

———— (1981b). "The Legitimacy of Political Institutions." *Polity* 14 (Fall): 51–69.

———— (1982a). "Structure and Structuralism." *Social Science Quarterly* 63 (December): 617–33.

———— (1982b). "The Search for Social Structure." *Social Science Quarterly* 63 (December): 640–42.

———— (1983a). "The Social Scientific Interpretation of Game Theory." *Erkenntnis* 20 (July): 27–47.

———— (1983b). "Taking Dworkin to Hart: A Positivist Conception of Institutional Rules." *Political Theory* 11 (May): 244–65.

———— (1986). "Political Freedom and Political Action." *Western Political Quarterly* 39 (September): 464–79.

———— (1988). "The Problem of Institutional Constraint." *Journal of Politics* 50 (August): 577–99.

———— (1989). "Getting the Whole to Play Its Part." *Social Choice and Welfare* 6 (January): 77–83.

———— (1990). "Missing the Archimedean Point: Liberalism's Institutional Presuppositions." *American Political Science Review* 84 (March): 177–193.

———— (1991). "An Evidential Decision Theory of Turnout." *American Journal of Political Science* 35 (November): 989–1010.

Granovetter, Mark (1985). "Economic Action and Social Structure: The Problem of Embeddedness." *American Journal of Sociology* 91 (November): 481–510.

Habermas, Jürgen (1971). *Knowledge and Human Interests*. Boston: Beacon.

Hacking, Ian (1983). *Representing and Intervening*. Cambridge: Cambridge University Press.

Hampton, Jean (1980). "Contracts and Choices: Does Rawls Have a Social Contract Theory?" *Journal of Philosophy* 77 (June): 315–38.

Hardin, Russell (1982). *Collective Action*. Baltimore: Johns Hopkins University Press.

Hare, R. M. (1974). "Rawls' Theory of Justice." In *Reading Rawls,* ed. Norman Daniels. New York: Basic Books.

Harman, Gilbert (1973). *Thought*. Princeton: Princeton University Press.

Harper, William L. (1985). "Ratifiability and Causal Decision Theory." *PSA 1984* 2: 213–28.

Harré, Rhom (1981). "Philosophical Aspects of the Macro-Micro Problem." In *Advances in Social Theory and Methodology,* ed. K. Knorr-Cetina and A. V. Cicourel. Boston: Routledge & Kegan Paul.

Harris, Marvin (1968). *The Rise of Anthropological Theory*. New York: Crowell.

Harsanyi, John C. (1969). "Rational-Choice Models of Political Behavior vs. Functionalist and Conformist Theories." *World Politics* 21 (July): 513–38.

———— (1967–68) "Games with Incomplete Information Played by 'Bayesian' Players, I–III." *Management Science* 14: 159–82, 320–34, 486–502.

Harsanyi, John C., and Reinhard Selten (1988). *A General Theory of Equilibrium Selection in Games*. Cambridge, Mass.: MIT Press.

Hart, H. L. A. (1961). *The Concept of Law*. Oxford: Oxford University Press.

Hechter, Michael (1987). *Principles of Group Solidarity.* Berkeley and Los Angeles: University of California Press.

Hellman, Geoffrey Paul, and Frank Wilson Thompson (1975). "Physicalism: Ontology, Determination, and Reduction." *Journal of Philosophy* 72 (October): 551–64.

——— (1977). "Physicalist Materialism." *Noûs* 11 (November): 309–45.

Hernstein, Israel, and John Milnor (1953). "An Axiomatic Approach to Measurable Utility." *Econometrica* 21 (April): 291–97.

Hinich, Melvin J. (1977). "Equilibrium in Spatial Voting: The Median Voter Result is an Artifact." *Journal of Economic Theory* 16 (December): 208–19.

Hirschman, Albert O. (1970). *Exit, Voice, and Loyalty.* Cambridge, Mass.: Harvard University Press.

Hirshleifer, Jack (1976). "Comment." *Journal of Law and Economics* 19 (August): 241–44.

——— (1987). *Economic Behaviour in Adversity.* Chicago: University of Chicago Press.

Hobsbawm, Eric (1971). *Primitive Rebels.* New York: Praeger.

Holmes, Stephen (1989). "The Lion of Illiberalism." *New Republic* (30 October): 32–37.

Horwich, Paul (1985). "Decision Theory in Light of Newcomb's Problem." *Philosophy of Science* 52 (September): 431–50.

——— (1986). "A Defence of Conventionalism." In *Fact, Science and Morality,* ed. Graham Macdonald and Crispin Wright. Oxford: Basil Blackwell.

Howard, Nigel (1971). *Paradoxes of Rationality.* Cambridge, Mass.: MIT Press.

Huntington, Samuel P. (1968). *Political Order in Changing Societies.* New Haven: Yale University Press.

Isaac, R. Mark, Kenneth F. McCue, and Charles R. Plott (1985). "Public Goods Provision in an Experimental Environment." *Journal of Public Economics* 26 (February): 51–74.

Jackson, Frank (1987). *Conditionals.* Oxford: Basil Blackwell.

Jeffrey, Richard C. (1974). "Frameworks for Preference." In *Essays on Economic Behavior under Uncertainty,* ed. M. S. Balch, D. L. McFadden, and S. Y. Wu. Amsterdam: North-Holland.

——— (1981). "The Logic of Decision Defended." *Synthese* 48: 273–92.

——— (1983). *The Logic of Decision.* Chicago: University of Chicago Press.

——— (1988). "How to Probabilize a Newcomb Problem." In *Probability and Causality,* ed. James H. Fetzer. Dordrecht, Holland: D. Reidel.

Kadane, Joseph B., ed. (1984). *Robustness of Bayesian Analyses.* Amsterdam: North-Holland.

Kau, James B., and Paul H. Rubin (1982). *Congressman, Constituents, and Contributors.* Boston: Martinus Nijhoff.

Kinder, Donald R., and D. Roderick Kiewiet (1979). "Economic Discontent and Political Behavior: The Role of Personal Grievances and Collective Economic Judgments in Congressional Voting." *American Journal of Political Science* 23 (August): 495–527.

Kirzner, Israel M. (1962). "Rational Action and Economic Theory." *Journal of Political Economy* 70 (June): 380–85.

Kluckhohn, Clyde (1951). "Values and Value-Orientations in the Theory of Action." In *Toward a General Theory of Action,* ed. Talcott Parsons and Edward Shils. New York: Harper & Row.

Kohlberg, Elon, and Jean-Francois Mertens (1986). "On the Strategic Stability of Equilibria." *Econometrica* 54 (September): 1003–37.

Kreps, David M. (1989). "Out of Equilibrium Beliefs and Out-of-Equilibrium Behaviour." In *The Economics of Missing Markets, Information, and Games,* ed. Frank Hahn. Oxford: Clarendon Press.

Kreps, David M., and Robert Wilson (1982). "Sequential Equilibria." *Econometrica* 50 (July): 863–94.

Kuhn, H. W. (1953). "Extensive Games and the Problem of Information." In *Contributions to the Theory of Games* vol 2, ed. H. W. Kuhn and A. W. Tucker. Princeton: Princeton University Press.

Ledyard, John O. (1981). "The Paradox of Voting and Candidate Competition: A General Equilibrium Analysis." In *Essays in Contemporary Fields of Economics,* ed. George Horwich and James Quirk. Lafayette, Ind.: Purdue University Press.

——— (1984). "The Pure Theory of Large Two-Candidate Elections." *Public Choice* 44, no. 1: 7–41.

Leeds, Stephen (1973). "How to Think About Reference." *Journal of Philosophy* 70 (6 September): 485–503.

——— (1978). "Theories of Reference and Theories of Truth." *Erkenntnis* 13 (July): 111–29.

Levi, Isaac (1975). "Newcomb's Many Problems." *Theory and Decision* 6: 161–75.

——— (1982). "A Note on Newcombmania." *Journal of Philosophy* 79 (June): 337–42.

——— (1983). "The Wrong Box." *Journal of Philosophy* 80 (September): 534–42.

——— (1985). "Epicycles." *Journal of Philosophy* 82 (February): 104–06.

Lewis, David K. (1969). *Convention.* Cambridge, Mass.: Harvard University Press.

——— (1975). "Languages and Language." In *Language, Mind, Knowledge,* ed. Keith Gunderson. Minneapolis: University of Minnesota Press.

——— (1976). "Probabilities of Conditionals and Conditional Probabilities." *Philosophical Review* 85 (July): 297–315.

——— (1979). "Prisoners' Dilemma Is a Newcomb Problem." *Philosophy and Public Affairs* 8 (Spring): 235–40.

——— (1981). "Causal Decision Theory." *Australasian Journal of Philosophy* 59 (March): 5–30.

——— (1983). "Levi against U-Maximization." *Journal of Philosophy* 80 (September): 531–34.

Lichtheim, George (1961). *Marxism.* New York: Praeger.

Lucas, Robert E., Jr. (1977). "Understanding Business Cycles." *Journal of Monetary Economics* 5 (supplement): 7–29.

——— (1981). *Studies in Business-Cycle Theory.* Cambridge, Mass.: MIT Press.

Luce, R. Duncan, and Howard Raiffa (1957). *Games and Decisions*. New York: Wiley.

Luhmann, Niklas (1975). *Legitimation durch Verfahren*. Darmstadt: Luchterhand.

——— (1976). "Generalized Media and the Problem of Contingency." In *Explorations in General Theory in Social Science,* vol. 2, ed. Jan J. Loubser, Rainer C. Baum, Andrew Effrat, and Victor Meyer Lidz. New York: Free Press.

Machina, Mark J. (1987). "Choice under Uncertainty: Problems Solved and Unsolved." *Journal of Economic Perspectives* 1 (Summer): 121–54.

McKelvey, Richard D., and Peter C. Ordeshook (1984). "An Experimental Study of the Effects of Procedural Rules on Committee Behavior." *Journal of Politics* 46 (February): 182–205.

Macpherson, C. B. (1962). *The Political Theory of Possessive Individualism*. London: Oxford University Press.

Mannheim, Karl (1936). *Ideology and Utopia*. New York: Harcourt, Brace & World.

Marcet, Albert, and Thomas Sargent (1989). "Convergence of Least Squares Learning Mechanisms in Self Referential Linear Stochastic Models." *Journal of Economic Theory* 48 (August): 337–68.

March, James G., and Johan P. Olsen (1984). "The New Institutionalism: Organizational Factors in Political Life." *American Political Science Review* 78 (September): 734–49.

——— (1989). *Rediscovering Institutions*. New York: Free Press.

March, James G., and Herbert A. Simon (1958). *Organizations*. New York: John Wiley.

Margolis, Howard (1984). *Selfishness, Altruism, and Rationality*. Chicago: University of Chicago Press.

——— (1987). *Patterns, Thinking, and Cognition*. Chicago: University of Chicago Press.

Marwell, Gerald, and Ruth Ames (1981). "Economists Free Ride, Does Anyone Else?" *Journal of Public Economics* 15 (June): 295–310.

Marx, Karl (1970). *A Contribution to the Critique of Political Economy*. New York: International Publishers.

Marx, Karl, and Frederick Engels (1947). *The German Ideology*. New York: International Publishers.

——— (1968). *Selected Works*. New York: International Publishers.

Mayhew, Bruce (1982). "Structuralism and Ontology." *Social Science Quarterly* 63 (December): 634–39.

Miller, Arthur H., Martin P. Wattenberg, and Oksana Malanchuk (1986). "Schematic Assessments of Presidential Candidates." *American Political Science Review* 80 (June): 521–40.

Millikan, Ruth Garrett (1984). *Language, Thought, and Other Biological Categories*. Cambridge, Mass.: MIT Press.

Mintz, Sidney W., and E. R. Wolf (1957). "Haciendas and Plantations in Middle America and the Antilles." *Social and Economic Studies* 6 (September): 380–412.

Morton, R. B. (1987). "A Group Majority Voting Model of Public Good Provision." *Social Choice and Welfare* 4 (June): 117–31.

Nau, Robert F., and Kevin F. McCardle (1990). "Coherent Behavior in Co-operative Games." *Journal of Economic Theory* 50 (April): 424–44.

Nelson, Dale C. (1979). "Ethnicity and Socioeconomic Status as Sources of Participation: The Case for Ethnic Political Culture." *American Political Science Review* 73 (December): 1024–38.

Newton-Smith, William (1982). "Relativism and the Possibility of Interpretation." In *Rationality and Relativism,* ed. Martin Hollis and Steven Lukes. Cambridge, Mass.: MIT Press.

Noonan, Harold W. (1980). *Objects and Identity.* The Hague: Martinus Nijhoff.

North, Douglass C. (1981). *Structure and Change in Economic History.* New York: Norton.

——— (1990). *Institutions, Institutional Change and Economic Performance.* Cambridge: Cambridge University Press.

Nozick, Robert (1969). "Newcomb's Problem and Two Principles of Choice." In *Essays in Honor of Carl G. Hempel,* ed. Nicholas Rescher. Dordrecht, Holland: D. Reidel.

——— (1974). *Anarchy, State, and Utopia.* New York: Basic Books.

——— (1981). *Philosophical Explanations.* Cambridge, Mass.: Harvard University Press.

Oakeshott, Michael (1962). *Rationalism in Politics and Other Essays.* New York: Basic Books.

Orbell, John T., Peregrine Schwartz-Shea, and Randy T. Simmons (1984). "Do Cooperators Exit More Readily than Defectors?" *American Political Science Review* 78 (March): 147–62.

Ordeshook, Peter C. (1986). *Game Theory and Political Theory.* Cambridge: Cambridge University Press.

Ostrom, Elinor (1986). "An Agenda for the Study of Institutions." *Public Choice* 48, no. 1:3–25.

——— (1990). *Governing the Commons.* Cambridge: Cambridge University Press.

Owen, Guillermo (1974). "A Discussion of Minimax." *Management Science* 20: 1316–17.

——— (1982). *Game Theory.* Orlando, Fla.: Academic Press.

Palfrey, Thomas R., and Howard Rosenthal (1983). "A Strategic Calculus of Voting." *Public Choice* 41, no. 1:7–55.

——— (1985). "Voter Participation and Strategic Uncertainty." *American Political Science Review* 79 (March): 62–78.

Parijs, Philippe Van (1984). "Marxism's Central Puzzle." In *After Marx,* ed. Terence Ball and James Farr. Cambridge: Cambridge University Press.

Parsons, Talcott (1935). "The Place of Ultimate Values in Sociological Theory." *International Journal of Ethics* 45 (April): 282–316.

——— (1951). *The Social System.* New York: Free Press.

——— (1954). *Essays in Sociological Theory.* New York: Free Press.

——— (1966). *Societies.* Englewood Cliffs, N.J.: Prentice-Hall.

——— (1968). *The Structure of Social Action.* New York: Free Press.

——— (1971). *The System of Modern Societies.* Englewood Cliffs, N.J.: Prentice-Hall.

Parsons, Talcott, Robert F. Bales, and Edward Shils (1953). *Working Papers in the Theory of Action.* New York: Basic Books.

Parsons, Talcott and Edward Shils (1951). "Values, Motives, and Systems of Action." In *Toward a General Theory of Action,* ed. Talcott Parsons and Edward Shils. New York: Harper & Row.

Parsons, Talcott, and Neil J. Smelser (1965). *Economy and Society.* New York: Free Press.

Pearce, David G. (1984). "Rationalizable Strategic Behavior and the Problem of Perfection." *Econometrica* 52 (July): 1029–50.

Peffley, Mark, Stanley Feldman, and Lee Sigelman (1987). "Economic Conditions and Party Competence: Processes of Belief Revision." *Journal of Politics* 49 (February): 100–121.

Peltzman, Sam (1976). "Toward a More General Theory of Regulation." *Journal of Law and Economics* 19 (August): 211–40.

Pettit, Philip, and Robert Sugden (1989). "The Backward Induction Paradox." *Journal of Philosophy* 86 (April): 169–82.

Phelps, Edmund S. (1983). "The Trouble with 'Rational Expectations and the Problem of Inflation Stabilization.'" In *Individual Forecasting and Aggregate Outcomes,* ed. Roman Frydman and Edmund S. Phelps. Cambridge: Cambridge University Press.

Plott, Charles R. (1972). "Individual Choice of a Political-Economic Process." In *Probability Models of Collective Decision Making,* ed. Richard G. Niemi and Herbert F. Weisberg. Columbus, Ohio.: Charles E. Merrill.

Polsby, Nelson W. (1980). *Community Power and Political Theory.* New Haven: Yale University Press.

Popkin, Samuel L. (1979). *The Rational Peasant.* Berkeley and Los Angeles: University of California Press.

Popper, Karl R. (1961). *The Poverty of Historicism.* New York: Harper & Row.

Pratt, John W., and Richard J. Zeckhauser, eds. (1985). *Principals and Agents: The Structure of Business.* Cambridge, Mass.: Harvard Business School Press.

Price, Huw (1986). "Against Causal Decision Theory." *Synthese* 67 (May): 195–212.

Przeworski, Adam (1975). "Institutionalization of Voting Patterns, or Is Mobilization the Source of Decay?" *American Political Science Review* 69 (March): 49–67.

——— (1985). *Capitalism and Social Democracy.* Cambridge: Cambridge University Press.

——— (1990). *The State and the Economy under Capitalism.* Chur, Switzerland: Harwood.

Przeworski, Adam, and Michael Wallerstein (1988). "Structural Dependence of the State on Capital." *American Political Science Review* 82 (March): 11–29.

Putnam, Hilary (1975). *Mind, Language and Reality.* Cambridge: Cambridge University Press.

Putnam, Robert D. (1971). "Studying Elite Political Culture: The Case of 'Ideology.'" *American Political Science Review* 65 (September): 651–81.

Quattrone, George A., and Amos Tversky (1986). "Self-Deception and the

Voter's Illusion." In *The Multiple Self,* ed. Jon Elster. Cambridge: Cambridge University Press.

———— (1988). "Contrasting Rational and Psychological Analyses of Political Choice." *American Political Science Review* 82 (September): 719–36.

Quine, W. V. (1951). *Mathematical Logic.* New York: Harper & Row.

———— (1960). *Word and Object.* Cambridge, Mass.: MIT Press.

———— (1961). *From a Logical Point of View.* New York: Harper & Row.

———— (1969). *Ontological Relativity and Other Essays.* New York: Columbia University Press.

———— (1976). *The Ways of Paradox.* Cambridge, Mass.: Harvard University Press.

———— (1981). *Theories and Things.* Cambridge, Mass.: Harvard University Press.

———— (1985). "Events and Reification." In *Actions and Events,* ed. Ernest LePore and Brian P. McLaughlin. Oxford: Basil Blackwell.

Rae, Douglas W. (1975). "The Limits of Consensual Decision." *American Political Science Review* 69 (December): 1270–94.

Rapoport, Anatol (1966). *Two-Person Game Theory.* Ann Arbor: University of Michigan Press.

Rapoport, Anatol, and Abraham Chammah (1965). *Prisoner's Dilemma.* Ann Arbor: University of Michigan Press.

Rawls, John (1971). *A Theory of Justice.* Cambridge, Mass.: Harvard University Press.

———— (1985). "Justice as Fairness: Political not Metaphysical." *Philosophy & Public Affairs* 14 (Summer): 223–51.

Reiman, Jeffrey H. (1972). *In Defense of Political Philosophy.* New York: Harper & Row.

Riker, William H. (1980). "Implications from the Disequilibrium of Majority Rule for the Study of Institutions." *American Political Science Review* 74 (June): 432–46.

———— (1990). "Heresthetic and Rhetoric in the Spatial Model." In *Advances in the Spatial Theory of Voting,* ed. James M. Enelow and Melvin J. Hinich. Cambridge: Cambridge University Press.

Riker, William H., and Peter C. Ordeshook (1968). "A Theory of the Calculus of Voting." *American Political Science Review* 62 (March): 25–42.

Roemer, John E. (1982). *A General Theory of Exploitation and Class.* Cambridge, Mass.: Harvard University Press.

———— (1985). "Rationalizing Revolutionary Ideology." *Econometrica* 53 (January): 85–108.

Rogowski, Ronald (1975). *Rational Legitimacy.* Princeton: Princeton University Press.

Rorty, Richard (1979). *Philosophy and the Mirror of Nature.* Princeton: Princeton University Press.

Rosenkrantz, Roger D. (1982). "Does the Philosophy of Induction Rest on a Mistake?" *Journal of Philosophy* 79 (February): 78–97.

Ross, Stephen A. (1974). "On Consumer Consumption and Portfolio Decisions with Transactions Costs." In *Essays on Economic Behavior under Uncertainty,* ed. M. S. Balch, D. L. McFadden, and S. Y. Wu. Amsterdam: North-Holland.

Rousseau, Jean-Jacques (1964). *The First and Second Discourses*. New York: St Martin's.

Rudin, Walter (1976). *Principles of Mathematical Analysis*. New York: McGraw-Hill.

Salmon, Wesley C. (1984). *Scientific Explanation and the Causal Structure of the World*. Princeton: Princeton University Press.

Sandel, Michael (1982). *Liberalism and the Limits of Justice*. Cambridge: Cambridge University Press.

Sartori, Giovanni (1969). "Politics, Ideology and Belief Systems." *American Political Science Review* 63 (June): 398–411.

Schick, Frederic (1987). "Rationality." *Economics and Philosophy* 3 (April): 49–66.

Schiffer, Stephen R. (1972). *Meaning*. London: Oxford University Press.

——— (1987). *Remnants of Meaning*. Cambridge, Mass.: MIT Press.

Schmidt-Trenz, Hans-Jörg (1989). "The State of Nature in the Shadow of Contract Formation: Adding a Missing Link to J. M. Buchanan's Social Contract Theory." *Public Choice* 62 (September): 237–51.

Schotter, Andrew (1981). *The Economic Theory of Social Institutions*. Cambridge: Cambridge University Press.

Schwartz, Thomas (1986). *The Logic of Collective Choice*. New York: Columbia University Press.

——— (1987). "Your Vote Counts on Account of the Way It Is Counted: An Institutional Solution to the Paradox of Voting." *Public Choice* 54, no. 2:101–21.

Scott, John Finley (1963). "The Changing Foundations of the Parsonian Action Scheme." *American Sociological Review* 28 (October): 716–35.

Searle, J. R., ed. (1971). *The Philosophy of Language*. London: Oxford University Press.

Seidenfeld, Teddy (1985). "Comments on Causal Decision Theory." *PSA 1984* 2: 201–12.

Selten, Reinhardt (1975). "Reexamination of the Perfectness Concept for Equilibrium Points in Extensive Games." *International Journal of Game Theory* 4, no. 1:25–55.

Sen, Amartya (1982). *Choice, Welfare, and Measurement*. Cambridge, Mass.: MIT Press.

——— (1986). "Foundations of Social Choice Theory: An Epilogue." In *Foundations of Social Choice Theory*, ed. Jon Elster and Aanund Hylland. Cambridge: Cambridge University Press.

Shepsle, Kenneth A. (1986). "Institutional Equilibrium and Equilibrium Institutions." In *Political Science: The Science of Politics*, ed. Herbert F. Weisberg. New York: Agathon Press.

——— (1989). "Studying Institutions: Some Lessons from the Rational Choice Approach." *Journal of Theoretical Politics* 1 (January): 131–47.

Shepsle, Kenneth A., and Barry R. Weingast (1981). "Structure-Induced Equilibrium and Legislative Choice." *Public Choice* 37, no. 3:503–19.

——— (1984). "Why Do Rules of Procedure Matter?" *Journal of Politics* 46 (February): 206–21.

Shoemaker, Sydney (1975). "On Projecting the Unprojectible." *Philosophical Review* 84 (April): 178–219.

Shubik, Martin (1982). *Game Theory in the Social Sciences*. Cambridge, Mass.: MIT Press.

Skocpol, Theda (1979). *States and Revolutions*. Cambridge: Cambridge University Press.

Skowronek, Stephen (1982). *Building a New American State*. Cambridge: Cambridge University Press.

Skyrms, Brian (1980). *Causal Necessity*. New Haven: Yale University Press.

Skyrms, Brian (1982). "Causal Decision Theory." *Journal of Philosophy* 79 (November): 695–711.

Smart, J. C. C. (1963). *Philosophy and Scientific Realism*. London: Routledge & Kegan Paul.

Smelser, Neil J. (1963). *The Sociology of Economic Life*. Englewood Cliffs, N.J.: Prentice-Hall.

Smith, Rogers M. (1988). "Political Jurisprudence, the 'New Institutionalism,' and the Future of Public Law." *American Political Science Review* 82 (March): 89–108.

Sobel, Jordan Howard (1985). "Not Every Prisoner's Dilemma Is a Newcomb Problem." In *Paradoxes of Rationality and Cooperation,* ed. Richmond Campbell and Lanning Sowden. Vancouver: University of British Columbia Press.

Squire, Peverill, Raymond E. Wolfinger, and David P. Glass (1987). "Residential Mobility and Voter Turnout." *American Political Science Review* 81 (March): 45–65.

Stalnaker, Robert C. (1984). *Inquiry*. Cambridge, Mass.: MIT Press.

Stich, Stephen P. (1983). *From Folk Psychology to Cognitive Science*. Cambridge, Mass.: MIT Press.

Stigler, George J., and Gary S. Becker (1977). "De Gustibus Non Est Disputandum." *American Economic Review* 67 (March): 76–90.

Strauss, Leo (1963). *On Tyranny*. New York: Free Press.

Sugden, Robert (1986). *The Economics of Rights, Co-operation and Welfare*. Oxford: Basil Blackwell.

Suppes, P. (1988). "Lorenz Curves for Various Processes: A Pluralistic Approach to Equity." *Social Choice and Welfare* 5 (April): 89–91.

Talbott, W. J. (1987). "Standard and Non-standard Newcomb Problems." *Synthese* 70 (March): 415–58.

Tan, Tommy Chin-Chiu, and Sérgio Ribeiro da Costa Werlang (1988). "The Bayesian Foundations of Solution Concepts of Games." *Journal of Economic Theory* 45 (August): 370–91.

Taylor, Charles (1985). *Philosophy and the Human Sciences*. Cambridge: Cambridge University Press.

Taylor, Michael (1987). *The Possibility of Cooperation*. Cambridge: Cambridge University Press.

——— (1988). "Rationality and Revolutionary Collective Action." In *Rationality and Revolution,* ed. Michael Taylor. Cambridge: Cambridge University Press.

Teixeira, Ruy (1989). "Registration and Turnout." *Public Opinion* 11, no. 5:12–13, 56–58.

Thompson, Earl A., and Roger L. Faith (1981). "A Pure Theory of Strategic

Behavior and Social Institutions." *American Economic Review* 71 (June): 366–80.

Tsebelis, George (1990). *Nested Games.* Berkeley and Los Angeles: University of California Press.

Turner, John C. (1982). "Towards a Cognitive Redefinition of the Social Group." In *Social Identity and Intergroup Relations,* ed. Henri Tajfel. Cambridge: Cambridge University Press.

Turner, Stephen P. (1977). "Blau's Theory of Differentiation: Is It Explanatory?" *Sociological Quarterly* 18 (Winter): 17–32.

Tversky, Amos and Daniel Kahneman (1987). "Rational Choice and the Framing of Decisions." In *Rational Choice,* ed. Robin M. Hogarth and Melvin W. Reder. Chicago: University of Chicago Press.

Tversky, Amos, Paul Slovic, and Daniel Kahneman (1990). "The Causes of Preference Reversal." *American Economic Review* 80 (March): 204–17.

Uhlaner, Carole Jean (1989a). "'Relational Goods' and Participation: Incorporating Sociability into a Theory of Rational Action." *Public Choice* 62, no. 3:253–85.

——— (1989b). "Rational Turnout: The Neglected Role of Groups." *American Journal of Political Science* 33 (May): 390–422.

Unger, Roberto Mangabeira (1987). *False Necessity.* Cambridge: Cambridge University Press.

Vanberg, Viktor (1986). "Spontaneous Market Order and Social Rules." *Economics and Philosophy* 2 (April): 75–100.

Vanberg, Viktor, and James M. Buchanan (1989). "Interests and Theories in Constitutional Choice." *Journal of Theoretical Politics* 1 (January): 49–62.

van Damme, Eric (1989). "Stable Equilibria and Forward Induction." *Journal of Economic Theory* 48 (August): 476–96.

Viscusi, W. Kip (1989). "Prospective Reference Theory: Toward an Explanation of the Paradoxes." *Journal of Risk and Uncertainty* 2 (September): 235–64.

von Neumann, John, and Oskar Morgenstern (1953). *Theory of Games and Economic Behavior.* Princeton: Princeton University Press.

Walzer, Michael (1983). *Spheres of Justice.* New York: Basic Books.

Watkins, J. W. N. (1968). "Methodological Individualism and Social Tendencies." In *Readings in the Philosophy of the Social Sciences,* ed. May Brodbeck. New York: Macmillan.

Weber, Max (1949). *On the Methodology of the Social Sciences.* Ed. and trans. Edward A. Shils and Henry A. Finch. Glencoe, Ill.: Free Press.

——— (1968). *Economy and Society.* Vol. I. Berkeley and Los Angeles: University of California Press.

Weir, Margaret, and Theda Skocpol (1985). "State Structures and the Possibilities for 'Keynesian' Responses to the Great Depression in Sweden, Britain, and the United States." In *Bringing the State Back In,* ed. Peter B. Evans, Dietrich Rueschemeyer, and Theda Skocpol. Cambridge: Cambridge University Press.

Williams, Donald Cary (1966). *Principles of Empirical Realism.* Springfield, Ill: Charles C. Thomas.

Williamson, Oliver E. (1985). *The Economic Institutions of Capitalism.* New York: Free Press.

Winter, Sidney G. (1964). "Economic 'Natural Selection' and the Theory of the Firm." *Yale Economic Essays* 4: 225–72.

Wolff, Robert Paul (1976). *In Defense of Anarchism.* New York: Harper & Row.

Wolfinger, Raymond E. (1971). "Nondecisions and the Study of Local Politics." *American Political Science Review* 65 (December): 1063–80.

Wolfinger, Raymond E., and Steven J. Rosenstone (1980). *Who Votes?* New Haven: Yale University Press.

Wood, Gordon (1973). "The American Revolution." In *Revolutions: A Comparative Study,* ed. Lawrence Kaplan. New York: Vintage Books.

Wrong, Dennis (1962). "The Over-Socialized Conception of Man in Modern Sociology." *Psychoanalysis and the Psychoanalytic Review* 49 (Summer): 53–69.

Zolberg, Aristide (1972). "Moments of Madness." *Politics & Society* 2 (Winter): 183–207.